AGITATED
GRUPOS AUTÓNOMOS AND ARMED ANTICAPITALISM IN SPAIN, 1974–1984
JONI D.

TRANSLATED BY PAUL SHARKEY

Agitated: Grupos Autónomos and Armed Anticapitalism in Spain, 1974–1984
2023 CC BY-NC 3.0, by Joni D.
Originally published as *Grupos Autónomos. Una crónica armada de la transacción democrática*
in 2014 by El Lokal, Barcelona

This edition © AK Press

ISBN: 978-1-84935-431-8
E-ISBN: 978-1-84935-432-5
Library of Congress Control Number: 2022935888

AK Press
370 Ryan Ave. #100
Chico, CA 95973
United States
www.akpress.org
akpress@akpress.org

AK Press
33 Tower St.
Edinburgh EH6 7BN
Scotland
www.akuk.com
akuk@akpress.org

The above addresses would be delighted to provide you with the latest AK Press distribution
catalog, which features books, pamphlets, zines, and stylish apparel published and/or
distributed by AK Press. Alternatively, visit our websites for the complete catalog, latest news,
and secure ordering.

Kate Sharpley Library
BM Hurricane
London, WC1N 3XX
UK
www.katesharpleylibrary.net

Thanks to John Barker for indexing
Cover design by John Yates (stealworks.com)
Printed in the Unites States on acid-free paper

CONTENTS

5. ARMED AGITATION

6. THE END OF A DREAM

7. THE DREAM LIVES ON

INTRODUCTION

The work of the Kate Sharpley Library has in many ways been guided by Edward Thompson's articulation of the necessity of rescuing groups and people from "the enormous condescension of posterity." We have also been driven in our publications to challenge the political amnesia toward those who were anarchist and libertarian—as well as the unaligned and unknown who allied with them to challenge the horror of capitalism. This book fits firmly in that tradition and offers us a compelling portrait of those in the Grupos Autonomos between, 1974–1984—a time of substantial change in Spain.

Franco died on November 20, 1975 after thirty-six years of brutality toward those who opposed him. His death, for some, signaled all sorts of radical possibilities. We might best characterize this period as what Alexander Berkman, when describing other times and places ripe with potential, described as "the psychological moment." If the time was seized, then another world was possible.

Of course, some Grupos members had been active well before Franco's death. They had been active in the MIL or its allies and were outraged by the state murder of MIL member Salvador Puig Antich on March 2, 1974.[1] Disdaining fixed organizations, their work in MIL prisoner support and resistance to the repression around them became the blueprint for actions over the next ten years. Agile and creative, working in small affinity groups, at times based in communities and workplaces, they showed a disdain for Parties and their lines even if they were sometimes members! Grupos members moved away from protesting and toward direct action as they upped the ante after the death of Franco. They sensed that this was their time and the possibility of the destruction of capitalism and the bringing in of a new world had never been closer since 1936.

We would do well to consider what they were up against. Plans for a move toward a constitutional monarchy and a parliamentary system based on

---

1. *Salvador Puig Antich: Collected Writings on Repression and Resistance in Franco's Spain* (Chico, CA: AK Press, 2021) ed. by Ricard de Vargas Golarons, trans. Peter Gelderloos, is essential reading for an understanding of this period of Spanish resistance to the dictatorship.

representative democracy had been quietly laid before the death of Franco and discussions were taking place between the Francoist regime and some of its opponents. The fear of violence and radical, revolutionary change was a real factor in these discussions and much effort over the next few years was taken to bind the political center together and diminish the effects of what were seen as "extremists." These moves were encouraged by the United States and Germany who had no desire to see Spain become destabilized. For them the creation of a capitalist democracy was essential.

By 1977 most trade unions and political parties had been legalized, including the Spanish Communist Party (as early as 1976 Santaigo Carillo, General Secretary of the Communist Party of Spain had spoken of an "an agreed break" in activity against the new government). An Amnesty Bill was also passed in 1977 where some political prisoners were released in exchange for no legal proceedings being taken by the new government against the perpetrators of human rights violations under the Franco regime.

The year 1977 also saw the first democratic elections since Franco's death as well as the signing of the Moncloa Pacts by many of the political groupings and trade unions. The pacts guaranteed increased unemployment benefits, new corporate taxes, and a permanent tax on wealth. Left-wing parties and trade unions were enthusiastic about the Pacts, seeing them as a substantial change for the better for the working class. Writing of the effects of these economic changes on working class life Joni D. writes, "As far as they were concerned (the working class) twenty years earlier they had been famished and this was a revolution in itself" (p. 74 below). Many of the Workers Assemblies set up in some factories to challenge management and economic structures soon became subsumed back into union and party structures.

On their return to Spain the CNT had experienced a renaissance in support. Its first meeting in Spain since 1939 was held on the July 2, 1977 in Barcelona with a crowd estimated at 300,000. Some of the Grupos were members of the organization and some supported the CNT without joining.

Their apparent popularity was seen as a major threat to governance. The CNT clearly opposed the Moncloa Pacts and on Sunday January 15, 1978 held a demonstration of between 10–15,000 people in Barcelona against the Pacts. Later that day the Scala nightclub in Barcelona was firebombed and four workers (two of whom were CNT members) died in the resulting fire. Some CNT members were quickly arrested. It was later proved that this firebombing was instigated by a police agent provocateur and there were always doubts about how the fire bombs could have caused the conflagration to spread as quickly as it did. All this would come out later but for the CNT the damage had been done. The Spanish state's position was made clear by the statement from Minister of the Interior Ricardo

Martin Villa who claimed that anarchist violence in the shape of the attack on the Scala and other incidents was the most worrying violence in Spain, its biggest challenge, and had to be eradicated.

In these cultural and political settings the Grupos carried on their activities. Now the fight was with capitalist democracy not the smothering brutality of the Francoist state. The conflict was between those whose saw the demise of Franco as a time to put their energies into the creation of a capitalist democracy in Spain and those whose energies went into the creation of a Spain based on economic and social equality and freedom from all hierarchies.

In our view, *Agitated* is a work of exemplary radical history. And it is exciting to have this work available in English where we can see a fuller picture of the Grupos than ever before. Their story is told blemishes and all, often using the experiences of some of the people involved to bring events and activities to life. Some may want to offer critiques in the future (and we have no doubt that Grupos participants have done that themselves) but we need this book to rescue the people involved, their stories, and their actions from the condescension of posterity and the political amnesia of history.

Kate Sharpley Library, July 2022

FOREWORD, BY MATEO SEGUÍ

"A realist novel." This book by Joni D. reads like a novel but a "realist" novel, it has to be said. Real since it focuses on setting out the evolution of the "*autónomos*." A fine effort to stop the historians from "historicizing" fiction and officialdom, to focus on knowing and revealing that a lot of people spent much of their lives in jails, asking nothing in return. Characters who troop through the book with some very clear-cut principles: defeating "the powers-that-be," but not in order to replace them and place themselves at the head of the citizenry, like the so-called "anti-Francoists" did during the Spanish political transition following the dictator's death, by coming to an accommodation with and drawing a veil over the damage done by the Civil War. No, defeating the "powers-that-be" in order to live differently.

I remember from the conversations I had with former autónomos that the roots of the *grupos autónomos* ran deep. During the Republic and especially in Catalonia, with the CNT (Confederación Nacional del Trabajo / National Confederation of Labor) being the majority (or quite possibly the only) trade union, grupos autónomos were set up, dedicated to robbing banks in order to use the proceeds to further the revolution. They operated along autonomous lines, tied to the CNT, but engaging in individualized activities outside of their trade union activities. We can see from the narratives in this book that the activity of members of the grupos autónomos was rooted in their repudiation of the official reality and rejection of what they were being taught, standing up to an imposed education in order to embark upon a different life. They reacted to their schooling and official cultural education by conjuring up alternatives, the underlying principle of which was rebelliousness plus fraternity, a preparedness to suffer imprisonment rather than be gobbled up by the prevailing system.

Through all the years when the grupos autónomos were most active, I can bear witness in my professional capacity to their altruistic and fraternal motives. Naturally, the official society made its mark on them, forcing them out of circulation and doing all it could to blacken their reputations. Joni explains the devastation caused by the drug culture and the infiltration of undesirable characters into the ranks of the autónomos.

I stated at the outset that what we have here is a novel, if by novel we mean an adventure that set out to destroy the official authorities, holding nothing back and putting one's own life on the line in order to achieve this. It is hard fighting against "giants." As explained in this book, the autónomos at least gave it a go and their spirit has imbued later generations. Power and authority are still vested in a few hands, but the lesson of brotherliness stands. No one will be able to argue that they did nothing; they did something, and the authorities came down on them like a ton of bricks, but their courage, their idealism can never, ever be destroyed.

I have used the term "fraternity" several times and have done so because the term was explained to me by our beloved Nunes. He stated, "these days there is much talk of 'solidarity,'" a notion that he understood as akin to doing somebody a good turn, but from above, rather than face-to-face, "but fraternity is what happens between human beings who are equals, with no one superior to anyone else." I learned this lesson from Nunes and, having observed it close up, it strikes me that the autónomos' chief ideal was to take action against the powerful by forming groups in which everyone was an equal.

One day "history" will tell us what influence they had on the way of life. This book is a first attempt to shed light on the human character of members of the grupos autónomos and is, I reckon, a starting point for anyone deluded, helping them to realize that the "official reality" is wrong and that there is more to life.

In the "Workers' Autonomy" section, there is a very interesting description of the impact on the world of work, trade union activity back in the day, the Moncloa Palace Agreements, the petrol pump attendants' struggles, etc.

There is also the very enlightening "Culture for Change" section. In my view, these are matters that cannot be set to one side but rather cry out for thorough exploration. As I have said, this book is a start and a reading of it is an invitation to study, positing that nothing is over, that there is a long way yet to go.

To conclude, allow me an anecdote. When the "work" issue was opened to debate inside the grupos autónomos, "work" being understood as a system of exploitation at the hands of capitalism, the autónomos came to the following conclusion: "Down with work" and, raising the issue at the time with autónomos who were serving time in Segovia Prison, I told them "I find your conclusion very interesting and I propose to make it mine," at which point they kicked up a stink and told me "Work on getting us out of jail."

I found the reading of this book a pleasure. Joni has done sterling work here and it is now up to somebody else to pick up the baton.

Mateo Seguí

AUTHOR'S INTRODUCTION

This story started many years ago—seventeen, to be precise—when, as luck would have it, I made the acquaintance of Irma. Irma was never a member of any of the grupos autónomos, but she was part of the support network and that was what led to her being arrested. Later, she was but one of the thousands of those damned for having lived through those heated years and, though a heroin addict, she worked a thousand and one wonders for the comrades prior to her leaving for exile. From that exile she fondly remembered those whom she could so easily have damaged.

Eleven years later, in December 2007, I lived through the second chapter of this story when, together with the comrades from the Associació d'Amics d'Agustín Rueda in Sallent and those from the Centre de Documentació Josep Ester i Borràs in Berga, we set about cataloging the archives of the Associació, which at the time were held at the Centre de Documentació. It was in Berga that the Sallent comrades expressed their wish to see a book published that would tell the story of those young dreamers who squandered their youth on a struggle that ended in a defeat, a defeat that translated into years in prison, exile, or, in Agustín's case, murder.

The final nudge came in September 2010 when, with the help of the internet, I tracked down Petit Loup, with whom I had identified back in my adolescent years as I pored over the letters he used to send to *La Lletra A*, letters always signed by "A Pyrenean native."

In the end, after an "investigation" begun in December 2007 but put on the back-burner for three years while I was writing, publishing, and distributing *Que pagui Pujol!*, I made up my mind in February 2012 that I would make a start on writing these pages, which make no claim to being a history of the armed grupos autónomos but are merely a first draft of one.

All throughout the work I have had to make decisions regarding the format of it. The first decision related to its boundaries. I had it clear in my mind that I wanted to write a study of the armed, libertarian grupos autónomos. The folks who had shunned even the historical libertarian organizations and employed armed agitation as a propaganda tool. I should like to stipulate something here.

3

There were libertarian grupos autónomos who steered well clear of the wide-spread recourse to violence. This study focuses on the ones that decided to practice armed struggle, albeit that the dividing-lines between the two camps may at times have been blurred, especially during the final years of Francoism when they all had to live under the same circumstances of clandestinity. At the same time, I decided that there were a couple of these groups—the MIL (Movimiento Ibérico de Liberación / Iberian Liberation Movement) and the CAA (Comandos Autónomos Anticapitalistas / Anticapitalist Autonomous Commandos—upon which I had no wish to dwell, since there were already several books in existence based on their experiences. Which is why this book begins with the dismantling of the MIL and makes only passing references to the Comandos.

The next doubt I had to clear up was how I was going to highlight the significance of the individual development of the young people behind these groups, while simultaneously touching upon the actual creation of the network, which came about almost casually over the passage of time. For that reason, this book is made up of two kinds of chapters, clearly differentiated but always interwoven throughout the text as a whole. One kind explores the personal evolution of some activists. The other depicts the social and historical context in which they were living. The former being based on the memories of the protagonists, albeit that the texts have been enriched by and assayed against newspaper archives. The second kind is the result of a historical study of the time period assembled through those same newspaper collections.

The third issue centered on names. Some of the comrades interviewed had no wish to see their full particulars given. I opted to use their nicknames in the case of the activists interviewed and those of some of their comrades in the more personal chapters, whereas I use their actual particulars in the historically contextualizing chapters where these have already been cited in print. I have, however, allowed myself the odd exception here and there.

Having decided on these matters, an emotional time came that I shall never forget. A minor discovery that weighed on my mind. Halfway through the book, just as I was tying up the loose ends, I was able to track down the person who had accompanied Agustín Rueda in his journey toward anarchism in the Modelo Prison, thanks to Manel Tirado's recollections, support from Iñaki García and with the aid of the internet (the internet again!). When I first called him, even though we were not then acquainted, I could hear the emotion in his words. Forty years after sharing a cell with Agustín, Andrés Grima had not been expecting the call. Over the summer of 2012, thirty-five years after his last glimpse of his friend's face, Andrés was able to fulfill a longstanding ambition. To meet María, the sister of his cellmate.

And now to finish, since this should have been quite a short introduction, allow me to thank all those nameless battlers whose names are not Petit Loup, Sabata, Roger, Llengües, Gerard, José, Dani, Juan, Felipe, Paco, Miguel, Juanjo, Michel, or Víctor, for having, in many cases for the very first time, filled me in on their story, or part of it.

This book would not be what it is but for the assistance of María Rueda, Andrés Grima, Iñaki García, Bombetes, Sebas, Vigo, Titina, Víctor Simal, Antonio, Francesc Llimona, Hortensia Inés, Enric Melich, Gonzalo Wilhelmi, Manel Tirado, René Álvarez, Daniel Pont, Jakue Paskual, David Fernández, and Mateo Seguí.

Very special thanks to David Castillo, Oscar Espuña, Marta Ch., Guiomar Rovira, and Txell Freixinet for their literary and grammatical support in the original edition. Olalla Castro has helped me enormously by proofing much of the Spanish-language edition.

Thanks also to the women comrades who see to the upkeep of the El Aurea Social library, the La Ciutat Invisible documentation center, and the Josep Ester i Borràs documentation center.

To Carlos Undergroove for his enthusiasm when it came to turning this book into something visually presentable.

Not that I have forgotten all those who egged me on throughout my research and have, in many cases, also had to suffer my one-track conversation, namely: Joan and Imma, Quim and Eva, Gregor, Chucho, Jimmy and Manoli, José Santainés, Raúl and Teresa, Pere Miralles, Dolors Marín, Carles Viñas, Jesús Rodríguez, Irene, and Janian.

Dedicated to Irma, El Jebo, Agustín Rueda, Joan Conesa, Miquel Mulet, Cri Cri, and all who gave their lives in so many different ways while dreaming of a different world.

But for the patience and unwavering support of Amparo, this would not have been possible.

Jara, don't let them push you around, but if they do . . . Think—and gather up the seeds.

To the comrades from the Associació d'Amics d'Agustín Rueda. To those that keep the memory alive.

PROLOGUE: IRMA

Viewed from the air, the city was more than the human eye could take in. The hundreds of thousands of buildings surrounded by the hundreds of thousands of shacks in the mountains around them, were too much for just two eyes. In the late-afternoon of that day in March 1996, the DF (Federal District) was teeming. A little over two years before, there had been the native uprising in Chiapas, and the two young people from Barcelona, in their thirties, were keen to see and experience the situation for themselves. A revolution in the twilight years of the twentieth century; the least significant folk in the land had said "Enough!"

The plane landed and once in the airport building the duo joined the appropriate queue to request an entry visa: "Reason for trip?" the Mexican official asked. "Tourism," they replied. They had never been to Mexico before but were very clear that if they were caught in possession of all the legal tender from several European countries that they had on them (French francs, German marks, Italian lire and Spanish pesetas), they would not be doing so on this occasion, and it would be hard for them to do so in the future. They passed through the first checks, having secured their tourist visas. Back in Barcelona they had been warned that they would then run into the "traffic lights." Traffic lights are the Mexican officials' curious method for deciding whether someone needs to be searched before entering the country. Every visitor has to press a button and if the traffic lights in front of him go green, he is free to enter Mexico unmolested; on the other hand, if the red lights up, the forces of law and order deploy to frisk the visitor. It was the only time they felt nervous. They had confidence that they would get over the border but leaving that decision up to a random traffic light was not to their liking. In the end, she was the one to press the button first. As the green lit up, they both crossed the supposed red line without giving the red light another chance to be triggered next time around.

Like so many other young activists from the 1980s and 1990s, they had come to the libertarian movement through music. Which ensured that their sole contact, the only address they had in the D.F., was that of an autonomous, libertarian music center on Calle Cuauhtémoc in the Roma District, the one known (as a

tribute to the northern Italian free radio station of the mid-1970s) as the Foro
Alicia.

The young couple, on leaving the airport, climbed into a taxi and gave the
driver that address. The traffic was chaotic and the distance enormous (given that
it was still within the same city boundaries) but the cab finally pulled up in front
of a graffiti-daubed wall which was obviously the entrance to the libertarian premises. As they ventured inside, they found themselves in a room ten meters long and
four wide, its walls and ceiling bedecked with posters produced by the same collective that ran the premises. Posters promoting concerts held at the Foro Alicia
and posters on political and social themes, printed up in support of campaigns
mounted in concert with other groups or to boost brand-new campaigns devised
by the "Alicia." Off to the left, stretching from just past the halfway mark in the
room as far as the rear wall, there was a bar behind which were some shelves displaying, not bottles of alcohol, but compact discs and other items for distribution,
many of them homemade. Between the bar and the shelves, a woman older than
themselves was in charge of serving up the beer and attending to whatever comrades stepped inside the Foro; hearing them converse in Catalan, she volunteered
to put them up at her place.

She said her name was Irma.

Irma had arrived in the DF in 1985, the year the earthquake struck, weeks after
the awful day when the earth moved beneath the city on September 19. She found
a city in rubble, shattered, families separated, a lot of folks eking out a bare living
on the streets, and broken lives galore. An effort was underway to return to normality, but it was not easy, the city had collapsed. Amid all the chaos, Irma found
it easy to pass unnoticed and embark on a new life.

She was born in 1957, lived out her youth in Barcelona and by 1985 had to flee.
Her collusion with armed sections of the libertarian grupos autónomos brought
about her "fall" (arrest in the jargon of the activists of the late 1970s and early
1980s) in a police operation picked up by the newspapers of the day because of the
high number of activists rounded up and the importance of a number of them.
The members of the Brigada were out to get Irma. She was one of the girls who
stood out most in the demonstrations. She was forever being spotted in the front
lines during clashes, something that the macho police officers could not tolerate
since they felt that they were being made to look ridiculous by someone they reckoned belonged to the weaker sex.

Her fall was triggered by an unwitting betrayal. Toward the end of 1980, the
members of one Valencian grupo autónomo crossed the border into France to
pick up some weapons for which a number of Barcelona comrades had placed an
order. They were to collect the gear, smuggle it over the border and, on reaching
Barcelona, hand it over. In the south of France there were still a few groups of

Spanish exiles and French libertarians who had arms caches that were often put to use on Spanish soil. In some instances, these were the very same guns as had been used by comrades from the libertarian maquis, who had packed it in after the murder of Ramón Vila Capdevila ("Caracremada") on August 7, 1963. However, the Valencian comrades decided to capitalize upon their possession of the weapons in order to mount an operation on home ground before passing them on to the Barcelona comrades. That operation went awry, and the group in Valencia was broken up at the beginning of October. The gear had been lost. With them was El Francés, an activist who often collaborated with the Barcelona comrades that had placed the order; once arrested, he let slip a name, a name that he thought was just a nickname, but which turned out to be a real name, although quite an unusual one, and this triggered the arrests in Barcelona. By means of rendezvous and precautionary phone calls, the Barcelona comrades who were waiting for the guns got wind of the arrests that same night and decided to make for the apartment of Irma and her comrades near La Ciudadela at the end of the Calle Princesa, to tip them off and help clear the apartment of incriminating materials, since they too had had dealings with El Francés. Unfortunately, they did not have much time and the very next day members of the security forces showed up. In the course of several searches, they made twelve arrests and confiscated numerous identity papers, traveler's checks, and savings books from the Caja Postal to the tune of five million pesetas, all of it counterfeit, plus a couple of revolvers. One of the people arrested had successfully infiltrated the FN (Fuerza Nueva / New Force) and it looked as if blowing up the FN headquarters in Barcelona had been under consideration. A few days later, on October 16, the chief of police called a press conference on the raid. By that time, half of those arrested had already been released, even though his briefing made much of the twelve arrests and not of the subsequent releases.

Shortly after that, Irma fell victim to the lure of escapism and began dabbling in heroin, which at that time rendered sterling service to the state by making nonsense of all the social prisoners' demands for a collective amnesty. Now suffering from an addiction that she could not shake, Irma kept in touch with the autónomo network, and a number of innocent comrades suffered the consequences when they entrusted her with cash meant for a number of struggles. By 1985, the situation had become unsustainable, and Irma fled. She had no desire to carry on with her life of deceiving and lying to her fellow activists.

Not that Irma forgot her past once in Mexico. Her home was open house for some comrades who passed that way, comrades such as Petit Loup, whom she taught how to move through the frenzied city during his first stay there. They used to do the shopping together or shared the cooking, preparing tasty dishes for sharing later with other comrades.

Inmaculada Ventura Llobet (Irma) died in Mexico on August 9, 2008.

1.

GRUPOS AUTÓNOMOS

ACTION GROUPS

"Insurrections in their beginnings are almost always like an adventure, with
a high likelihood of one's getting lost or coming out of the attempt defeated.
The advantage of defeats of that sort is that they can never be final, because
they represent instructive chapters that are added to the history of proletarian
struggle."

—BUENAVENTURA DURRUTI

The grupos autónomos were the 1970s equivalents of the historical anarchist
affinity groups of the first third of the twentieth century—obviously with
differences resulting from the stark contrasts in the way of life during the two
periods. Whereas the affinity groups evolved in a working-class society that
aspired to purity in order to shrug off the whole brutalizing burden of centuries
of oppression, and which had molded itself with the tools that the anarchist labor
organizations had made available to it (*ateneos*, libraries, rationalist schools, etc.),
the grupos autónomos were mostly recruited from among educated but greenhorn youngsters, utterly without expertise and with no experience to fall back
on (except in a few isolated cases) in relation to the everyday reality of struggle,
things like clandestinity, arms procurement, or self-organization. Furthermore,
after nearly forty years of repression at every level (educational, religious, sexual,
cultural, etc.), these youngsters wanted to learn for its own sake rather than simply
for an ideal. They not only welcomed but were grateful for any sort of impurity,
seizing upon any chink that might allow them to enjoy life in the raw, if only for a
few minutes. They had no taboos, no inhibitions, no rules, no gods, and no mas-
ters. Running away from everything that had been inculcated into them up to that
point: "You could say that we were all running away from something: military

service, the factory floor, the worksite, the lecture halls, family, religion, ideology, prison, society."[1]

Those youngsters were madly enthusiastic and often failed to foresee the consequences their actions were going to have for themselves, such as the time one group in Valencia was dismantled after its members were arrested sleeping in a vehicle laden with weapons on the very doorstep of a bank they had set out to expropriate. Or that time in late 1977 or early 1978 when Petit Loup was strolling through the narrow streets of the Barrio Gótico in Barcelona and came upon a silhouette that was oddly familiar to him. That gait, that back, it had to be El Moro; there was no doubt about it. Just before stepping up to hail him, Petit Loup realized that El Moro was carrying in his hand a plastic bag from some major store, and, in that bag, the barrel of a submachinegun was poking out through a hole. Petit Loup picked up his step and when level with his comrade, and without as much as glancing in his direction, he surreptitiously whispered to him: "Your iron is showing," before striding on, slightly shocked by his friend's carelessness.

They wanted to break with everything that they had experienced since they were young and at one point they believed that their resolve could tip the scales in the direction of global liberation; this was something they needed as human beings at any rate: to fight for absolute liberation, meaning educational, religious, sexual, cultural, work-based, political liberation. They were committed to the extent of being ready to offer up their lives for what they believed in, but, on the other hand, such was their lust for life and their craving to live that, at the last moment, after the battle was lost, they were quite capable of slipping back into the normality imposed by the capitalist system without in any way feeling rueful for having fought it so fiercely: "It never occurred to us that our struggle would be setting an example; it went no further than being simply ours; we were not embracing it for life; it just struck us as the most effective option RIGHT NOW. That was all."[2] Some of them, like Juan, once the fight had ended and the PSOE (Partido Socialista Obrero Español / Spanish Workers' Socialist Party) was in power, when he had the chance of getting out of jail early in return for his signature on a piece of paper disavowing his actions, decided to serve out his legal term rather than abdicate his own dignity. They gave their lives, neither lapsing into playing the martyr nor going on to renounce their ideas just to save their own necks. Not all of them, though, made it home again after the fray. The winner

---

1. M. Amorós et al., *Por la memoria anticapitalista: Reflexiones sobre la autonomía* (Barcelona, Klinamen, 2009), 188.

2. Barcelona Grupo Autónomo, "Comunicado a la Opinión Pública," March 1978, in *Comunicados de la prisión de Segovia y otros llamamientos a la guerra social* (Bilbao: Muturreko Bututazoiak, 2005), 19–20.

did not make do with winning the battle and provided his warriors with all the weapons in his arsenal to ensure that there would be no repetition: "And what was the upshot of it all? A certain illusory feeling, disproportionate police and court repression, a return to order and the advent of hard drugs like heroin, a snare that did it in for many of the activists that refused to be cowed by the orders coming from the powers-that-be."[3]

The earliest known groups, the MIL and the so-called OLLA (Organització de Lluita Armada / Armed Struggle Organization), which emerged during the first half of the 1970s, at a time when the dictator was still alive, were a synthesis of the spontaneously libertarian forms of action of the youth with the maverick Marxist ideology that had spread through the workplaces and state universities. A lot of them, Roger for one, were drawn to the libertarian movement as a natural reaction against the centralism and authoritarianism of Leninists, Stalinists, Maoists, Trotskyists, and other orthodox communists striving to lead the everyday mini-revolts that were beginning to spread through the length and breadth of the Iberian peninsula. Situationism opened new doors beyond which struggles were more fun, satirical, and provocative. Meanwhile, young people rejected inflexible arrangements that did not sit well with the frenzied times in which they were offered a self-indulgent, consumer society. A motley crew of students, workers, philosophers, and activists swayed by the worldwide counterculture, Llengües's generation was drawn mainly to propaganda to spread the revolt in order to, as a first step, topple the fascist regime, and later, to end capitalism.

The second cohort of autonomous groups was very different. It emerged in 1974, during actions in support of the MIL prisoners, and activists like Michel and Sabata never lost sight of that. Their aim was to "demonstrate, as the MIL had intended, that the level of violence that could and therefore should be deployed in answer to capitalist violence was much greater than commonly believed."[4] On the night of March 2–3, 1975, a year on from the murder of Puig Antich, a device exploded at the foot of the Monument to the Fallen in Madrid. In 1976, on Friday, February 27, a group of youngsters intercepted a bus on Barcelona's Calle Pelai, forced all its passengers to step off and set it on fire, while a second group threw Molotov cocktails at the branch of the Banco Hispano-Americano in the same street. On March 2, again in Barcelona, there were several attempts to mount demonstrations (one of which drew in excess of three thousand people, according to La Vanguardia) in the course of which several bank branches were set on fire. The media reported simultaneous acts of vandalism and propaganda distribution

---

3. D. Castillo, *Barcelona: Fragments de la* contracultura (Barcelona, Ajuntament de Barcelona, 2010), 14.

4. M. Amorós, *Por la memoria anticapitalista*, 185.

on Calle Canaletas, on Calle Hospital, at the intersection of the Rambla de
Catalunya and Calle Aragón, at the intersection of Calle Urgell and Calle de la
Diputación, and in the Calvo Sotelo area (today's Plaza de Francesc Macià).

Such coordinated acts were one of the characteristic features of those years of
clandestinity when demonstrations were banned. They were referred to as "leaps"
(*saltos*) and required no more than twenty or so people; once the demonstrators had assembled at a given location, traffic could be stopped, leaflets setting
out demands could be flung into the air, graffiti daubed, and hand-picked targets
attacked, whereupon the crowd would evaporate, having arranged to reassemble at
the next targeted location. Mobility and the absence of any pre-announced gatherings thwarted any police response.

In Valencia on February 27, 1977, several branches of the Banco de Vizcaya,
Banco de Bilbao, Banco Hispano-Americano, and the Levantina Insurance
Company were targeted; in Madrid on March 1, a device exploded at the headquar-
ters of the Justice Ministry; and in Barcelona on March 2, Molotov cocktails were
thrown at the police station on Calle Santaló, along with the Liceu and branches
of the Banca Catalana, Banco de Bilbao, and Banco Español de Crédito. Again
in Valencia, on March 5, Molotov cocktails touched off fires at three branches of
Banco Popular, Banco Santander, and Banco de Vizcaya. Four days after that, in
Madrid, the branches torched belonged to the Banco Popular, the Banca March,
Banesto, and the Banco de Vizcaya. And the day after that, it was a branch of the
Banco Occidental.

And the anniversaries of the last firing squad executions carried out by the
Franco regime were red-letter days. On September 27, 1976, the headquarters of
the Telefónica company in Valencia came under attack; the following day, Molotov
cocktails rained down on the El Corte Inglés department store in Madrid, and
the day after that, four Civil Guard barracks in the national capital came under
the same sort of attack. On September 27, 1977, an explosive device attached to a
placard protesting against the death penalty and placed on a bridge on the Mataró
motorway was defused; responsibility for the planting of it was claimed in a telephone call by "Badalona anarchists."

It was no coincidence that actions of this sort, marking the anniversaries
of incidents that had left a deep impression on that generation of youngsters,
were being set aside from 1978 onward, when the sheer dynamic of direct confrontation forced them to park the historical demands that had emerged under
Francoism and focus instead upon their day-to-day struggles; from the start of
1978 onward, the activities of informers and infiltrators triggered an unrelenting
series of falls that forced them to step up their precautions. The dates in question
were also red-letter days in the calendars of the security forces, who were ready
and waiting.

These were youngsters who, like the Valencian Paco, had already read the classic anarchist authors, who were in touch, most of them, with the historical Spanish libertarian structures in exile (albeit that they were aware of the great differences between themselves and the elderly activists belonging to these structures), and who very quickly were drawn into a spiral that hardly ever allowed them to seize the initiative.

After an initial year-long apprenticeship, driven by the stark reality with which the murder of Puig Antich had confronted them, these groups experienced 1975 as a sort of a period of truce, but by the beginning of 1976, after the death of the dictator, they were throwing everything they had into an all-out war. They were far-sighted. They saw and had a very clear picture of the system that was being assembled around Franco's graveside: "These days there is no one so naive . . . as to dare deny that we under a despotism as tough and degrading and hard to bear as the one that existed in Franco's day, and, as time wears on, it is going to get worse."[5] They were not fighting the dictatorship now. They were fighting the establishment of the Bourbons to the throne and a capitalism imposed by the United States and by the big capitalist transnationals, a capitalism hell bent on perpetuating state oppression of the citizenry by circumventing any chance of a clean break and any attempt to open the gates to a revolt that might usher in any political and, more specially, economic change: "It was the only possible endeavor worth undertaking, if we take 'possible endeavor' to mean the only thing that needs doing in this modern age—destruction of the capitalist mode of production."[6]

Their struggle was characterized by a constant learning process. Students from the chemistry departments were the ones chiefly responsible for the earliest experimentation with explosive devices, in many instances carried out in disused former quarries, while students from the departments of medicine took care of certain complicated situations arising out of clashes with the police or lack of expertise in the handling of dangerous materials. Training with firearms was not carried out in remote logistical bases in the backside of nowhere, but took place in our forests, at rapid pace, and, by implication, was inadequate, exploiting hunting seasons when a couple of gunshots might go undetected. Clandestinity forced them into continual improvisation, although they did try to establish sound bases to sustain what might turn out to be a protracted struggle. Weapons were often passed from hand to hand and had no owners and, whenever the members of one group had need of one in order to mount some operation, it was normal practice for activists from a better equipped group to lend them one. Víctor's group

---

5. Guy Debord, "A los libertarios," September 1980, in *Comunicados de la prisión de Segovia,* 76.

6. Grupos Autónomos, "Presentación," in *Comunicados de la prisión de Segovia,* 14.

lent him a pistol so that he could hold up a police officer and thereby acquire his first proper firearm. Whenever repression from the state apparatus was unleashed with full force, solidarity was vital if any minimally effective effort was to be made. The support of numerous comrades to help get those in jeopardy over the border was vital.

Another constant factor, again by way of a response to repression, was solidarity with various armed resistance groups such as the RAF (Rote Armee Fraktion / Red Army Faction) in Germany; on May 13, 1976, following activist Ulrike Meinhof"s death in prison, an attack with incendiary devices burned out two floors of the Hoechst Ibérica company premises in Barcelona. A year later, on April 21, 1977, the Lufthansa offices in Barcelona suffered an attack mounted in solidarity with the RAF members undergoing trial in Stammheim, and on October 20 of that year, the deaths in prison of other militants led to a Molotov cocktail attack on the German consulate in San Sebastián. In Madrid, on November 11, Molotov cocktails targeted the outlets of Porsche and Mantequerías Alemanas in the city and, on November 19, a dynamite charge went off at the German School in the city. Nearly four years later, the Hoechst company's Barcelona offices came under attack again, this time in the shape of an explosive device, by way of a response to the death on hunger strike of the activist Sigurd Debus; that operation was claimed by the EAA (Escamots Autònoms Anticapitalistes / Anticapitalist Autonomous Commandos). Such solidarity actions were a two-way street, since, on August 10, 1978, a French libertarian *groupe autonome* demanded the release of autonomous activists jailed in Barcelona and Madrid by mounting an attack on a police station in Montpellier.

Solidarity was the number one driver behind the various groups that coalesced into the EAA, of which Miguel was a member. One of those groups, named after Oriol Solé Sugranyes, in homage to the MIL comrade murdered years earlier, claimed responsibility in July 1980 for the attack mounted against the Banco Comercial Español in the Paseo de Gràcia in Barcelona, in response to the conviction of some ERAT (Ejército Revolucionario de Ayuda a los Trabajadores / Revolutionary Army for Helping the Workers) members tried some days earlier. Another group planted a TNT charge in the office of the Crédit Lyonnais on February 18, 1981, in response to the arrest in France four days before of fourteen activists with ties to the CAA (Comandos Autónomos Anticapitalistas / Anticapitalist Autonomous Commandos). Also part of this dynamic were operations in the summer of 1977 designed to thwart the extradition of the ETA (Euskadi ta Askatasuna / Basque Homeland and Freedom) militant Apala. In Barcelona on August 29, during one of the earliest demonstrations, Molotov cocktails were thrown at the SEPU shopping center on the Ramblas. A few days later, on September 3, two Barcelona buses were torched while a third was sent careering into the Banco Popular Español branch on the Ronda de San Antonio. Not that these were the only actions. The daily tension in the city center ensured that between September 13 and October 8 the media reported the arrest of twenty-seven youths in connection with urban guerrilla actions mounted in the city at the end of that summer; these youngsters were linked with the FIJL (Federación Ibérica de Juventudes Libertarias / Iberian Libertarian Youth Federation).

This was another peculiarity of these youngsters, the persistent linkage made between them and outfits in which they were not involved. The media were forever reprinting police reports tying the grupos autónomos to the FAI (Federación Anarquista Ibérica / Iberian Anarchist Federation), CNT or FIJL, to start with and, later, to supposed organizations styled as the Grupos Específicas Anarquistas (Anarchist Specific Groups) or later, the Grupos Autónomos Armados (Armed Autonomous Groups). While it is a fact that many of them, especially in Barcelona, at some point became CNT members and even, as in José's case, acquired a certain profile inside the union, most of them remained aloof and generally withdrew from membership before moving on to armed agitation.

Elections were also red-letter days. On June 13, 1977, two days ahead of the first general elections under the brand-new democratic regime, a dynamite charge went off at the courthouse in Barcelona. Eight months later, one grupo autónomo that was linked to the operation was dismantled. The night before election day, two devices exploded in Córdoba, one at the city courthouse and the other at a building housing several ministerial agencies. A device exploded in Seville at the courthouse there, while in Málaga the target was an electricity pylon. Another pylon was damaged by a bomb attack in Madrid and in Alcorcón an explosive device underneath the desk at a polling station was defused. In Valencia, several Molotov cocktails were thrown. On March 1, 1979, during the next round of the elections, a bottle filled with incendiary materials was thrown at the Sant Josep de la Muntanya Civil Guard barracks in Barcelona. In all likelihood, not all of the actions were the handiwork of grupos autónomos or libertarians but the very fact that there were no claims of responsibility made inclines us to believe that most of them were.

Indeed, one factor at the time was the determination of the police when it came to trying to play down the activities both of the anarchist groups and of the autónomos, especially outside of the Barcelona area, ascribing actions mounted by these groups to other, armed, authoritarian Marxist organizations: "On occasion, the failure to claim responsibility for some of these (attacks, expropriations, etc.) leads to some organizations or grouplets claiming them in order to create the illusion of a potency they do not possess and earn themselves recognition as the most effective in their competition with the state."[7] This modus operandi on the part of the police and other armed groups particularly affected the Madrid groups. Some of the actions in which Juanjo was involved were claimed by or attributed to the FRAP (Frente Revolucionario Antifascista y Patriótica / Revolutionary Antifascist Patriotic Front).

All in all, the struggle was an existential one, and the dynamic of it prioritized individualism within the voluntary collective over hierarchization and any sort of pecking order within the groups themselves. The autonomy of the individuals making up the groups was one of the core conditions of their actions. Although there were some groups which were fairly stable, this being a boost to their security, there were others in which activists participated sporadically. There were situations where a four- or five-man group carried out an action that required participation by several dozen comrades. This was an important part of networking as well as the most fragile aspect of it: this ability to mobilize unconnected people who ultimately linked up, albeit without any real appreciation of the extent of the action. The best known of such actions were, of course, the various organized, cross-European campaigns to cash phony checks, but there were others at the local level that used the same approach without their being made public by the police since that would have meant an implicit acknowledgment of the ease with which such expropriations were being carried out.

There was also "personal" action, meaning active engagement by youngsters who, while not signed up with any specific group, took part in the actions of various groups, using different names in each. This would ensure that they could not be tracked down should any of the groups be dismantled. French activist Alain Drogou provides one example of this: in 1980, he was arrested with a Valencian grupo autónomo. He had previously taken part in actions carried out by a Barcelona-based group and later, in 1985, was arrested again for his ties to the FIGA (Federación Ibérica de Grupos Anarquistas / Iberian Anarchist Groups' Federation). This was also the case with Manuel Muner, who was arrested in 1979 with a Barcelona grupo autónomo. Two years later, he fell in Errenteria and was linked to the Catalan EAA. In 1985, he was again arrested, this time in the Basque Country, and linked with the CAA.

This mobility between groups also applied to cities that were far apart. A lot of youngsters, after having exposed themselves too often in one town would move away to a different city in order to join local comrades there in carrying on the struggle. This was a necessary precaution, particularly when friends and acquaintances were arrested. One such example was Paco from Madrid when he moved

---

7. Grupos Autónomos, "Comunicado de los grupos autónomos," January 1979, in *Comunicados de la prisión de Segovia*, 23–24.

away to Lisbon. But such mobility was not to be found only in such cases; entire groups or significant numbers of their members moved around in order to mount activities far from their own home ground.

There was political mobility as well. A far cry from orthodoxy, communication, and collaboration with other sectors of the revolutionary left was a reality: "It wasn't a matter of ideological choice but of practicality."[8] During the most pugnacious Barcelona demonstrations, Dani used to rub shoulders mainly with members of the PCE(i) (Partido Comunista de España [internacional] / Communist Party of Spain [international]). This engagement during street activity sometime used to create ties of affinity which then carried over into other, riskier sorts of activity where the improvisational approach used on the streets was not feasible. This situation was replicated in Catalonia as well as in the Basque Country, especially between the libertarian movement and the pro-independence left. Such collaboration came from afar, from exile and, in the Catalan case, especially, it dated back to Perpignan where, between 1973 and 1977, a lot of these young people had rubbed shoulders with one another. This was no blinkered collaboration: every so often, it created sparks. Like when, right there in Perpignan, during a Lluís Llach concert in 1976, a bunch of young libertarians unfurled a black *senyera* (the Catalan flag) on stage and some pro-independence revolutionary groups went ape at that sacrilege. But, aside from any theoretical arguments, there were comrades from both camps who had no problem collaborating actively. Such was the case of José Digón, an ex-member of the FAC (Front d'Alliberament Català / Catalan Liberation Front) who was arrested in 1983 during the breakup of a Barcelona-based grupo autónomo. After linking him to Terra Lliure, the police reported that he was the link between the pro-independence armed organization and the libertarian grupo autónomo. Digón had lived in Perpignan in the dying days of Francoism. A joint campaign was mounted in order to avoid his extradition to Belgium as well as to demand the release of a couple of pro-independence prisoners and a libertarian prisoner—Gerard—who also had that threat hanging over him. Digón was jailed and tried for his part, alongside members of the grupo autónomo, in three bank holdups. Pro-independence militant Joan Carles Monteagudo also took part in one of these holdups.

The grupos tended to be short-lived and their lives were marked chiefly by imminent police repression, but a few comrades managed to stay active for about five years without mishap, like the group in which El Profe was involved. The media reported on August 4, 1979, that a dozen anarchists had been arrested in Barcelona and that they were being linked with armed raids mounted five years previously—the first of which was on December 12, 1974, when a gang of

---

8. M. Amorós, *Por la memoria anticapitalista*, 185.

youngsters held up the Roca gun store on Calle Aribau. But some of those arrested had been involved in armed agitational actions ever since the dismantling of the MIL and were publicly linked to the odd OLLA action. The most extreme case of which we have knowledge is that of a comrade who was a member of the OLLA and who had first been jailed after he was arrested on February 5, 1984. A member of one of the very first grupos, he was one of the last Catalan autónomos to fall.

One of their inviolable principles was that there was to be no spilling of blood: "Our greatest concern was always that we would claim no innocent victims. Actually, in that we were successful. Our preference was to abort an operation or take additional risks rather than place a life in jeopardy."[9] One such youngster, put in charge of the planting of explosive devices (against financial targets for the most part), set off his last bomb one hapless afternoon when the timer switch failed to work properly. The device went off prematurely and injured a woman. Never again did the youngster have any further dealings with such actions. Not that operations always went off as planned. Not everything was within their control. On August 5, 1976, during a holdup at the Caja de Ahorros y Monte de Piedad in the Saconia neighborhood in Madrid, its security guard was shot dead; years later that raid was linked to a dismantled grupo autónomo. The same thing happened in Barcelona on July 27, 1979, when four activists from a grupo autónomo held up the Banco Central branch at 186 Calle Pere IV, just as an armored van carrying twenty-five million pesetas (some 150,000 euros) was arriving. The three guards from the Esabe-Express company resisted the raiders and a shootout erupted, in the course of which one guard died and another was wounded along with one of the raiders. These were the only two killings connected to the libertarian grupos autónomos (if we except the CAA in the Basque Country and the Scala affair) over the ten years of operations carried out between early 1974 and late 1983, although, in the case of Madrid, those indicted were acquitted of all charges in the subsequent trial.

They were loyal to their comrades, very loyal. Even to the extent that one of them, after having been sentenced to a three-month prison term for the preparation of an escape tunnel dug from the streets outside into the prison precincts, declared: "If it turns out that the sentence for trying is three months, I'll leave Spain like a Gruyère cheese." In fact, prisoner comrades were often critical of this policy. Not on account of the loyalty being shown, obviously, but because this commitment to escapes took time away from other political actions.

The most spectacular escape attempt involved the tunnel on Calle Vilamarí right beside the Modelo Prison in Barcelona. Dozens of people, some of whom had traveled in from Madrid, Valencia, and France, spent upward of six months at work on it without any information leaking out to the informers who had infiltrated the

---

9. Barcelona Grupo Autónomo, "Comunicado a la Opinión Pública," 20.

libertarian movement. This was in 1979, and the Modelo held a dozen comrades from the autónomo network. Using phony papers, Felipe had rented a ground floor flat on Calle Vilamarí and the digging began. When the escape plan was eventually uncovered, all of those involved managed to escape without arrest, but yet again the state's massaging of the news came into play. Within a few days, with parliamentary elections looming, the media announced that an ETA tunnel had been uncovered and that the plan had been to attack an army barracks right there on Calle Vilamarí. A month and a half after that, by which time the elections were over, this switched to reports of an escape bid, and the tunnel's true purpose was revealed. Yet Felipe had been in custody for nearly three weeks by then.

Not that that was the only escape attempt; not by a long shot. In addition to the Modelo tunnel dug during 1979, or the attempts to break out the comrades captured in Girona a year earlier, in January 1979, four activists were detained in Valencia for trying to break out their comrades in the same way, and in Madrid a further five comrades were arrested in May 1981 for the very same reason.

"The grupos autónomos were the hardest hit sector of the Libertarian Movement. But they were a sector that was very hard to pin down; and attempts to catalog them would be a waste of time. Such was their diversity in terms of their discourse and performance. Their power was rooted in that very diversity."[10]

---

10. L. Andrés Edo, *La CNT en la encrucijad:. Aventuras de un heterodoxo* (Barcelona: Flor del Viento, 2006), 303.

PETIT LOUP

Petit Loup was first arrested in Toulouse on September 14, 1974. He had been born in Barcelona's Calle Carders in 1954, but three years later his parents moved to France. They had been part of a network supporting the maquis coming down from France, and by the start of the decade, their home had come to police attention. There was not enough evidence to charge them, but after plenty of searches, their position became unsustainable. In March 1957, the parents, their two children, and the maternal grandmother left for exile and the family settled in the capital of the Languedoc, where Petit Loup spent his youth. At the Lycée Berthelot he was a contemporary of a whole cohort of youngsters who, especially from May 1968 onward, felt impelled to help their comrades on the far side of the Pyrenees in their fight against the fascist dictatorship. They found the inward-looking French democracy to be wanting. The activism of his parents, the personal contact with all the elderly (or not quite so elderly) Spanish exiles, and the day-to-day conversations with the latter's children—in short, the solidarity network—were no hindrance to his own activism. Quite the opposite. But that was not his sole concern; he liked to sing, just the same as he enjoyed nature, animals, and freedom, and it was not unusual for him to spice up meetings with Spanish exiles with his singing.

Along with his fellow students, he set up the Vive la Commune affinity group and they began to engage in direct action. One of the group's first actions consisted of an attempt to burn down the Spanish consulate, but the Molotov cocktail failed to ignite. In demonstrations, hand-to-hand grappling with fascist militants and members of the security forces was commonplace, as was demonstrators' use of urban guerrilla tactics. Shortly after that, at the age of sixteen, he found that he could stand his dogmatic education any longer and he made up his mind to quit high school, but French law forbade anyone of his age from working, and even though he tried for an apprenticeship as a lathe operator, he left for Andorra where he found work in the La Massana quarry between Andorra la Vella and the Spanish border. It was there that he learned all he needed to know about handling explosives. It was his task to dangle himself over the rock face and place the charges that would produce the quarry's raw materials. A year after that, his health affected by the dust thrown up from explosions at the quarry, he returned to Toulouse to find the situation greatly changed. Disillusionment had become widespread among young people, who had been hopeful in the wake of May '68. They had broken with the protest politics of previous years, the upshot of which had been the imprisonment of dozens of young people, prompting some comrades (including some friends of his who went on to join the MIL after 1971) to switch to armed struggle. Not that he was ever a member of that armed group although, if the need arose, he lent it structural support. But when Puig Antich was murdered in 1974, and he was faced with the looming threat of some of the MIL members having to face another military tribunal, Petit Loup was unable to remain on the fringes any longer. He took part in the launch of the GARI (Groupes d'Action Révolutionnaires Internationaliste / Internationalist Revolutionary Action Groups).

The GARI were made up of a coalition of several affinity groups, some of which (such as the GAI—Grupos autónomos de Intervención / Autonomous Intervention Groups—which machine-gunned the car of the Spanish consul in Toulouse and blew up several railway lines leading to the Spanish border) had by then already taken autonomous action in support of the MIL prisoners, prior to the abduction of Baltasar Suárez, an operation that gave the network its public profile. Among these affinity groups there were two quite distinct platforms: one was more intellectual and political; the other spoke to young enthusiasts itching for practical responses. After the abduction failed, those members who escaped arrest, members from the younger sector, came up with a short-term plan to sabotage the Spanish state and the French state's collusion with it. This was the most spectacular aspect of the grupos : attacks with explosives designed to highlight the repression within the Spanish state as well as holdups of financial bodies in support of the prisoners' families and to cover the prisoners' needs. In one such action, which actually had no public acknowledgement on Spanish soil, they blew up a high-tension electricity pylon in the Cerdanya, leaving the Barcelona area for weeks without the 380 volts required by major industries, which were brought to a standstill. They knew that the failure to report their action was due precisely to the fact that it was doing damage. Finally, in August 1974, the network decided to call a halt to its activities, barely a month before the arrests began (with the exception of the arrest of Tonton, a comrade who had fallen in the wake of a holdup on July 29). Petit Loup was the first to be arrested and was detained in Toulouse on September 14; the six days that he spent at the gendarmerie post proved hellish; in one of the explosions targeting the Spanish consulate in the city over the preceding months, an explosion that they blamed him for, a superintendent had sustained an arm injury.

Once the gendarmes had completed their preliminary inquiries, he and fellow prisoner Ratapignade were removed to the La Santé prison in Paris, where they joined another two GARI prisoners who had been caught subsequent to their own arrest. Once the majority of the GARI prisoners were together (except for Tonton, who was still being held in Toulouse, and Sabata, who was in Fresnes) on December 27, they embarked on a hunger strike and cold-shouldered the examining magistrate, in the aim of securing political prisoner status. The boycott of the examining magistrate consisted of a refusal to make declarations to him. Every week, he asked that they be transferred from prison to the courthouse. As for the hunger strike, Petit Loup managed to keep that up for forty-three days, as did most of his comrades. They were all held incommunicado, but they knew that on the outside, their comrades standing in solidarity with them were overwhelming the forces of the French state and that their popularity was growing. In the end, they achieved their purpose. As a result of the hunger strike, Petit Loup lost a number of teeth, but secured recognition as a political prisoner.

He served nearly three years in preventive custody with his comrades Sebas and Ratapignade, and the following year they locked horns with the state again, mounting a second hunger strike that lasted for thirty days when an attempt was made to strip them of political prisoner status. At which point the solidarity from other inmates and, yet again, support on the outside was unconditional. They were dubbed the "Three Musketeers" and turned out to be likable dynamiters who had not claimed a single victim. While in prison, however, he saw one small teenage dream come true: his first record was released, a little 45 rpm with four songs, the profits from which were to go to support for GARI prisoners. The disc carried two songs from the late-nineteenth-century singer-poet Aristide Bruant, looked upon as the founder of French realist songsters and "the voice of the people," plus the popular Mexican Revolution song "Carabina 30/30" and an Atahualpa Yupanqui song entitled "Little Queries About God," which closed with these lines: "I sing along the highway and when in prison, I hear the voices of the people singing better than I do. If there is one thing on earth more important than God, it is that nobody should be spitting blood just so that somebody else can live better. God watches out for the poor? Maybe yes, maybe no. The fact is that He dines at the boss's table."

During his stay in prison, up in the north of France, members of another *groupe autonome* styling itself the MATRA (Mouvement Armé Terroriste Révolutionnaire et Anarchiste / Armed Revolutionary Anarchist Terrorist Movement) had fallen. These young people languished in prison in Le Mans, forgotten and unable to secure political prisoner status while they still enjoyed some popularity. After they were discharged from prison in 1977, Petit Loup and his comrades decided to gather information and to try to rally people to support them. This campaign led to their setting up a whole network of autonomous groups, particularly in and around Paris. They started working in concert with these groups while also starting up a correspondence with similar groups in places like Germany and Italy.

Alongside this, the trio, who were awaiting trial, had to report every Friday to the gendarmerie in Toulouse at 5:00 p.m., so surreptitious trips made to other countries had to be brief. On July 2, Petit Loup arrived in Barcelona with Cri Cri and Sebas. They had been helped across the border by Víctor Simal from Perpignan and traveled via a farmhouse used as a base in Maçanet de Cabrenys. On arrival in Barcelona, they thought they were living in a dream. It was the day of the CNT's rally in Montjuic and red-and-black flags were flying throughout the city. On one of the days in early September when they were required to check in, they decided to rob a bank just before reporting to the gendarmes. The holdup was a success and after reporting to the gendarmes, with nervous policemen sallying forth in search of the bank robbers, all three sat down on the terrace of a nearby brewery to toast their success. It was not long before one of the vehicles regularly used by the Renseignements Généraux—the French political police—sailed up, at which point shots were fired at the drinkers. It was an unmistakable warning: they had no evidence to go on but had their suspicions as to who had been behind the robbery. The three comrades realized that the sense of humor demonstrated previously in GARI operations and the years long lampooning of the French police had not been well received by the armed agents of the state.

Petit Loup decided to return to Spain something over a year later, after making a number of hush-hush trips south of the Pyrenees where, through El Moro, a member of a Montpellier group, contact was made with the grupos autónomos operating in the Barcelona area. The Montpellier autonomous network had not yet established AD (Action Directe / Direct Action), which they did after their discharge from prison. Petit Loup settled first in Barcelona for about a year and then moved to a farmhouse in Elizondo (Navarra), where he was in direct touch with nature and living alongside his neighbors in the rural setting that he loved. It was there that his eyes were opened to the stark facts of life in the Basque Country: the ongoing military presence and the state oppression of an occupied territory. In Barcelona, though, he had prepared a structured support network around some comrades from the Plataformas de Comisiones Obreras and, together with several French activists, set about funneling financial support—raised by expropriations carried out along the Mediterranean coast—to comrades who were being captured in France. At the same time, the facts of life in the Basque Country brought him into contact with folk who did not identify with ETA but who were very actively involved in social struggles: they belonged to the CAA.

Back then there were frequent border crossings of both materials and people. Petit Loup used several Pyrenean passes between the Cerdanya and the Valle de

Arán. On one such crossing, with Salardú as the final destination, he came within an ace of being arrested by French gendarmes. In the Uretz pass, he had made the acquaintance of a French shepherd by the name of Birou, who spent six months of the year living on the first floor of a mountain refuge, the ground floor of which was set aside for hikers, among whom Petit Loup was able to pass unnoticed. On the nights when he and Birou were the only ones there, they swapped stories, food, and wine. On one such night, Birou told him that the forest rangers had stumbled upon a small munitions dump and reckoned that it belonged to a bunch of poachers. At 5:00 a.m., Birou came downstairs, woke him and told him that two men were coming up the mountainside and, judging by their gait, he had a sense that they were rangers. Petit Loup leapt out of his sleeping-bag and bade Biro farewell. He trekked for about an hour until he came to an old mine where he hid the twenty kilos of firearms he was transporting and then headed back to the refuge. Birou told him that day that he could rest easy because he already knew that Petit Loup was no poacher. He went on to tell him the story of his own brother who had cut the fingers off one of his hands in order to get out of serving in the war and he also admitted that for many years he and the brother had spent their time smuggling refugees across the mountains in both directions.

On March 19, 1984, arriving back in the village after several nights up in the mountains, Petit Loup found out that the Civil Guard was looking for him. Within moments he was under arrest. Three days earlier, two members of a Barcelona-based libertarian grupo autónomo had been arrested. He was accused of a bank holdup carried out in December the previous year along with these two comrades. In the same crackdown, between October16 and 19, four CAA activists were arrested in the Basque Country and the day following publication of that news, on October 22, members of the Civil Guard mounted the notorious "Pasaia (Pasajes) Ambush," in the course of which four Basque autónomos were shot dead and another one arrested, an operation that signaled the dismantling of the coordinated Basque autónomos.

Petit Loup was taken to the Civil Guard barracks in Vitoria, where the beatings began, but that night Civil Guards arrived to take him to Madrid, where his interrogation started. During the course of it, they strove to link him to the statewide libertarian autónomo network, a network of which he did not have much knowledge, since his activism had always been in association with the French groups. He was relentlessly tortured: they used the *barra* and the *quirófano* techniques on him and applied electrical shocks to his genitals. Then, in an effort to relieve the pressure, he "sang" (confessed, in police slang), giving the locations of two arms dumps, one at 36 Quai des Orfèvres in Paris and the other in the Rempart de Sant Etienne in Toulouse. 36 Quai des Orfèvres was the main headquarters of the French Police Judiciaire and the Rempart de Saint Etienne was the central headquarters of the gendarmerie in the capital of the Languedoc, the very two locations where GARI members had been tortured years back. The gambit worked—momentarily. After ten days, he was hauled before a judge. Just at the point when he was about to be seen by him he was approached by Lieutenant Garmendia, whose name had carelessly been dropped another Civil Guard during the interrogations; Garmendia said to him: "You may have tricked us, but did you never hear of the GAL [Grupos Antiterroristas de Liberación / Antiterrorist Liberation Groups]?" Realizing that right at that moment there was nothing that they could do to him, Petit Loup replied blithely, "No, I don't read the papers." "You'll find out soon enough," the lieutenant menacingly remarked.

In Carabanchel Prison at around this time the political factions had achieved a degree of autonomy and had secured certain rights from the administration. When Petit Loup showed up there, the comrades from the libertarian faction insisted that he be moved immediately on to the Sixth Landing and exempted from routine isolation. It was there that he bumped into Juan and other autónomo comrades with whom he shared some very heart-warming times; cleaning duties, cooking duties and protection against possible assaults by other inmates in the service of the jailers. It was actually Juan who told him when he arrived that they had a problem. The comrade arrested in Barcelona had arrived a short time earlier and, under interrogation, he had stated that Petit Loup had "sung" and pinned the holdup on him. This police ploy, however, was swiftly exposed.

On October 4, after upward of six months in prison, he was placed on conditional release and traveled up to Barcelona where his parents were living. One day, just as he was considering returning to Elizondo, he had a phone call from a friend who explained that the *picos* were already asking about him and that it might be better if he were not to return. So that is how things were. Remembering Lieutenant Garmendia's veiled threats just prior to his appearance before the judge, Petit Loup decided to return by clandestine means to France where he applied for political asylum. His application and thus a temporary grant of asylum were granted. But there was no respite. One day, toward the end of the summer of 1985—he had found work as a painter in Muret, a town thirty kilometers outside of Toulouse—he realized that he was being tailed by a number of men who did not look like gendarmes. He fell back on his old safety precautions and started watching his back, making his timings and movements very methodical. Even so, one midday, while he was eating in his usual restaurant, he spotted two men approaching his car. Both were wearing leather jackets beneath the blazing sun and, after a quick glance at the car, he saw them signaling to somebody who was out of sight. He got up from the table and headed for the back door, telling the waitress that he was just off to make a phone call and would be back. No sooner had he stepped into the kitchen, which is where the back door was, than he caught sight of another two men entering the premises with automatic pistols in their hands. He managed to get across the street and slipped into the post office, where he called a former comrade in Toulouse who was also son of a Spanish refugee. This comrade happened to be in the company of a Basque activist and another French comrade at the time. Petit Loup asked them to come to his aid, to step on it and to come prepared. But by the time they got there, the men had vanished. After thoroughly searching their car, they decided to go looking them. The French comrade drove his car and the other three followed in the other car. However, the men had evaporated and Petit Loup returned to Toulouse with his friends. From there he put a call through to his former lawyer Marie Christine Etelin, whom he knew from back in the GARI days, and he filled her in on what had happened. Two days after that the lawyer confirmed his suspicions; the Spanish police, acting incognito, had been mounting an operation in Muret at the time. He had survived a GAL operation, just the sort of thing that Lieutenant Garmendia had warned him about a year earlier.

He did his best to rebuild his life and considered a return to the Pyrenees, this time on the French side. But in order to be in a position to work the land he needed a qualification, so he moved to Couiza in the Aude Department to attend agricultural college and secure his diploma in six months. At the college his classmates were twenty-four students made up of old hippies who, in view of the new working regulations, needed a diploma if they were to carry on working the land the way they always had done and he quickly fell in with the gang. On February 3, 1987, as he was leaving the college, Petit Loup told one comrade who had a broken leg to wait by the gate for him while he went to fetch the car to ferry him home. He was making his way to his car when he was grabbed by four men who bundled him into a vehicle. As he swept past his comrades, the best that he could do was to gesture with one finger that he was about to have his throat cut.

His friends jotted down the license number of the car and immediately called through to the gendarmerie. But the gendarmes had a surprise coming to them. On checking the vehicle register, they discovered that the license plate was phony and so they set about tracking down the vehicle. Meanwhile, the kidnappers pulled the vehicle up on the hard shoulder and explained to Petit Loup that there was a warm welcome waiting for him in Spain; at the same time, they questioned him about his dealings with Sebas, to which his answer was that he had not set eyes on him in eight years. Whereupon, explaining that they were French police officers, they put it to him that he should get in touch with Sebas, in return for which they would sort out his papers in France once and for all. Plus they would turn a blind eye if he were to decide to do a little job on his own. If he refused, he would be handed back to the Spanish Civil Guard which, three years earlier, had made him impotent after ten days of questioning under the Antiterrorist Law. Even as he was trying to think of some way out of this delicate situation, two gendarmerie vehicles pulled up and parked, one in front and one behind, and two gendarmes alighted from one of them with their holsters open.

The gendarmes looked at their papers and asked what was going on, to which one of the kidnappers replied that they were "specials" on an operation. The lead gendarme, outraged, replied that he knew nothing of any such operation, that they were on his turf and were displaying phony license plates without having informed him of this. Given the delicacy of the situation, the kidnappers' leader chose to explain that they were merely carrying out an identity check, and the gendarme told him that if they were done, they were to drop the identified suspect back to the agricultural college, whereupon they were all to go to the gendarmerie so that the entire story could be checked out. En route to the college, the kidnappers guaranteed him that they would see one another again; that they were letting him have some time to think things over. Once back with his comrades and after the latter had been briefed on the situation, they forbade him to go home and put him up at one of the communes they had around the town while taking safety precautions and keeping a watch. Over the ensuing weeks, all these old hippies attended class with cameras at the ready, just in case the "specials" showed up again: they wanted to document the harassment.

That being the situation, Petit Loup was once again caught in a dead end and decided yet again to call his old lawyer friend. Marie Christine urged him to report the whole affair. Two days after the complaint was submitted, the judge sent for the lawyer and informed her that, on grounds of "national security" he had been prohibited from opening an investigation. Petit Loup reacted extrajudicially by making what had happened public knowledge. Over the ensuing days, they learned that what had happened to him had happened also to several former comrades. The state was ready to go to any lengths to entrap the AD activist.

A short time after that, he took a phone call from a former comrade, a member of the NAPAP (Noyaux Armés pour L'Autonomie Populaire Armé / Armed Nuclei for Popular Autonomy) who had belonged to the autonomous network set up ten years previously when Petit Loup was freed from his first prison term. The comrade told him that they were preparing a documentary on the murder of General Audran, an operation carried out by the AD but regarding which there were suspicions that the French secret services were involved. Petit Loup took part in the documentary. A couple of days after it was screened on public television the director called to tell him that his home had been searched and, as the authorities were leaving, they warned him that they were now going after Petit Loup This was how they finally forced him into going on the run again. He went underground, heading for Finland, arriving there on August 26. On arrival, he applied for political asylum and Amnesty International and a number of student groups looked after his needs and his defense.

A month and a half after arriving on Finnish soil, on October 8, he was arrested and, despite the many demonstrations and messages of support that flooded in, on March 28, 1988, he was forced on to a plane that flew him directly to Madrid where he was handed over to the Spanish police. Whereupon the torture started all over again. There was, however, a soupçon of Spanish comedy about the flight: before reaching Helsinki, the air force plane headed for Hamburg where it sought permission to land, a permission that was refused on the basis that it was a military plane. The Spanish pilot explained to the control tower in Hamburg that they were there to pick up a prisoner, but the response from there was that Hamburg had no record of that. Next, the flight crew provided the particulars of the prisoner, and the Germans stated that they had no such person on their soil. The misunderstanding was eventually cleared up from Madrid, and after several hours over German territory, the plane eventually landed in the Finnish capital.

After spending a night in Carabanchel, where nothing was as it had been four years earlier, due to the PSOE's new prison policies, he went before Judge Garzón, who informed him that he could not guarantee his safety. Petit Loup then arrived in Alcalá Meco. He was held for a further six months until being provisionally released in September. A month after that, he was brought before the National High Court, but sentencing was postponed, which led to yet another provisional release. By the time a phone call came through from his lawyer Fernando Salas on October 14, 1988, telling him that he had been sentenced to seven years in prison for the holdup allegedly carried out in Barcelona on December 2, 1983, Petit Loup had already made up his mind that going back to jail was not for him and he vanished.

In April 2005, he was intercepted at the Canadian border while trying to enter Canada from the USA. Questioned by the border police, he stated that in the 1970s he had been an anti-Franco activist, that he had been living in the Canadian town of D'Arcy for years and was on his way back from Mexico where he had been on holiday. There were no warrants outstanding for him anywhere in the world. In 1997, when he was finally acquitted by the Spanish Supreme Court (where his lawyer had argued his case) on grounds of lack of evidence, he had approached the Spanish embassy in the Mexican capital and been issued with a passport. During his stay in the Federal District of Mexico, his host had been Irma, who by then had been living in the country for twelve years, and she put him in touch with a network of political refugees from the Spanish state. In Canada, Petit Loup enjoyed life. He had Roma ancestry and the years of tranquility he had enjoyed after dropping out of sight in 1988 had allowed him to explore his human side.

Back in 1988, he had gone from Barcelona to France, France to Switzerland and from there on to Canada, where some comrades from a squat in Montreal provided him with his initial cover. Months later they suggested to him that he

join a native community in central Quebec and there, in the Atikamekw community, surrounded by dense forests, he spent a year and a half where the winters
plunged to forty degrees below and where he picked up some real survival skills.
From there, it was on to another community, this time on the coast, the Micmac
community, spending a further year and half there until, in 1994, he decided to
head west and made the trip out to Vancouver.

In Vancouver, he was also able to rediscover his natural calling, which he had
glimpsed in the 1970s in France: singing. He formed a musical group whereby he
was able to show the public the *duende* that he had always been carrying inside.
He became Lolo: "When I sing, I am just the vessel of my ancestors. I did not
choose to sing; they are the ones who chose me." Los Canasteros, the group with
which Lolo sang, cut several records. They often performed at the Kino Café in
Vancouver and at the prestigious Vancouver Folk Festival. A leading member of
the Romany people, he was interviewed in 1999 for a documentary about the
Roma people in Canada. Over time, he once again shied away from large crowds
and, with his partner, moved to the town of D'Arcy where they set up a bed-and-
breakfast establishment known as La Grange de la Lune. On Saturday nights, Petit
Loup would cook up Mediterranean dishes and after dinner Lolo would stage a
flamenco recital to guitar accompaniment. Patrons enjoyed his simplicity and his
human touch, but even in that corner of the planet, in those remote mountains, he
was dogged by his past.

When he was questioned at the border in April 2005, agents from the
Canadian Border Agency took careful note of his erstwhile activism and let him
know that they would be reviewing his file. On July 14 he crossed the border with
the USA, heading south, his plan being not to turn back. On the basis of personal
experience, he had the measure of the justice in the capitalist democracies and
embarked upon yet another flight, pressing on in search of a freedom that was his
birthright but which he had scarcely ever been able to savor.

A year and a half later, in September 2007, his name loomed large in the
Canadian press headlines: two ETA activists had been arrested in Canada and, in
the course of searches carried out, they turned up a snapshot taken in La Grange
de la Lune, showing the two nationalist militants together with Petit Loup, sun-
bathing in the garden over a relaxing cup of coffee. One newspaper ran with the
headline "*Wanted*" alongside his name, while another wondered, "In post-9/11
Canada, how can terrorist suspects go into hiding in this country for such a long
time?"

After crossing through the USA, he returned to Mexico where he found stability. At one point he began making his living by teaching classes in Mediterranean
cooking while helping to organize an inter-continental Romany get-together
held that October. Once the get-together ended, he resumed his study of cranial

osteopathy and delved deeper into quantum medicine. After submitting a thesis at the University of Morelos, he was awarded a university lecturer's qualification. This stability also helped improve his knowledge of the body; his natural curative gifts and self-knowledge allowed him to develop into an acknowledged healer.

2.

AFTER THE MIL

SOLIDARITY WITH THE MIL PRISONERS

In September 1973, about ten ex-members of the MIL were rounded up in a range of police operations. The MIL had disbanded itself a month earlier but some of its activists decided to carry on with their actions while attempting to put together a network of grupos autónomos with an eye to coordinating capacity for armed resistance to international capitalism. To that end, they decided to carry on using the initials GAC (Grupos autónomos de Combate / Autonomous Combat Groups) that they had been using during the lifespan of the MIL. The arrests put an end to the history of a group that sought to bring fresh practices to the workers' struggle in Spain and which described itself as autonomous in terms of its political and social ties to the old practical and theoretical structures dating back to the Civil War. But this finale also ushered in the start of a brand-new story that ran with many of its approaches and, especially, its modus operandi.

Solidarity networks started mobilizing from the moment when news of the arrest of Salvador Puig Antich, Josep Lluís Pons Llobet, Oriol Solé Sugranyes, and their comrades broke in the peninsula and across Europe, especially in France. These networks drew in youngsters who took the MIL as their example and who had no hesitation in employing armed agitation as a propaganda weapon. Among them were GAC members who had dodged the crackdown as well as groups that had already begun operating in coordination with them, groups that in some cases, were part of the Catalan structures that had not been dismantled.

On January 4, 1974, a device planted at the Policía Armada barracks in the Sant Andrés barrio in Barcelona exploded, causing considerable damage. Four days after that, on January 8, a military tribunal sat in judgment of Puig Antich, Pons Llobet, and María Angustías Mateos Fernández. The verdict, though, was a foregone conclusion and like every political trial under Francoism, its sole purpose was to impose legalized revenge. The verdict was announced the next day and on January 10, the newspapers reported that the death penalty had been imposed on Salvador Puig Antich. The support network went into overdrive. The next morning, on the 11th, three almost simultaneous bombings rocked Barcelona. Explosions struck both the Banco Popular Español and Banco de Vizcaya near the Sagrada Familia. Half an hour later, another mighty explosion caused serious damage to the Monument to the Fallen, felled five streetlamps in the vicinity and shattered many windows in the adjacent Faculty of Sciences. Hours before that, other devices had gone off near the Spanish consulates in Zurich and Turin. On January 15, solidarity efforts switched to Madrid with two bank branches being targeted.

In France, GAC comrades mobilized in an attempt to engage the maximum numbers of groups and individuals in a desperate race against time to thwart the murder of their friend and comrade. On January 15, clashes during a violent demonstration outside the consulate in Toulouse left six police officers injured. The next day, in Ivry, in the outskirts of Paris, four young people were arrested: they included the MIL activist Jean Claude Torres. Two comrades, Michel Camilleri and Pierre Roger, were released, but in the pockets of the fourth, Ángel Moreno Patiño, they found instructions for the assembly of a suitcase bomb. They had just stolen a car, were armed and produced phony papers. The fact of the matter is that they had it in mind to bring pressure to bear by kidnapping the Spanish representative to UNESCO. Just minutes earlier, they had left the courtyard of Ivry church, where the priest, the son of a CNT member from Llagostera, had provided them with logistical backup. In Strasbourg on January 17, the Spanish consul's home was overrun by a group of youngsters calling for the release of the MIL prisoners, while in Brussels a large number of people locked themselves inside the La Chapelle church and announced that they were on a hunger strike. Two days after that, also in Brussels, a demonstration was held and the Spanish Tourist Office in Marseilles was occupied at the same time. On February 28, the car of the Spanish consul in Toulouse was machine-gunned.

Solidarity activity spread through Spain. In the early morning of January 17, two devices went off at the Faculty of Economics in Bilbao. A couple of days later, on January 19, concerted action by several grupos around Spain led to the destruction of the Monument to the Fallen in Mataró. Meanwhile several Molotov cocktails were hurled at the Iberia offices in Valencia, and in San Sebastián there was a further Molotov cocktail attack on the offices of the *Unidad* and *La Voz de España* newspapers. On February 8, it was the turn of the Monument to the Fallen in Badalona and the Policía Armada barracks in Mataró. Three days later, on February 11, a huge demonstration made up of upward of two thousand young people set off from the Autonomous University and an eighty-vehicle motorcade arrived in Barcelona. On February 22, a group of youngsters used chains to shut down the main thoroughfare in San Sebastián, calling for prisoner releases. On March 1, a gathering of demonstrators triggered a number of clashes in Barcelona, but the latest chants calling for a pardon went unheeded.

On March 2, Puig Antich was murdered. The whole of Europe ignited in fury. That same night some CNT-connected libertarians organized a group to attack several barracks in the Vallés Occidental area which were raked with gunfire. After the funeral on March 3, a spontaneous demonstration was dispersed by the police in Barcelona. That afternoon, two bank branches in Barcelona's Via Júlia came under Molotov cocktail attack and, after nightfall, an explosive device was planted in the vicinity of the Sant Andreu army barracks. The façade and all the glass in the windows of the officers' residence sustained damage. In universities across Spain, there were endless meetings and demonstrations, with the Policía Armada on continual alert. On Monday, March 4, Barcelona, Valencia, Bilbao, Granada, Madrid, and Zaragoza, among other places, ground to a standstill and the police were deployed on various campuses. In Barcelona, a demonstration set off from the Faculty of Medicine, bound for the Diagonal; a more violent march started up on the Ramblas before being broken up in the Calle Ferran, where the police used their firearms. That night, a third and much larger demonstration started off at the intersection of Paseo de Gràcia and Diagonal, and incendiary devices were thrown at Banco Atlántico and Banco Comercial Transatlántico. The next day, several Policía Armada jeeps came under Molotov cocktail attack in Valencia. A youngster was later arrested and charged with involvement in that attack. On March 15, a device exploded at the courthouse in Barcelona.

Across Europe, the same dynamic was at work and the largest cities witnessed a flurry of sabotage acts and attacks on Spanish economic interests. The regime's press, which usually played down such reports, found themselves obliged to catalog some such actions: no longer could they hide the international facts. On March 4, there were Molotov cocktail attacks on two Banco Popular Español outlets, one Banco Español branch, and at the Spanish Welcome Center, all in Paris; in Genoa, a device went off at the entrance to the Spanish Chamber of Commerce. In Rome, a sizable demonstration tried to reach the embassy and the impressive police deployment to prevent this triggered a pitched battle. Three days later, a Spanish bank was attacked during a demonstration in Grenoble, at the same time as the Spanish Tourist Office in The Hague was on fire after several Molotov cocktails were thrown. On March 8, the Banco de Bilbao branch in Hendaye was utterly destroyed as a result of arson. The following day, during a demonstration in Lisbon, the police used their firearms to thwart an attack on the Iberia offices, which nevertheless sustained serious damage. This was replicated in Bayonne and Lyon, and in Nîmes there was a temporary takeover of the consulate.

Across Spain, the grupos autónomos continued to organize; many comrades were behind bars by then and some attempt had to be made to break them out, but police activity was also escalating. On March 22, the press reported the arrest of twenty-two activists in Catalonia; they included Enrique Conde Martínez in Port Bou and Núria Ballart Capdevila; both were alleged members of "two independent anarchist groups" responsible for armed operations carried out in the Barcelona area since the beginning of 1974.[1] For the first time, the media cited a brand-new set of initials—OLLA. That very night, three devices exploded in France; one on a motorway leading to the border with Spain, where a bridge was blown up after the motorway had been closed off by placards reading "Attention: Bridge Mined"; the other two went off on rail lines leading to Spain. These three attacks were claimed by yet another new group, the GAI. It looked as if the dismantling of the MIL had prepared the way for a proliferation of grupos autónomos. Two weeks after that, on April 7, three comrades—Joan Jordi Vinyoles Vidal, Georgina Nicolau Millà, and Ramón Carrión Sánchez—were arrested in Barcelona as the high-speed train from Geneva, Switzerland, arrived there. A suitcase filled with explosives was discovered in one of the carriages. On March 20, the police announced that they had broken up an organization launched with the financial and logistical backing of the MIL: this was the OLLA, the aim of which was "to establish a series of 'self-defense' nuclei in industrial complexes through the proliferation of Grupos autónomos de Combate."[2] The same bulletin also reported that those arrested on March 22 were part of that group.

September 23 saw the arrest in Barcelona of Roberto Safont Sisa on his arrival from France. He was on his way to keep a rendezvous with two comrades, Pedro Bartres Ametller and José Ventura Romero Tajés, who had been arrested just days earlier. The media reported again on October 17 that the organization had been smashed once and for all and four further arrests were made—including Raimón Solé Sugranyes (brother to three MIL members, Oriol having been in custody for over a year and Jordi and Ignasi having both dodged the 1973 crackdown)—but its definitive dismantling was announced yet again on November 6, with the two latest falls of members of the OLLA, which was "considered the continuation of the Movimiento Ibérico de Liberación."[3] That pair was Ricard de Vargas Golarons and Guillem García Pons. In six months, upward of thirty-four individuals linked with the MIL Prisoners' Solidarity Committee had been arrested and fourteen of them were, according to the police, involved in OLLA activities.

Even as these crackdowns were devastating the solidarity network in Catalonia, on May 3, the Banco de Bilbao director Baltasar Suárez was abducted in Paris. The police started lashing out blindly. Four days later, the operation was claimed by another hitherto unknown group, the GARI, which, in a statement

1. *La Vanguardia*, March 22, 1974.

2. *La Vanguardia*, April 21, 1974.

3. *La Vanguardia*, November 6, 1974.

issued to a French news agency demanded, among other things, the release of Santiago Soler Amigó, a gravely ill MIL comrade held in prison. At the same time, in a bar in Barcelona's Calle Pelai, a clandestine press conference was called to ensure that the group's demands would be made known inside Spain too. While the reporters were waiting for their hosts to make themselves known, two people showed up, introducing themselves as members of the Libertarian Antirepression Committee and handed out some envelopes to the waiting journalists before leaving. The next day, a further communiqué addressed to the Agence France-Presse added the demand for a further four MIL prisoners to be set loose.

The Groupes d'Action Révolutionnaire Internationaliste (GARI) were simply a brand-new network of groups and activists set up by former MIL members for the purpose of trying to secure the release of their comrades by bringing pressures to bear on French soil. Apart from actual MIL members, they also included some Spanish activists living in France, members of the First of May Group and a range of libertarian collectives made up of young French students and the children of Spanish exiles. One member of the network, Telesforo Tajuelo, wrote: "Without question, the most sizable group, was characterized by its theoretical muddle-headedness, besides a palpable contempt for all ideology."[4]

On Sunday May 12, the *Sunday Mirror* in the UK carried a photograph of the kidnap victim. It had been bought from David May, director of the London magazine *Time Out*, which had received it from an anonymous sender a couple of days before. The journalist May was arrested and charged with withholding evidence. A crackdown was set off against libertarian activists in Britain. The following day, on the Lyon-to-Geneva motorway, six Catalan comrades were arrested, one being Ignasi Solé Sugranyes. However, they were released after a few days, although two of Ignasi's companions—José Ventura Romero Tajés and Pere Bartres—were arrested in Barcelona four months later, as we have seen, and included in the OLLA indictment. On May 21, a group calling itself the "Puig Antich Commando" torched the premises of the French newspaper *L'Est Républicain*. Finally, on May 22, after picking up the ransom, the GARI released Baltasar Suárez. Within hours, seven activists were arrested—Lucio and Anne Urtubia, Octavio Alberola, Ariane Gransac, Jean Helen Weir, George Rivière and Annie Plazen. A significant portion of the ransom sum was recovered from them.

That same day, a car bomb went off at the entrance to an Iberia branch in Brussels and identical vehicles were located outside the company's offices in Liège and Antwerp. The cars had been stolen in Amsterdam, and on May 27, the GAI claimed responsibility for these attacks. On May 23, Pierre Guibert and Danièle Haas were arrested, charged with having harbored some of those arrested the

---

4. T. Tajuelo, *El MIL, Puig Antich y los GARI* (Paris: Ruedo Ibérico, 1977), 105.

previous day. On May 29, two further arrests were made in Paris; the couple Armand and Chantal Chestel were accused of having allowed their flat to be used in the Suárez kidnapping. Despite these arrests, the police were unable to trace the activists who had carried out the operation. They were merely dismantling the support network that had claimed the kidnapping and received the ransom payment. By July, the arrests had spread to Barcelona. On July 7, the Spanish press reported the arrest of eight anarchists, four of whom were imprisoned—Luis Andrés Edo, Lluís Burró Molina, and the pair who had attended that press conference on May 7 on behalf of the Libertarian Antirepression Committee, David Urbano Bermúdez and Joan Ferran Serafini.

But the GARI went marching on and, after two months' truce—two months that afforded the government time to honor what was demanded of it, although all it did was release Santiago Amigó—the actions resumed: on July 15, two devices exploded in Andorra at the premises of the Episcopal Magistrate and at a Spanish savings bank. Several power lines across the Pyrenees were attacked and the Paris-Irún train was damaged when a bomb went off just before it passed. The next day, thirteen coaches for pilgrims were torched in Lourdes, a number of cars from the Tour de France were burnt out, and several trees blocked the access leading up to the mythic Mount Tourmalet. Barely a week after that, a military tribunal sat in judgment of Oriol Solé and Josep Lluís Pons Llobet, who were sentenced to forty-eight and twenty-one years respectively. On July 27, a device exploded next to the wall of the Spanish consulate in Toulouse. The following day, two more bombs were placed in the same location in the Hendaye train station. A telephone call warned that a device had been planted and it was cleared prior to its detonation. That night in Paris three explosive devices were planted in coaches belonging to the Société France-Espagne-Portugal, and two cars blew up near the border crossings in Le Perthus and Bourg-Madame. All of these actions were claimed by the GARI, but other groups also had a hand in the struggle. On July 25, a device had gone off outside the Banco Popular Español branch in Nîmes, but no one claimed responsibility.

In Toulouse on July 29, the police arrested Pierre Roger: he was accused of a bank robbery. The following day, several explosive devices were planted at the entrance to La Grande Motte, sinking several luxury boats and yachts. On August 5, three car bombs went off in Brussels, one outside an Iberia office and the other two outside two branches of the Banco Español. Toward the end of August, the various members of the coordinating body met in Toulouse and decided to wind things down after having ensured that the Spanish state would not be imposing any more death sentences. That, however, was no impediment to a fair number of its members and members from other *groupes autonomes* pressing ahead with armed actions and the expropriations on French soil that had funded the struggle since the network was launched. On the other hand, the gendarmerie was still pursuing those responsible for all these actions.

On September 18, it was announced that four individuals accused of membership of the coordinating body had been arrested in the French Pays Basque and in Toulouse. These were Víctor Manrique and Jean Michel Martínez (arrested in Hendaye on September 15) as well as Mario Inés Torres and Michel Camilleri (arrested the previous day in Toulouse). The Pays Basque comrades had fallen due to a mistake on the part of the Toulouse comrades. The gendarmes had no need to make them "sing"; at the point of arrest, one of them had on him a letter from the former complete with address, a letter that should never have left the empty apartment occupied by the Toulouse people.

On October 9, several explosive devices were planted at a soccer field in Paris where FC Barcelona was due to play a match against a Parisian club; the devices were defused by the police after they had been alerted by a phone call claiming the action on behalf of the new GAI (Groupes d'Action Internationalistes / Internationalist Action Groups). The perpetrators later released a statement claiming that the devices had been planted but at no time activated. On October 14, at the conclusion of the trial of the duo arrested on January 16, Josep María Condom Bofill was arrested and charged with having had a hand in various actions of the coordinating body; he had attended the trial without realizing that he was a wanted man. Weeks later, on the night of November 2–3, a self-styled Groupe d'Action Révolutionnaire Occasionnellement Terroriste (Occasionally Terrorist Revolutionary Autonomous Group—GAROT) cut the head and hands off the effigy of Spanish Prince Juan Carlos de Borbón at the wax museum in Paris. On November 8, several French media outlets received, along with a claim of responsibility for the move, a selection of the missing fingers, and the Spanish embassy in Paris received one of the ears. On December 3, in Paris, Jann Marc Rouillan was arrested along with Floreal Cuadrado and Raymond Delgado. They were caught in possession of a photocopy of Baltasar Suárez's papers. All three were accused of involvement in several GARI actions.

Judicial proceedings arising out of all these actions in solidarity with the MIL comrades in Spain as well as in France were far-reaching. The comrades charged with membership of the OLLA were ten in number: Enrique Conde Martínez, Núria Ballart Capdevila, Joan Jordi Vinyoles Vidal, Georgina Nicolau Millà, Ramón Carrión Sánchez, Roberto Safont Sisa, Pere Bartres Ametller, José Ventura Romero Tajés, Raimón Solé Sugranyes, and Guillem García Pons. On May 17 and June 10, 1975, they were put through various proceedings in the TOP (Public Order Tribunal), and, later a joint military tribunal for membership in an armed band, in which sentences in excess of five hundred years' imprisonment were sought. In the end, after various convictions in the TOP, all of the prisoners were provisionally released when in 1976, having served about two years in preventive detention and since the dictator was now dead, the military tribunal was dismissed and the case was referred back to the ordinary courts.

In France, over the period between August 27, 1974, and February 13, 1975, the eleven prisoners arrested in the wake of the Baltasar Suárez kidnapping were released. On October 14, 1974, the first pair jailed (Jean Claude Torres and Ángel Moreno Patiño, on January 16, 1973), stood trial; the sentencing was announced the very next day—ten months in prison. They had already served nine months and walked out of La Santé prison that afternoon. On December 27, the remaining GARI prisoners still awaiting trial declared a hunger strike, insisting that the political motives for their accusations be recognized. On January 5, an explosion hit the Naval Museum in Paris during an exhibition of Spanish art. The attack was claimed on behalf of the "Kronstadt Sailors" in support of the imprisoned comrades' hunger strike. Three days after that, a tear-gas grenade was tossed into the courthouse in Toulouse, an action claimed by "The Friends of Puig Antich and Heinz Chez." On January 13, 1975, Pierre Roger and Michel Camilleri were tried after being arrested on the outskirts of Paris on January 16, 1974. On January 16, 1975, the Paris courthouse was paid a visit by the GALUT (Groupe Autonome Libertaire des Usagers du Tribunal / Court Users' Autonomous Libertarian Group), which left a little present that damaged the statue of Saint Louis, patron saint of the French courts. The group's choice of name was not unconsidered; the judge charged with the trial of the GARI suspects was called Gallut. Nearly two weeks later, a horse race being broadcast live on several TV channels was interrupted due to the throwing of flares. That action was claimed by a hitherto unknown GALOP (Groupe Autonome Libertaire Occasionnellement Parieur / Occasional Libertarian Autonomous Gambling Group). There was plenty of humor. On January 23, Floreal Cuadrado was released. Within days, another group interrupted a live French TV program and, before the connection could be cut off, it unfurled a placard in support of the campaign of the imprisoned comrades. Finally, on February 7, the Court acknowledged the political nature of the incidents. The hunger strike was maintained for between thirty and forty-three days.

At that point, eight of the activists were still behind bars, seven in Paris and one in Toulouse. The latter, Pierre Roger, embarked on a hunger strike on February 27 to press his demand to be moved to La Santé where all his comrades were still being held. Finally, Josep María Condom Bofill, Víctor Manrique, Jean Michel Martínez, and Raymond Delgado were released during April. On July 9 it was Pierre Roger's turn. The brunt was borne by Mario Inés Torres, Michel Camilleri, and Jann Marc Rouillan, who were still in prison by May 1976 and were only released a year later on May 25, 1977, having served about two and a half years in preventive custody without ever having been tried.

Even one year later in Spain, on January 3, 1976, the sentence was passed on those accused of having had a hand in the May 7, 1974, press conference in Barcelona. Luis Andrés Edo, Lluís Burró Molina, and David Urbano Bermúdez were sentenced to five years and Joan Ferran Serafini to three.

By the time the trial of those charged in relation to GARI actions opened in Paris in May 1981, every one of them was acquitted.

SABATA

Sabata (Catalan for "shoe") was going into the priesthood. He entered the seminary as a child, but in the belief that he was not cut out for a celibate existence, he decided to pack it in. Born in 1953 into a Catalan Catholic bourgeois family from La Bisbal, he was a restless child who, influenced by the personality of the local priest, decided to follow in his footsteps, despite some misgivings on the part of his father who reckoned that, aged nine, the boy did not know enough to make such a significant decision. The town priest was very active and his world captured the boy's enthusiasm: the hiking, the Catalanism, the brotherhood with his comrades. It was then that he tasted repression at first hand. One night, camped out near the border, their camp was surrounded by Civil Guard personnel: on another occasion, during a nighttime hike, he received a slap in the face for an offhanded response to a challenge from two policemen. His political awareness started in the seminary and, thus, he progressed from boyhood to adolescence. Worker priests showed the way, attentively following the development of liberation theology, while the youngsters were starting to read some banned writings from France. In the border districts, pretty much everybody had some relative in France, and the proximity of the border facilitated contact.

At the age of fifteen, he tried to follow the events of May '68 in France through French broadcasts that could readily be accessed from the comarcas of Girona. He was keen to check out the news that had reached his home through some French friends of his parents, supermarket owners, according to whom those behind the upheaval were Spanish workers. Though pained by the turn taken by events, his parents offered to take their friends into their own home should that upheaval turn into revolution. In the end, he decided to quit the seminary, although he hinted to his parents that he was going to study medicine before going off to serve in the African missions. Within months, Sabata had moved away to Barcelona, first to take some pre-university courses and later to pursue a career in medicine.

In Barcelona, he finished up in the Residencia Universitaria Ramón Llull, a division of the *Diputación*, into which he gained admittance thanks to family connections. The director, an acknowledged supporter of the regime, had been a

deputy in the Cortes and was friendly with Narcís de Carreras, a family acquaintance from La Bisbal. Carreras was the former chairman of FC Barcelona and was
a serving as a deputy in the Cortes at the time. Once he had settled in, his interests
led to his working with student drama groups while simultaneously furthering his
education by dabbling in his first ever criminal ventures: his specialty was stealing
books from a range of bookstores. A methodical sort, he used to jot down notes
in a little book regarding the best times to drop in on each store, along with his
itinerary and the methodology to be employed in each one. The Residencia was
prey to the same ferment as the high schools and universities, with the students
pressing for greater and greater freedom. Those were the years of the counterculture and the sexual revolution. Among the most restless students, Wilhelm Reich
was all the rage; he was a mold-breaker, politicized and, in addition, had had his
own difficulties with bureaucratic, orthodox communism.

Having passed the *Preu* (pre-university), he started university. There was a
set number of admissions and while he, from a family of doctors, managed to
get through and embark upon a career in medicine, hundreds of youngsters were
arbitrarily denied the opportunity to pursue their studies. Which explains what
was behind the earliest student protests. The students who had been turned down
started attending lectures as auditors, but it was not long before strikes erupted
and the department was shut down, with the lectures relocating to the Sant Pau
Hospital. It was at this point that the director of the Residencia was replaced by a
pro-communist director. Sabata then pinched a book that would leave its mark on
his political evolution, to wit, *From Proudhon to Cohn-Bendit*, something along
the lines of a history of anarchism written by Heleno Saña. The book had slipped
past the dictatorship's censor. At the same time (this was in 1972), his parents got
wind of his literary tastes and his special visits to bookstores. This led to a family row, which meant that he was cut loose, gave up on a career in medicine, and
embarked on a study of philosophy, although communal living and his early political activities left him little time for attending lectures.

The mainstay of the opposition to the dictatorship was the Communist Party
(the PSUC in the case of Catalonia—Partit Socialista Unificat de Catalunya /
Unified Socialist Party of Catalonia). Its fringes were teeming with all sorts of
groups critical of its centralistic policies but subscribing to Marxism—groups
such as the PCE (i), Bandera Roja, and many others which were trying to gain
control of the university student platforms. For some months, he flirted with the
Trotskyists and started taking part in the earliest demonstrations as a marshal, to
which end he was prompted to learn how to make Molotov cocktails. But Heleno
Saña's book prompted him to delve more deeply into the shelves of the Biblioteca
de Cataluña where he stumbled upon his first book on the Civil War with a particular analysis of the CNT's role. That book was followed by others with the same

or kindred themes, until one day he made up his mind that it was time to stop borrowing books of that sort for fear that borrowers were being monitored and that somebody might be alerted to his special interest. By then, though, the young man had come to a decision.

In the autumn of 1972, an unexpected dispute erupted in the department. Food prices in the university canteen were on the rise and several students decided to picket the entrance. It was then that he came into contact with the first organized anarchist groups. At the outset, these youngsters called a daily meeting just as the doors were opening, and once the meeting was over, they would flood inside, refusing to pay. This led to the collapse of the canteen and the first direct talks with its management, who, for some days, chose to let this bunch of youngsters through in an attempt to avert any obstruction of service. However, once they realized that the number of youngsters was growing considerably day by day, they decided to switch off the benevolent approach and attempted to bar the protesters from access. On that day the youngsters, without any prompting, took over the canteens and for some days kept them under occupation while serving the rest of the student body free of charge. They would enter the kitchens and serve the food up to their comrades themselves. When, in view of the protest action, the canteen was shut down, the youngsters decided to hold a demonstration march and bring their demands to the kitchens at the Industrial School. That everyday struggle was the springboard to militancy for a goodly number of young people.

Sabata started taking part in student demonstrations. These were no longer the initial demonstrations orchestrated by political groups using the students as an advance guard. Rather, the students themselves were running things. They would assemble somewhere, hand out leaflets, and daub graffiti. On hearing the sirens approaching, they would bring traffic to a standstill by parking cars across the road or tossing a few Molotov cocktails before arranging to rendezvous elsewhere in the city forty-five or sixty minutes later to replicate the action. 1973 was a year when such actions were relentlessly on the increase. They would enter the factories in an attempt to strike up direct connections with the working class while calling for general strikes that were taken up only in a few of the departments. But the death of a worker in Sant Adrià del Besòs expedited a connection with the Assemblea de Catalunya which, for the very first time offered them its backing for the ensuing demonstration. One day, Sabata traveled up to the University of Girona to hand out propaganda along with a couple of comrades. After chatting with several students, he began daubing graffiti. The police turned up, and he and a female comrade were arrested. A third comrade took to his heels and managed to get away. Sabata was locked up in Girona, in a prison that inmates who had sampled other establishments referred to as "family-sized." The cook said that it was more like a hotel than a proper prison. Three or four months later he was given a provisional release. Awaiting trial and expecting to be called up for his military service, he decided to go on the run. The outcome of the trial could not be predicted but he was convinced that, having sampled prison for political reasons, he had to act with caution. On the other hand, he did not feel that he had it in him to live under Franco's heavy hand without getting involved in struggles and had no reason to expect that anything good would come of time served in military barracks. No doubt, he would finish up in a disciplinary battalion.

Toward the end of that spring, he crossed the border along with his friend Roger, with Toulouse as their final destination. He crossed over on his own passport without a hitch. As he was awaiting trial, the regime did not put too many obstacles in the way of youngsters who were unwelcome on account of their political aspirations. In Toulouse, they were taken in by members of the CNT and spent a few weeks working at the union's printshop. It was a time of discovery of a world of which they had hitherto known nothing, a world that started the moment they crossed the Pyrenees and which struck them as boundless. In late June, they moved on to Paris, making straight for the anarcho-syndicalist premises at 22 Rue des Vignoles, where they met some young people with situations like their own, as well as others who, although they had not gone on the run because of any earlier political activities, had been prompted to do so because of their individual need for liberation, youngsters such as Michel. They also ran into the veteran libertarian militant Abel Paz, who found them work in the factory where he was employed. By then, it was July and they were to stand in for regular staff on their holidays. It was at this point that Sabata had his first clash with the authoritarian communists.

His political education having begun on the campuses in Barcelona, he had always looked upon the members of such dogmatic groups as fellow barricade fighters, but in Paris he realized that they were the first line of the capitalist system's emergency firefighters; a strike erupted that month at Lip, and the workforce took over the factory. The youngsters from Spain had no hesitation in siding with them and daubed graffiti over several factories, including their own. Whereupon the bureaucrats from the French Marxist trade union, the CGT, irked by such maverick activity, summoned them to a meeting to charge them with acting in defiance of national sentiment and having declined to sing the French national anthem on Bastille Day, July 14. They even accused them of having been sent in by the Spanish regime. At that point, there was increased pressure brought to bear at their workplace, and the union leadership threatened to dock their wages the costs of a fresh coat of paint for the entire plant. In the end, they were sacked by those very same trade unionists who were powerful enough to be in a position to decide who could work and who could not. However, these youngsters did not meekly leave the factory; one day, in the factory canteen, a CGT member called one of the young girls from the group a "hippy" and a "whore" and, without a moment's hesitation, Sabata leapt to her defense. A fight erupted, in the course of which chairs were sent flying in all directions.

A couple of months later, he learned, along with Michel and a couple of other comrades, of the fall in Barcelona of some young militants from the MIL, and they decided to set up a support committee in Paris. First, they assembled in the FL (Frente Libertario—Liberation Front—analogous to the Spanish Libertarian Movement in France) premises in the Rue Saint Denis. Later they met on the premises of the ORA (Organisation Révolutionnaire Anarchiste / Revolutionary Anarchist Organization) and CNT in the Rue Vignoles. Eva turned up during one of these meetings, an activist close to the MIL whom Sabata knew from the campuses in Barcelona. The meeting was also attended by Sebas and Cri Cri, Boni and they decided to start working together. Some of their Parisian ORA friends had been in contact with them down in Toulouse and had already broached the possibility of joining the MIL prior to the September arrests. This cooperation brought them to Toulouse so that they could outline their plans for action. While their first political action was in the planning stages, on January 16, 1974, Michel was arrested in Paris along with another three French comrades, two of whom were released after a short time. Michel and Cri Cri were jailed.

Sabata was still at university, having matriculated at the beginning of his course and, when the students learned about the execution of Puig Antich, fury erupted. The young people were ready for anything and that very night two Spanish banks and the Spanish Welcome Center in Paris came under Molotov cocktail attack. From that point on, they began linking up with a range of libertarian groups with an eye to preventing the military tribunal that some of the members of the MIL were facing from handing down further death sentences. They joined forces with veteran Spanish libertarian activists, with French militants, and a significant faction of Spanish students eager to do their bit. One of their regular rendezvous was the La Boule d'Or bar in the Rue Saint Michel, where university professor Agustín García Calvo held his weekly gatherings. It was a mixed bag of exiles, young students, girls who had traveled up from Spain to have abortions, and recent undocumented arrivals eager to regularize their status. In short, it was a place in constant ferment up until the owners called a halt to the gatherings. At the same time, one of the comrades who was living in a student residence, contrived to take charge of a section of the student halls where the young activists could lie low when they needed to make themselves scarce.

That May, as other comrades were abducting Baltasar Suárez in Paris— which was the springboard for GARI actions—one of the groups in the network, made up of four or five activists including Sabata, relocated to Amsterdam. The GARI was a network of groups that only claimed actions in its name when all of its component groups acknowledged them. In the meanwhile, each individual group operated along autonomous lines and remained free to carry on acting as it wished, claiming its own actions under other names if that was their preference. When Sabata's group moved to Amsterdam, it detonated the first car bombs to target Spanish economic interests and claimed responsibility in the name of the GAI. These bombings were carried out on the same day that Baltasar Suárez was set free and seven comrades were arrested in France. The targets had been the Iberia offices in Brussels, Liège and Antwerp, all in Belgium.

That was followed by a couple of months of truce until, that July, the GARI embarked upon a fresh phase marked by a more frenzied pace. On July 29, following the holdup of a bank, one of the French youngsters who had been arrested on January 16 and freed within days was rearrested. This was Tonton, but this time he was not so lucky. In the course of the tough questioning to which he was subjected over the ensuing days, the name "Zapata" came up (a French version of the nickname Sabata filtered through Spanish). After two months of uninterrupted direct action, in late August the GARI disbanded, each component member getting on with things, but a few weeks later the arrests started in Toulouse. Sabata, unaware that he was being sought by the gendarmerie, got his turn as he was leaving the trial of his friend Michel: on August 14, he had gone to the courts in Paris along with several other activists to support his comrade and, once the hearing concluded and he was having a beer in an adjacent bar, he and some other comrades were arrested. Some of the latter, like Benito, could not be connected to any action and were released, but in the course of a number of searches carried out in these young people's apartments, a French comrade, Jacques Lescouet, was discovered; he had been in hiding as he was a draft dodger and was taken away to a military prison. Sabata was held by the gendarmes for five or six days. During the first three days he was bound and brutally beaten by forces brought in especially from Toulouse; on one occasion he was beaten senseless. From day four onward, he was guarded by Parisian police who stopped their colleagues from Languedoc from wreaking their personal revenge. As we have seen already, in one of the GARI actions, a police inspector from Toulouse had sustained an injury to his arm. Over this time, Sabata was also questioned by police drafted in from Brussels and Amsterdam, but they were unable to indict him for the first actions claimed on behalf of the GAI. Then he was placed in the prison in Fresnes in the Paris area, charged with the holdup that had led to the arrest of Tonton, a holdup in which Sabata had had no hand, act or part.

In Fresnes, he mounted his first hunger and thirst strike to assert his innocence but was unprepared, so, seven days in, he gave up. A month and a half after he was arrested, other comrades who had been involved in GARI actions were arrested. All the prisoners from the network were concentrated in the prison in Paris, except for Tonton, who was down in Toulouse, and himself. This was the point at which they decided to launch a hunger strike to press for recognition as political prisoners. During the first few days, Sabata, who was isolated from his comrades, was none too strict in his observance of the strike. His lawyer would surreptitiously slip him the odd egg which he would swiftly gobble down. But before long his self-control got the better of him and he kept up the strike for twenty-three days, at the end of which time the judge gave in to his demand. Eight months after that, he was transferred to the St Michel prison in Toulouse, where he served a few weeks before being released.

On his release, he moved up to Paris where he carried on with his studies while distancing himself from armed struggle, although he still felt a deep friendship with all the youngsters with whom he had risked his life in the spring and summer of 1974. From Paris, he made frequent trips down to Perpignan to meet with relatives and friends who crossed the border just to see him. During one such trip, he ran into some comrades from Girona and escorted them to the Librería Española where they bought several books that were banned in Spain. Within days those friends got word to him that they had been detained on the border where they had been expected. They advised him to take care if he was visiting the Librería. In 1977, he finally returned to Catalonia, where the only thing still hanging over his head was his military service obligation, which he wriggled out of by claiming to be an epileptic.

For many years, he divided his time between Catalonia and Paris, although in 1978 he was arrested again, in Stockholm this time. Determined to open a libertarian school, he chose to get involved in an international operation involving the passing of phony checks in order to raise the necessary funds. Sabata decided to operate in Sweden where his friend Michel had been arrested a year and a half before for the same reason, because he had some friends in that country. Among those involved in the operation were some former social prisoners, one of whom, a member of the COPEL (Coordinadora de Presos en Lucha / Prisoners-in-Struggle Coordination), acted as his partner. When his comrade was arrested in Stockholm, he, having changed his checks without mishap, returned to the hotel where they were staying to pick up his passport. He had intended to make for the airport, but they were waiting for him. He spent six months in complete isolation in the Stockholm police cells and was then jailed in Kumla, a high security prison where his fellow inmates for a further six months included dangerous prisoners, repeat offenders, and high-flying criminals.

THE CATALAN NETWORK

In Catalonia, much of the old logistical network underpinning the libertarian armed struggle had been dismantled back between 1957, the year Facerías was murdered, and 1963, when they murdered Caracremada. El Quico had also been murdered at the halfway point, in 1960. However, during the 1960s, direct action was still being used by a couple of groups linked to the historic organizational structures of the Spanish Libertarian Movement: the CNT-linked DI (Defensa Interior / Internal Defense) and the Frente Libertario-linked First of May Group, which also had ties to brand-new international libertarian networks. Some years later, the influence of May '68 in France was felt in a new generation of youngsters. In the universities and high schools, these youngsters were starting to get themselves organized.

In the comarcas of Girona Province, the nearness of the French border and contact with the first waves of French tourists were making themselves felt: some youngsters had begun to daub graffiti and carry out token actions on red-letter days like the First of May, July 19, October 1, etc. Little by little, the web was being rewoven and contacts were widening despite the enforced clandestinity. In the end, those youngsters came to Barcelona, where other youngsters had also been drawn in by the writings of the Situationist International (writings that surreptitiously circulated on several Barcelona campuses). Nineteen sixty-nine saw the establishment of the Bakunin Anarchist Group made up of youngsters from Empurdà, a bunch of young students from the schools in Barcelona, and some members of the FIJL. By 1970, coordination had been boosted by the creation of Negro y Rojo, a group amalgamating several collectives from around the metropolitan district. One year on, Negro y Rojo was meeting in Valencia with the Ácratas group from Madrid and Bandera Negra from Valencia, and, between them, they set up the first body coordinating the libertarian grupos autónomos among that upcoming generation of youngsters. That coordinating body's reach even extended to Zaragoza through the Aragonese group, Acción Directa.

In October 1972, a dispute erupted in the university city on Barcelona's Diagonal. Several student organizations, Negro y Rojo for one, picketed the entrances to the canteens due to the exorbitant pricing. Unexpectedly and spontaneously, one comrade from Girona, Josep María Condom Bofill, from the Faculty of Letters, urged everyone to take over the canteen, shouting "Eat for free!" This move was embraced by a large number of students, and the organizations sponsoring the pickets found themselves swamped. Their picket quickly turned into a sit-in. This entailed meetings and day-to-day distribution of food free of charge in the canteen on the Pedralbes campus and later at the Industrial School. Months later, Josep María was arrested and sent to prison for daubing graffiti at Girona University. He was given a provisional release, but, prior to his appearance before the Public Order Tribunal, he crossed into France, where he joined the GARI and was jailed a second time. The sit-ins at the canteens dragged on for two months and, as they ended, the Manifest d'Estudiants Llibertaris de Catalunya i les Balears (Manifesto of the Libertarian Students of Catalonia and the Balearics) emerged; this was the coordinating body set up some months before to coordinate the high schools and university departments.

This student coordinating body, which had a presence in Gironès, Garrotxa, Empordà, Osona, Barcelonès, and Baix Llobregat as well as in the Balearics, lasted for about two years. September 1973 saw publication of the first edition of its bulletin; this coincided with the fall of the MIL comrades and the creation of the MIL Prisoners' Solidarity Committee. At which point a substantial number of its activists decided to join the grupos autónomos and withdraw from the student network. And six months after that, the coordinating body was dealt a heavy blow by the forces of repression, one that would effectively kill it off. In March 1974, when the police first reported on the dismantling of the OLLA and the arrest of twenty-two anarchists in Catalonia, they were in fact referring to the dismantling of one part of the MIL Prisoners' Solidarity Committee, made up of various armed grupos autónomos along with members of the Estudiants Llibertaris and the group that published the *CNT-Informa* bulletin.

Between September and December 1973, the committee's activities had been confined to propaganda. Three dossiers had been prepared as a briefing on the struggle waged by the comrades from the MIL, their ideological tenets and their prison conditions, but at a meeting held on the very day that Carrero Blanco was murdered, the decision was made to deploy armed action as a solidarity tool as well. The committee divided its efforts: on the political side, the aim was to mobilize the various factions of the organized opposition in case of heavy sentencing, while the technical side would carry out spectacular armed actions in order to draw public attention to the case.

The comrades that the police had arrested and whom they were linking with this brand-new armed organization going by the name of the OLLA were in actual fact members of the armed groups going by that name (they had been operational for at least three years and had occasionally coordinated with the members of the now defunct MIL in carrying out armed actions), plus Estudiants Llibertaris activists like Eugeni Méndez and Enric Casasses, sympathizers, and friends who had nothing to do with the armed struggle linked to a recently raided libertarian commune in Mirasol (Sant Cugat). When, one month later, on April 20, the media reprinted the photograph of three arrested comrades they also tossed in snapshots of other supposedly highly dangerous activists who had gone on the run: Ignasi Solé Sugranyes, a MIL member who had crossed the border; Miquel Didac Piñero Costa, an Estudiants Llibertaris member who had slipped into France on April 28 using the libertarian border network in the Cerdanya; Felipe Solé Sabaté, cousin of the Solé Sugranyes brothers, a member of the grupos autónomos who had taken part in the odd joint operation with the MIL and who made it out to France on January 3; and Genís Cano, who was being hidden for a few months in the family home in Vilanova by Pau Maragall Mira until the heat died down a bit.

There is a measure of confusion surrounding the OLLA. One faction of activists asserts that it never existed as such and that the name was concocted by a regime which was in need of brand-new organizations through which to exploit the public's fear of terrorism against the established order. According to them, the police seized upon an internal document of the grupos autónomos that was in the possession of some MIL members and that had been confiscated when the MIL was being dismantled; it claimed that the activists were not part of any armed-struggle organization. The point, as far as the regime was concerned, was to render comprehensible what its own bureaucrats could not understand. In the view of that faction, the groups that were dismantled under the designation OLLA, were in fact part of a network of small grupos autónomos.

There is another faction that contends that the OLLA did exist as an organization and that there are documents signed with those initials.

Be that as it may, whether it existed as an organization or did not, the fact is that there was a series of three- or four-man groups interlinked by a go-between, making the dismantling of them a very complicated affair. Those cells were scattered across the territory (in Mataró, Badalona, Terrassa, Santa Coloma, Nou Barris, Sant Andreu, etc.) and the vast majority of their activists, who numbered around forty, were not living below the radar but were working or studying. Such was the affinity between the youngsters belonging to these groups that it entirely precluded the possibility of police infiltration; in fact, in some instances we can speak of shared development rather than affinity; there were no misgivings of any sort between them. They were motley groups, like so many other youth groups that emerged during the latter days of the dictatorship under Francoism's iron hand, and they had no structural ties to any of the older organizations that had figured in politics prior to or contemporary with the Civil War. Impelled by the need to educate themselves politically, these youngsters read everything they could get their hands on, starting always with the Marxist classics and, little by little, going in the direction of the anarchist classics that were harder to get hold of back then. In that, they were like the MIL: a breath of fresh air for anti-authoritarianism in Spain.

The network was formed around three former members of the PSAN (Partit Socialista d'Aliberament Nacional / Socialist National Liberation Party) on the basis of theoretical notions like autonomy and anticapitalism. Back then, all the underground groups and political parties, including the PSAN, had their own self-defense groups, some more armed than others. These three young people, members of one of the PSAN self-defense groups, carried out some propaganda operations that were disowned by the Party, for which reason they were prompted to carry on as an independent group under the name "Resistencia." In the summer of 1972, two of the activists, Felip Solé and Joan J. Vinyoles met up with Jann Marc Rouillan and Oriol Solé in the Sierra del Moixeró and they decided to bolster the links between them: on November 18, members from the two groups mounted their first joint expropriation, robbing the Savings and Pension Fund in Barcelona's Calle Escorial. Ten days after that, on November 28, their collaboration was repeated at the Banco Central branch in the Paseo Valldaura. Up until the arrest of the members of the MIL in September 1973, they carried out another two joint expropriations, but these grupos autónomos did not need the MIL in order to act. In January 1973, three of the youngsters (with support from other comrades from abroad) raided the offices of the Banco de Vizcaya in the Calle Manel Girona and, on July 2 that year, two comrades carried out a riskier action by robbing the Telegraphs office at the Central Post Office.

When it came to their activities, they were rather more methodical than their MIL comrades who, as professional militants, were always short of cash. They did not have the same financial urgency and this allowed them to carry out much safer actions. They even managed to plant a female comrade of theirs, Núria Ballart in an official printer's involved in the printing of national identity cards, and this enabled them to secure about five thousand ready-to-use documents. A further novelty, one of the many they brought to the history of armed movements in Spain, was the role played by women. The female comrades used the Sten gun just like their male comrades, and every aspect the struggle was shared 100 percent.

The arrest of the MIL comrades left its mark on the future of this network. The involvement of its activists in the Solidarity Committee (which entailed dealings with other political and social factions) meant that in some instances they had to come out of the closet. By the autumn of 1973, two of the ex-members of the MIL, Ricard de Vargas and Ignasi Solé Sugranyes, had joined these groups. Meanwhile, by way of a rapid response to the arrests, several dossiers were printed up in Felip Solé's home explaining the actions and theoretical beliefs of the MIL, whose members were being depicted by the media and a fair proportion of the orthodox left parties as "gangsters." That November, in Barcelona, they held the first ever congress of grupos autónomos, intending to expand the coordination of the network and widen their actions in support of the prisoners. A couple of months after that, on January 19, by which time Puig Antich was under a death sentence, they held a second congress to coordinate how they were going to respond to this threat and to explore the chances of an escape. Among the actions planned by these grupos autónomos, which never came to fruition, there was the plan to attack the police van ferrying the prisoner comrades from the Modelo Prison to the Captaincy-General building on the day of the military tribunal (this plan was rejected by Puig Antich himself because of the risks to which it would have exposed so many comrades). Another plan was to break out of the Modelo through the sewers, to which end a comrade crept through the underground network for almost twenty hours before coming up empty-handed. Finally, on the day of the execution, they planned to attack the police station in the Via Laietana and wreak revenge for the killing, but this action was rejected at the last moment by the activist themselves who could see the negative fallout from that sort of operation.

The police forces ran into stark reality when they proceeded to dismantle the committee. They found themselves faced with a bunch of young people engaged in armed direct action, especially expropriations and attacks on symbols of the state, army, and capital: these were the groups responsible for the attacks using explosives and incendiary devices against banking institutions, army barracks, police stations, and fascist monuments, attacks mounted from Mataró all the way down to Barcelona between January and March 1974. During the dismantling of the committee, which news was released on March 22, 1974, two activists from the network were arrested: Núria Ballart and Enrique Conde. Conde had links to the Mirasol libertarian commune and was a member of the Estudiants Llibertaris at the Faculty of Fine Arts. On April 7, another three comrades were caught trying to collect a suitcase packed with explosives that had been supplied by a Swiss libertarian group and which had arrived on the TALGO (high-speed inter-city train) from Geneva. The suitcase, supplied by comrades from Zurich had, even though it had started on its journey in Switzerland, not reached the TALGO until Ignasi Solé Sugranyes brought it on board in Narbonne. He had alighted in Perpignan and the suitcase made the border crossing unaccompanied. When it was detected by Spanish police, they mounted discreet checks in the main stations and, once it arrived in Girona, they watched as a couple of young people approached the suitcase. On arrival in Barcelona, they were arrested along with a third person who was waiting for them on the platform. Felip Solé, who was also in the France station in Barcelona managed to slip away undetected. Which was the point at which the dictatorship's police forces caught on to the dimensions of the grupos, tracing thirteen empty apartments and nearly a dozen vehicles, as well as plentiful weaponry and documentation identifying potential targets.

The Zurich group that had supplied the mines was the very same one that had, on January 10, 1974, attacked the Spanish consulate in the Swiss city after the news broke that Puig Antich had been sentenced to death, setting off two grenades in a phone box situated opposite the diplomatic legation. Some of these young Swiss even traveled to Barcelona on several occasions, the first being in 1973. They then took part in a Molotov cocktail attack on a bank over the death of a worker. A year later, they partook alongside the Barcelona autónomos (part of the network had been dismantled by then) in a bank robbery carried out at the Banco Central branch in the Calle Girona on April 27.

Following the first two crackdowns, the actions continued: on April 26, a Catalan Railways train on the Vallès line was halted at Muntaner station by a sizable bunch of young people close to *CNT-Informa* who distributed leaflets and daubed lots of propaganda slogans before taking to their heels. This led to the line's being closed in both directions for some hours, as the authorities decided to clean up the convoy before anyone could read the youngsters' demands. The following day, the Calle Princesa branch of the Banco Guipuzcoano came under Molotov cocktail attack and, four days after that, on the First of May, five banks in Poble Nou sustained damage following the explosion of several dynamite charges and the hurling of Molotov cocktails by other groups that once again daubed libertarian demands.

CNT-Informa purported to be a wide-ranging libertarian network linked to the CNT, yet unconnected with the divisions within the CNT abroad. Outside of Spain, the libertarian movement organized in large structures (CNT, FAI, and FIJL) had suffered a crisis that had resulted in splits. In the specific case of the CNT, the split resulted in there being two structures; on the one hand the official CNT, and on the other, what later came to be called the CNT-Narbonne Congress, linked to the FL (Frente Libertario). Activists from both factions out to create a network inside Spain were involved with *CNT-Informa*. They reckoned that the CNT was an organization capable of galvanizing the social struggle rather than just the trade union struggle. Their activists were the ones chiefly responsible for the various clandestine press conferences called during 1974 in order to publicize actions mounted in solidarity with the MIL prisoners. The first such press conference was held in a bar in the Gràcia barrio, regarding the blowing up of the Monument to the Fallen in Barcelona. The second was called following Baltasar Suárez's abduction in Paris and led to the arrest of two of their members along with a comrade from abroad and a member of the NAP (Nucleos de Acción Proletaria / Proletarian Action Nuclei), a revolutionary Marxist group that sided with the MIL comrades.

In a little over six months, about a dozen people connected with the network of grupos autónomos were arrested (in addition to another thirty young libertarians belonging to other factions—mainly Estudiants Llibertaris and *CNT-Informa*), yet the network had not been smashed, not by a long shot. The cell-based structure enabled many young people who had taken an active part in direct actions in support of the MIL comrades to keep operating, although in some instances, due to the fall of their go-betweens, they had to remain disconnected from the other groups. They even launched brand-new cellular structures, some of which remained active for several years. Some of the youngsters took the precaution of slipping into France temporarily, and other activists, such as the brothers José and Francisco García Huertas, though exposed during questioning of indicted comrades, also successfully evaded arrest.

Although the outrageous repression led to the arrests of forty-two comrades in Catalonia between March and November 1974, and the flight to France of a number of others, both Estudiants Llibertaris and the OLLA were back in the media headlines after the arrest of Miquel Mulet Nicolau, Josep Illamola Camprodón, and Margarita Pla Consuegra on August 6, 1975. The latter two were linked to the student organization and Josep Illamola was connected to the Organització de Lluita Armada (OLLA).

Just one month later, on September 15, the police reported the arrest, in an apartment at 117 Calle Urgell in Barcelona (where several weapons had been found) of four young anarchist students—Ricard García Salacort, Núria Aleu Sanfeliu, Marina Peña Carulla, and Ana Ferrer Agell. The same statement reported the dismantling of the propaganda and defense machinery of the libertarian movement in Catalonia, with the arrest of Gerard Jacas, Eduard Domènec, and Vicente Iglesias, from whom three Sten submachine guns and three thousand kilos of subversive propaganda was seized.

ROGER

In 1968 he began studying for his *bachillerato* at Vic high school and, driven by his concerns, he made his initial contacts with several political groups. The social repression and, above all, the religious oppression enforced in the small towns around the comarca was very harsh, and the priest became the number one casualty of the craving for liberation felt by the young during their adolescent years. He represented the regime, and social control began with the Church. Those not attending Mass were marked, and residents were obliged to go through the motions in order to avoid being stigmatized. In Vic, Roger started off as an acquaintance of underground militants of the PSUC, but membership failed to satisfy him since he felt that it replicated the dogmatism of the Church, albeit with a different pantheon. It was then that he began to hear of anarchism and, together with Miquel and other comrades, he began to feel an attraction to its essential ideas.

After the summer of 1972 he moved away to Barcelona to embark on his university education and there he came into contact with the Estudiants Llibertaris, more at a human level than because of any ideological affinities. Estudiants Llibertaris was an informal bunch demanding no rigid commitment and even though there were comrades striving toward a more broadly-based organization, most of the young people there were looking for changes in their everyday lives rather than to develop any deep-seated ideology. That was a disputatious year in the universities and, come the summer, Roger decided to venture abroad to see the wider world, along with Sabata, a fellow student with whom he had struck up a friendship. Together they made their way via Toulouse to Paris, where they made contact with the two libertarian structures, the classical CNT and the FL, and made the acquaintances of those grandfatherly sorts wistful about times past and ignorant of the social reality in which people inside Spain had been living during the early years of the 1970s. It was in Paris that they met two youngsters from Madrid who had nothing to do with the libertarian movement, one of whom wanted to go and work in the United Kingdom. Sabata decided to remain in Paris, but Roger headed off to London with his two new traveling companions. On arrival at customs, they were questioned by the British police. The Madrid comrade who wanted to enter the country in order to settle down and find a job was denied entry, whereas Roger and the other youngster, who claimed they were there on holiday, faced no such impediment. And so, they both found themselves in the United Kingdom, without any contact address and knowing barely one word of the language. In the port of Dover, somewhat at a loss, they considered doubling back, but in the end, they made up their minds to press on and look for some anarchist collective that might take them in. Which is how they came to be acquainted with Miguel García, an anarchist who had been part of the maquis and served many years in Spanish prisons. They also met Stuart Christie, who had sampled Franco's prisons in the 1960s, and Albert Meltzer, a British journalist who lived with Miguel García. It was García who urged Roger to go to Liverpool, where there was a Girona-born anarchist by the name of Enric Tremps, with whom Roger became fast friends. After a few weeks in the British Isles, Roger decided to travel on and, after passing through Cologne, he arrived back in Barcelona by the end of the summer.

That was an autumn of changes in the city. The arrest of the MIL members was a watershed moment. Hard reality required greater commitment from the young activists who had hitherto focused mainly on propaganda, and the out-and-out boycott of the campaign to support the arrested comrades on the part of the PSUC-led classical left pushed them into make a decision: along with Enrique, a Boltaña-born comrade from Estudiants Llibertaris, they made up their minds to join the grupos autónomos which were resorting to armed agitation and coordinating around the MIL Prisoners' Solidarity Committee. From that moment forth, they went underground and the actions began. They had the use of a safehouse where the group's members would gather to plan actions and stash weapons and underground propaganda materials. Where their fellow members of the group lived, they did not know. They moved around using phony papers supplied by activists who had already been at it for two years and who had managed to plant a female comrade, Núria, in a firm that legally produced ID cards. On January 11, 1974, two days after the military tribunal passed the death sentence on Puig Antich, Roger was involved in the planting of explosives in two Banco de Vizcaya and Banco Popular Español premises on Avenida Gaudí. There were also incessant border crossings, generally via Bourg-Madame and on foot, over mountain trails. They also crossed via a mountain trail known by mushroom-gatherers (that trail allowed them to travel the whole way by vehicle without having to run into any customs posts).

When, three weeks after the murder of Puig Antich, Enrique was arrested on the border and a clamp-down hit dozens more comrades from the Catalan network, Roger made up his mind to drop out of sight for a while and fled to France. Not that he was the only one. In Barcelona, there was Eva, an activist with MIL connections who, in the face of the crackdown, also decided to go on the run. It was around then that she learned from the media that she was part of a network that the police had dubbed the Organització de Lluita Armada (Armed Struggle Organization). Before the month of March was out, they orchestrated a climbing expedition to Puigmal. Surrounded by comrades, they set off from Núria, aiming to flee, but, instead of pressing on to the peak itself, the goal was to slip across the border unmolested. It was no cakewalk. It was heavy going. They had to trudge through the snow that covered the entire course, but their efforts succeeded and they arrived in France without any surprises. It later came to light that Roger had not been detected by the police but, even so, he stayed on in Europe for a few months. After passing through Perpignan along with Sancho, a comrade of Eva's and a member of the MIL himself, it was then on to Toulouse, but Roger settled in Montpellier where he was put up by a local libertarian group made up of native-born French and the children of Spanish émigrés. He also popped across to England to see the comrades he had met the previous summer. In addition to working, these months were spent mainly on attempts to get hold of a professional laminating machine so that the group could be autonomous and equip itself with phony papers. Eventually, once the pressure on his circle of activists had eased somewhat, he decided to return to Barcelona.

This was point at which he contacted a former Estudiants Llibertaris comrade known as "El Profe" and, as well, Miquel, the friend alongside whom he had studied for his *bachillerato* back in Vic; both chose to join the group. The earliest grupos autónomos, the ones whose operations had begun two years earlier, had been hard hit by the repression, but other youngsters decided to carry on their struggle. On December 12, Roger took part in a holdup at the Roca gun store in the Calle Aribau, and a couple of weeks after that, on December 27, he and some other comrades raided the Banco Hispano-Americano branch in the Zona Franca. Actions carried on over the ensuing months, but the situation was becoming complicated. Given the pressures implicit in clandestine living and with many of the comrades with whom they had launched the struggle now under arrest, they found themselves obliged to carry out holdups just to get by. On May 9, 1975, Roger took part in a holdup at the Sabadell Savings Fund in the town of Martorelles, but he was beginning to lose faith in what he was doing and his misgivings were multiplying. He felt like he was turning into a mere criminal and that there was no clear-cut social strategy behind it all. He eventually made up his mind to pack in armed action and he said as much to his Liverpool friend, Enric Tremps, in a letter, a letter that he never got to send. On August 6, he was arrested along with Miquel, his school pal, and another female comrade.

His arrest was not especially violent, but he had the bad luck to be leaning down when one of the Civil Guards threw a mighty punch in his direction so that the guard's fist smashed into the jeep, causing him to break some bones, and so assault charges and resisting arrest were added to charges of terrorism, theft, and unlawful association. Knowing that they would have a hard time charging his comrades with anything, he decided to take the blame and clear them. Under questioning, he managed to be evasive by providing information about old safe apartments that were already "burnt" (i.e., that the police had already traced). During searches the letter he had written to his friend in Liverpool in which he explained that he was packing in armed action was discovered. The police reckoned that he did not know anything more and so he avoided being tortured. Two days after that, he was in the Modelo Prison.

In prison, he bumped into the comrades that had been arrested during 1974, Enrique—the comrade from Estudiants Llibertaris with whom he had gone underground—for one. Francoism was on its last legs, the prison officers were worried about their future prospects, and the political prisoners wielded power within the prisons. Change was in the air and the jailers were trying to cover their own backs. A couple of months later Roger took part in a hunger strike by political prisoners demanding an amnesty. They were all moved to isolation cells for forty days, although the isolation, as such, was scarcely effective, given the large number of inmates who had been involved in the protest. As luck would have it, he was in isolation with Lluís Burró, the comrade who had had a hand in the press conference held in support of the very first GARI action, and with an inmate from Granollers. One day, from the cell just below the one in which they were, they had an indication that the occupants wanted to communicate with them, and so, as was always the case in such situations, they drained the water out of the toilet so that the pipework could be used as a means of communication. This was how another inmate was able to pass on to them the news that Franco was dead. With no cakes on hand, they celebrated by feasting on some biscuits.

Half a year later, in May 1976, those comrades involved in the OLLA indictment were released, but Roger, having been arrested a year after them, was not able to benefit from this move. Months later, in February 1977, by which time he had served eighteen months, into the Modelo came a sizable group of libertarians as a result of a crackdown mounted in Barcelona during the FAI's peninsular conference. A few days later, he was in the Fifth Ward, which was occupied by what were regarded as the dangerous inmates. Making his way to the usual movie show through a corridor leading from the First Ward, he was summoned by one of the new arrivals. It was a comrade with whom he was not acquainted but with whom he had a few mutual friends. While they were chatting, up came Miquel Inglés, a PCE(i) prisoner who had served many years in prison, and Inglés gave them a queer look. Minutes later, he was telling Roger that the inmate right beside the comrade to who he had been chatting was an informer. It was Joaquín Gambín, a common law prisoner who had been rounded up with some comrades from Murcia. Roger passed this information on to the comrade who was with Gambín and, during a visit, he asked his sister to also let Luis Andrés Edo know. Edo had been released a few months earlier.

Within weeks of that, on March 11, 1977, both Roger and Miquel were hauled in front of a military tribunal. It was a sham, designed to demonstrate the good-will of the military courts. They were not tried for the planting of explosives on January 11, 1974, nor for the bank holdups on December 27, 1974, and May 9, 1975, of which they had been accused, but did face charges of insulting and resisting the lawful authorities during their arrests. That way they were able to be acquitted, and the military tribunals, which were normally harsh in its sentencing policy, could be portrayed in a good light. Whereas Miquel was released, Roger, though acquitted, was sent back to the Modelo pending trial for all the actions of which he stood accused. In the end, on May 25, he was provisionally released, which meant that he was now on the outside waiting for the amnesty to come through.

But there was a debt still unpaid. Roger had yet to perform his compulsory military service. Now ready to start a new life with no quarrels outstanding with the military courts, one day he approached the Captaincy in Barcelona to establish where he stood. He was dealt with by a major visibly under the influence of alcohol and was told that because he was on provisional release, he needed permission from the judge before he could be called up. That was a weight off his mind, and obviously he never applied for the requisite permission. Then he headed back to the family farmhouse in San Martí Sescorts, where he was born in 1955, to tend the livestock and, with the support of his family, get back to life on the outside.

A couple of years went by until, one afternoon in late July 1979, he was contacted by some of his former comrades. They were still on active service and that very morning, in the course of a holdup, things had gone contrary to expectations. The security guards had drawn their weapons, a ferocious shootout ensued and one of the comrades, Pep, had been wounded. They were in urgent need of a doctor. Roger managed to get in touch with a doctor in Lérida who tended to the injured comrade, but, in the course of the shootout, one of the guards had been killed, and the police were in hot pursuit. On July 31 the police arrested one of the members of the gang, and five days after that, the media reported the arrest of eleven people, including the physician Roger had contacted and his high-school pal, Miquel. Roger feared the worst, but the days passed and none came looking for him, nor did he pick up on any strange movements around the farmhouse. It took them a month and a half.

One day in mid-September nearly a dozen police showed up to place him under arrest. Despite the overkill, all he was charged with was the holdup at the Roca gun store on December 12, 1974, almost five years earlier. The group in question had remained active five years. It had begun taking action to demonstrate solidarity with Puig Antich, and even until it was dismantled in 1979, some of the actions it had carried out at the time had not been cleared up. Under questioning, when they made the connection with Miquel, they were able to confirm Roger's role in the raid on the gun store. In any event, he was not worried. That action, like all the others in which he had had a hand, had not caused any physical injury and, having been mounted prior to the death of the dictator, they were covered by the amnesty. Roger was held in the Modelo from September 15 to October 13. The situation inside the prison was not as it had been during his first stay there, a couple of years before. Whereas, during that first stint there, he had come across only one junkie, the prison was now full of them. Even his pal Miquel was completely addicted to heroin.

Miquel Mulet, his high-school pal, was just one of the many victims of the dirty war, having succumbed to the blandishments of artificial paradises.

WORKERS' AUTONOMY

It was the assembly that was in control
It was the workers who gave the orders.
You felt alive.

—ROSA TORTOSA MACIPE, *SETENTA Y DOS HORAS*

Labor struggles bounced back with a vengeance at the beginning of the 1960s. As the Workers' Commissions coalesced into a labor front headed by the PSUC and PCE, the various currents that argued on behalf of assemblies as the ultimate expression of the workers (Plataformas Anticapitalistas, the CCOO de Empresas, the Grupos Obreros Autónomos, etc.) together with other groups unconnected with trade union bureaucracy (anti-authoritarian Marxists, councilists, libertarians, etc.) took shelter under the umbrella of Autonomía Obrera (Workers' Autonomy). These labor organizations gained ground in the larger firms. Disputes were assuming greater and greater autonomy and achieving levels of horizontalism unthinkable nowadays. The sole legal trade union was the CNS (Central Nacional Sindicalista—National Syndicalist Center—known as the Vertical Syndicate) and maneuvers of the other organizations were still merely internal as they competed for members. In those circumstances, it was very hard to manipulate the numerous assemblies of workers: "In terms of an organized mass movement, there was no union movement prior to 1976. There were huge strikes, but the unions existed in only embryonic form within the CNS. As far as workers were concerned, the only choice was between state-run trade unionism and the wildcat strike."[1]

It all kicked off with the Harry Walker strike in Barcelona, mounted from December 1970 to February 1971, but in its wake came lots of other disputes, like

---

1. *Los incontrolados: Crónicas de la España salvaje 1976–1981* (Seville: Klinamen / Biblioteca Social Hermanos Quero, 2004), 13.

the one at CEMOTO, the firm manufacturing the Bultaco motorcycle in Sant Adrià del Besòs, in April and May 1976; or the Roca dispute in Gavà from 1976 to 1977; right up to the gas station workers' strike in September–October 1978. In Madrid there were the Metro strikes in January 1976; the Induyco dispute (at a subsidiary of El Corte Inglés) in January–February 1977; and the Shopworkers' and Construction workers' disputes. There was outstanding solidarity and collaboration by the grupos autónomos in these disputes, but as far as a significant portion of the workers were concerned—those that actually worked for the firms on strike—they were none too enthusiastic about their performance.

At the time, workers were embarking upon disputes mainly in pursuit of work demands, but in many cases the workers' demands acquired a political hue due to the repression (the essential point being that all strikes were forbidden) and the consequent need for solidarity. The Roca company dispute was a fine example of this: this dispute lasted a year and became radicalized due to the inflexible stance adopted by the management and the choice by some of them to have recourse to force.

Between March and April 1976, the Roca workforce mounted an initial forty-one-day strike in pursuit of wage improvements; during that initial dispute the workers were aware of the need for them to elect representatives outside of the Vertical Syndicates and they began organizing themselves on the basis of assemblies. Six months after that, they mounted two new twenty-four-hour strikes, to which the management replied by suspending one of the representatives elected by the assembly for seven days without pay. The workers decided to dig in for an indefinite strike from November 9 onward when the plant was taken over, only to be cleared by the security forces: "The town of Gavà was brought to a complete standstill by workers' barricades, and for a week the police did not dare set foot in the town. When they did enter, battering anyone and everything on the streets, it was a sheer miracle that no life was lost, although there were injuries galore and, naturally, two hundred arrests were made, thirty of them being sent to prison."[2]

The Civil Guard began using a heavy-handed approach in its treatment of assemblies held on the streets, while parapolice gangs attacked the homes of some workers in the working-class community in Gavà (known as Poblado Roca), where many of the employees' families lived. For its part, the management took action against the workers and the numbers sacked rose to forty-six. On November 24, *La Vanguardia* reported that the day before, only 228 out of a complement of 4,809 workers had reported for work, and that figure included management.

In December, in view of their being ignored by the media and by certain left-wing parties and unions ("One of the first successes of the Roca proletarians was

---

2. L. Andrés Edo, *La CNT en la encrucijada*, 265.

to spur the parties and unions into speaking out against them in the wretched way they did"[3]), they decided to launch Roca Support Committees, which held briefings and drew other sectors of the population into the dispute. At the same time, on December 2, the drugstore owned by the family of the representative sacked at the outset of the dispute was attacked with Molotov cocktails, an action that had been attempted previously in November, when his home had also come under attack. Also on December 2, the home of another delegate came under incendiary attack. On January 11, the unions, which were still illegal but were being tolerated, legally summoned a demonstration in Cornellà. The demonstration ended with heavy clashes with the Policía Armada, and ten of the factory's workforce under arrest. The unions had canceled the protest just hours before, but no one had informed the people primarily concerned, the actual striking workforce. On February 1, 1977, the courts declared that thirty-five of the forty-six dismissals were null and void, and on that very day a heavily armed, far-right commando attacked the home of one of the workers who had been arrested, sending two of his comrades—who belonged to the self-defense groups organized in the wake of the initial attacks in November and December—to the hospital. That attack was claimed a couple of days later on behalf of the Triple A (AAA—Alianza Apostólica Anticomunista/Apostolic Anticommunist Alliance). On February 11, the workers went back to work after upward of three months on strike, the company having welcomed back all but one of its dismissed employees.

The strikes spread from firm to firm. A strike in one factory might very well turn into a sectoral stoppage and spread even beyond that. This was the case with the Metro strike in Madrid: on January 5, 1976, the Metro workers went on strike; the dispute quickly spread through the industrial belt in the city, attracting solidarity from the services sector in the city center. Within days the dispute had spread to the Banking, Insurance, Printing Trades, Postal Service, and RENFE employees. By January 14, the strike was being backed by four hundred thousand workers.

The operations of the grupos autónomos were designed to lash out at employer bodies and to afford financial support to the strikers, but although strike funds normally welcomed the proceeds from expropriations into their shrinking coffers, the workers were trying to detach themselves from the action of these young people who, in some instances, came, not from working-class circles but from the more radicalized student quarters. Essentially the criticisms were of two sorts: on the one hand, certain groups viewed as intellectuals eager to influence the working class while not part of it, came in for criticism; and, on the other, there was criticism of the violence employed by certain groups which certain

---

3. *Los incontrolados*, 23.

worker sectors were quick to condemn, especially from the mid-1970s onward. The dilemma was mainly strategic and class-based: in those disputes, groups of workers drawn from the striking factories themselves were carrying out actions very much akin to those of the grupos autónomos (typical of this were the actions of the ERAT, a group raised in the Seat plant in Barcelona and made up mostly of the plant's own workers). These actions derived a sense of legitimacy from the fact that they were carried out by members of the working class, whereas they regarded the actions of the youngsters as dangerous meddling. In the course of strikes, it was a common occurrence to find the workers using violent direct action on company property and also for them to take organized action against strike-breakers. Finally, over time, criticisms also surfaced of the vicious cycle of spiraling violence, especially in the Basque Country:

> There was one frustrating and dramatic point when we began to see that what these actions were doing was supplanting the movement at the grassroots level. That had a big impact on us. You're in your workshop pressing ahead with the movement, opening folks' eyes and all that and next thing you see is a boss killed). . . . And then it's all over: now it is all action-repression, dead bodies . . . the whole thing winds up revolving around that. And that is the most irksome paradox: rather than our speaking for ourselves, instead of dealing with the issues that affect us, the way we used to, for the sake of our freedom and for the sake of people's freedom, we end up talking about the problem of the state and the problems of the folk taking on the state with its own weapons.[4]

Hard reality entailed a constant clash between two contending worlds, one that was sinking as a result of capitalism's evolution, coming to the end of the line after nearly a hundred years, and the other that was just starting out. It was "Work for all" versus "Down with wage slavery." The workers were out to uphold the status they had inherited from their fathers and grandfathers, their membership in the working class, while securing improvements for workers. The young people wanted to live life, enjoy it and secure a certain measure of joyful existence while shunning the alienation involved in the concept of toil. That joyousness was utterly incompatible with the system of ongoing toil and exploitation by the powerful classes. A paradigm shift was beginning. In both groups, the strategy and the historical analysis were the same, or very nearly so: what would never be the same again were the options, or visions, for the future.

---

4. Espai en Blanc, *Luchas autónomas en los años 70* (Madrid: Traficantes de Sueños, 2008), 193.

Many of these young activists had no hesitation in dropping out of their studies so as to be able to form an effective part of the working class (this was termed "proletarianization"), but their practical ideas regarding the latter's demands would be wholly unacceptable to those whose entire lives had been lived within the same paradigm and with one single purpose: improving working conditions, sure, but to continue working. This was a prospect to which the young were steadfastly opposed (during an interview given for this book, Petit Loup reminded me that *trabajar* (working) derives from the Latin *tripalium*, which was a method of torture. How could they consent to working?) Strikes were popping up, seemingly out of nowhere, out of a subterranean process of worker analysis or material necessity. In some instances they turned into wildcat strikes that added on radical demands in pursuit of revolutionary changes, but the youngsters always had the same sensation about these strikes: all of a sudden, the revolutionary bubble would burst, and, if they were lucky, those initially sacked were rehired and all the workers would troop back into work (this is not to sneer at those strikes that concluded with workers' victories). Although on many occasions those initially dismissed were the scapegoats in disputes that insisted upon improvements all round, as in the case of the Induyco dispute in Madrid.

Induyco was the textile plant belonging to El Corte Inglés, its workforce made up mostly of women. In January 1977, an assembly presented its platform of demands going into collective bargaining, and four employees (three women, one man) were sacked. The workforce reacted by calling for intermittent stoppages and holding a demonstration that was brutally dispersed by the police; in response to these partial stoppages, the management sacked seven thousand workers and closed down the factory for some weeks, alleging that anybody wishing to return to work would be required to apply in writing, explaining the reasons why they wanted to go back to work. On February 14, 2,500 workers attempted to return to work, but only 1,000 were taken back. The assembly then decided to organize pickets to prevent strike-breakers from accessing the plant and, at the same time, it rejected a suggestion from the Workers' Commissions (CC.OO) that the strike be ended. The management's reaction was to send in security forces to disperse the pickets. In the end, in mid-March, after two months of conflict, the workers went back to work without having secured the rehiring of the four individuals dismissed at the outset of the dispute.

Worker autonomy was a real option in the factories between 1972 and 1977, when the trade unions were legalized and state-wide representation accorded exclusively to the CC.OO and the UGT (Unión General de Trabajadores / Workers' General Union). The CNT's refusal to negotiate with the state regarding working conditions in the private sector was exploited to that end. The CNT was out to negotiate directly with entrepreneurs the way it had done before the

Civil War. Up to that point, the workers, unrepresented except for the delegates from the CNS, reckoned that they were equipped to take charge of their own demands and paid a high price for that, due to the repression. The numbers murdered for demanding better working conditions were high, much too high, but the state had a feeling that the campaigning was not just designed to obtain better working conditions but that what these workers were starting to demand, unwittingly in many cases, was a paradigm shift. In the case of the groups supportive of Workers' Autonomy, this approximated the abolition of the state and its replacement by workers' councils. Hence, the fierce violence of the repression. But that violence did nothing to halt the demands. Quite the opposite. It breathed life into them.

The demands increased up until the month of March 1976. In Vitoria, on March 3, in a city at a standstill due to strikes, where the entire life of the society revolved around the workers' assemblies, violence was unleashed by the forces of order and five workers were murdered. There was an exemplary response from the workers, nationwide strikes, assemblies, demonstrations—followed by more deaths—many more deaths. The authorities were well aware of what the working class was asking for and what the repressive measures against their justified demands had achieved. From that moment on, the strategy of the capitalists accelerated. Also that March, the top leader of the Communist Party, Santiago Carrillo, spoke for the very first time of an "agreed break"; four months later, Adolfo Suárez was appointed prime minister and, by 1977, the trade unions and political parties had been legalized, including the Communist Party (but nothing further to its left). A little over a year and a half after the incidents in Vitoria, the Moncloa Agreements were signed. The media fell over themselves to query the legitimacy of the assemblies as a method of labor organization: "The assembly—a haphazard body, its manipulable attendees bereft of control, bereft of rules, and in the minority—plays a negative role by scorning and, in some instances, even actually thwarting the growth of the trade union centrals. Assembly-ism refuses to appreciate that its heroic era of struggle against fascist syndicalism is now a thing of the past."[5]

However, from mid-1976 onward, many of those same autónomo workers flooded into the CNT, especially in Catalonia, Valencia and Andalusia, in search of a strong platform that might allow them to have a say in labor policy in Spain. In Catalonia, the CNT's support for the Roca workforce was the springboard: "Only the CNT of all the unions had backed the Roca workers' strike from start to finish and made no attempt to supplant or set itself up as the leadership of the strike. That was a significant factor in labor circles linked to the autónomo movements or

---

5. *Diario 16*, November 27, 1977, in *Los incontrolados*, 37.

merely workers with some feeling for an uncompromising, participationist trade unionism flirting with the stances that the CNT of Catalonia championed."[6]

The gas-station workers' strike in Barcelona Province highlighted this new situation. From September 28 to October 26, 1977, the very first strike was won by the workers, most of whom decided to join the CNT as a body during a sector-wide assembly held on July 4 (of the twelve representatives elected by the assembly, seven belonged to the CNT). The employers responded to an initial demand for a wage of a thousand pesetas a day (about six euros) by offering seven hundred (a little over four euros) and the workers reduced their demand to nine hundred pesetas (just over five euros). By the time the strike finished, the workers had secured a wage of 881 pesetas (a little over five euros), or almost double the rate of pay they had been receiving at the outset of the dispute, when they were earning 458 pesetas (under three euros): "The strike boosted the CNT's prestige in a labor scene battered by a ferocious economic crisis and betrayed by trade union centrals that had underhandedly agreed to wage cuts with the political authorities."[7]

A year later, the leaderships of the CC.OO and UGT signed on to a national agreement slashing by about 30 percent the economic conditions secured by the workers in Barcelona Province, who, after a number of assemblies, decided on September 2 to launch a fresh strike to win back what they had won a year before, what the CC.OO and UGT leaderships had deprived them of by of signing the nationwide agreement. The dispute was truly harsh. The first thing agreed between the government and the employers' body was that members of the armed forces would replace the workers so as to deprive the strike of any practical impact. The workers' reaction was unambiguous; service stations came under all sorts of attacks; there were gunshots, Molotov cocktails were thrown, they were attacked with explosives. At the same time, dozens of workers were arrested during many actions, and CC.OO and UGT representatives unconnected with the gas station workers were assaulted by strikers when they attempted to negotiate on their behalf. After a lengthy dispute, during which the state mobilized all its forces, a rehiring agreement was accepted on October 20—the gains made in the province-wide strike back in 1977 were honored.

To all practical purposes, the anarcho-syndicalist confederation had vanished from the workplace after the end of the Civil War, especially during the 1960s, but when Franco died, the union enjoyed a sudden spurt of growth, given the need by a significant section of the population to recover its history and the hostility toward the use of the workers for political purposes. And yet, because of the

---

6. J. Zambrana, *La alternativa libertaria: Catalunya 1976–1979* (Barcelona: Edicions Fet a Mà, 2000), 91.

7. J. Ribas, *Los 70 a destajo: Ajoblanco y libertad* (Barcelona: RBA, 2007), 520.

Scala affair as well as internal squabbling and the absence of any practical trade union alternative to the brand-new social conditions—conditions enforced by those wielding power and enjoying the backing of the trade union and political bureaucrats—the libertarian trade union found, equally suddenly, that it had lost all ability to represent the bulk of the working class.

The grupos autónomos carried on supporting the strikes, but, little by little, social and work-related changes inexorably distanced them from the working class, and from 1979 onward, they drifted apart: labor disputes were forgotten about, and when they did crop up they were systematically defused by the official trade unions, while the youngsters pressed on with their fight against capitalism and the abolition of wage slavery, although that fight too had been undermined by social reality.

"Prior to '77, all the major Barcelona firms struck, striking for between fifteen days and two months, and they secured wage rises far superior to any secured by the trade unions over the following twenty years."

—DANIEL CANDO, *SETENTA Y DOS HORAS*

LLENGÜES

Llengües (Tongues) had a hand in the relaunch of the CC.OO from a church in the La Borderas barrio of Barcelona in 1966, when he was seventeen years old and working in a printing firm where he had come into contact with some sections of the politically organized proletariat. Those were the years when the groundwork of a new working class was being laid. In recent years, hundreds of thousands of workers had arrived in Catalonia from various locations around the country. Many of them were from rural areas and devoid of any political grounding. At the time, the CC.OO was split into two main factions, one controlled by the PSUC and the other under the sway of the FOC (Frente Obrero Catalán / Catalan Workers' Front). From 1968 on, a third path emerged, and this was the one he sided with: it embraced anti-authoritarian workers supportive of workers' autonomy, and within the year had started calling itself Plataformas. Some of these groups, though, like the Comisiones Obreras de Barrios, realized the need for self-education and made it their priority. Born in Barcelona in 1949, Llengües lived in the El Clot barrio. He started to develop an interest in French, attracted by the events of May '68 in Paris and by the ease with which he could pick up other languages.

In Spain, the working class had suffered a breakdown since the war. Up to that point, the trade union organizations had preserved an organizational and educational continuity, even during the Primo de Rivera dictatorship, but the thirty years of Francoism amounted to a stone slab separating experiences prior to the war from contemporary ones. That slab needed blowing asunder. Llengües quickly felt attracted to the group of workers that was out to supply books about worker consciousness and political action to members of the new proletariat from the greater Barcelona area. He then started helping to create a clandestine labor library. The first book he translated into Spanish was Paul Lafargue's *The Right to be Lazy*, but that was followed by a good number of revolutionary and political analytical texts. It was this library that would later give way to Ediciones Mayo del 37.

In contact with Emili Pardiñas (who had been an eyewitness to May '68), Santo Soler Amigó (who had a particular interest in the education of workers),

and Oriol Solé Sugranyes (a man of action working on behalf of the militant proletariat), the tentacles of the network started to spreads wider, and Llengües made
contact with some French comrades. At the time, he was working in a Barcelona
hotel, but a time came when he decided to take a step forward, keeping pace with
the organization he had joined—the MIL—and in 1972 he gave up work. He was
part of what was known as the "theoretical team," the group tasked with choosing
the political texts to be distributed to the workers. This was the beginning of a
period of clandestinity, or semi-clandestinity since, even though he was not working and was wholly committed to the struggle, he still lived at home and, having
no record, he could move around freely, using his own papers.

For some months and years, the differences between the laboring masses
and the slightly reckless groups of youngsters had been widening. The impact of
May '68 in France and of Situationism were discernible in a whole new generation of fighters who decided to make the revolution in their day-to-day lives, in
their everyday existence (and not merely in matters relating to work or politics).
Meanwhile the bulk of the labor movement was dazzled by the PSUC's proposals
for averting splits and being content with a gradual increase in the proletariat's
purchasing power. The new breed of workers emerging from the abject poverty
caused by the war were beginning to feel content if they could buy themselves an
apartment, kit it out with a television set, a fridge, and a washing-machine and
take three or four weeks' holidays in their Seat 600. As far as they were concerned,
twenty years earlier they had been famished and this was a revolution in itself.

In Catalonia, the members of the GAC, who came to serve as the MIL's armed
wing, were starting to carry out expropriations while Llengües focused on logistical support, coordinating with workers' groups, and his translation work. Even as
he was preparing his first texts for publication, he was busy with the comrades
from the same team building up the workers' library; alongside which members of
the outside team, the ones who made up the GAC, were making contact with the
incipient network of armed Catalan grupos autónomos.

When, after two years in action, the bulk of his comrades had been arrested
and the MIL's Barcelona network smashed, Llengües manage to slip away. First, he
spent a couple of weeks in hiding in an apartment in the Calle Providencia. Then
he crossed the border and headed for Italy, where he spent a couple of months
with the comrades from Lotta Continua. In Barcelona, as the person in charge
of some of the organization's safehouses, he let a couple of apartments be rented
in his own name. One was in the Calle Girona, used mainly by Puig Antich, and
the other in the Calle Cerdaña where, in order to avert suspicions on the part of
neighbors and the landlady, he passed himself off as a young bohemian artist keeping unusual hours and equally bohemian company. From Italy he would call the
family which was clueless as to his clandestine activities. When some weeks passed

and the police had not turned up at his home, he realized that his name had not come out during interrogations. The comrades had managed to shield him and he was free to return to Barcelona.

On his return, he made contact with the grupos autónomos that had set up the MIL Prisoners' Solidarity Committee and carried on with the struggle alongside them. He reluctantly took part in some public actions in support of his comrades, particularly demonstrations, and in the clandestine distribution of propaganda in the barrios, but they were hard hit that April, following the very first fall of one of the female activists from the grupos autónomos in March 1974. Their cell structure had been compromised by the arrest of three of their go-betweens, three members of different groups arrested while trying to collect that suitcase carrying mines shipped in from Switzerland. The network was in jeopardy when some of its members went public in support of the jailed comrades, and it was beginning to pay the price. It was in April 1974 that Llengües met some anarchist comrades from Zurich who were bringing in arms for the Catalan groups and who had come down to Barcelona to take part in a bank expropriation. Shortly after that, that spring, he had his eyes opened to the underground reality of the first organized groups of young Barcelona anarchists. First there were the publications: *CNT-Informa* and *Tribuna Libertaria*, and then in early June, at the invitation of Joan Ferran and Lluís Burró, he and a comrade from the groups attended a meeting held in the mountains of central Catalonia. There they both met up with around forty young anarchists who had little connection with the grandfatherly types that were the mainstay of the CNT in exile. These youngsters, who put together the *CNT-Informa* bulletin, shared the same experience of oppression, both in social and generational terms as well as in cultural and political terms. That was the day he made the acquaintance of the libertarian militant Luis Andrés Edo, the oldest attendee. A month after that, both the two youngsters who had invited him to the meeting and that veteran anarchist militant were arrested for having taken part, directly or indirectly, in the clandestine press conference mounted a couple of months earlier in Barcelona in connection with the Baltasar Suárez abduction.

Comrades involved in the armed autónomo network continued to fall in September and October. In November, it was the turn of Llengües and his comrade. The media reported their arrests on November 7. No weapons were found at the time of arrest, and all they could do was seize clandestine propaganda from his home. His comrade, on the other hand, was caught in possession of a key about which he declined to provide any information. For two days, that comrade withstood violent police bullying (he spent those two days buying his brother and another comrade enough time to go and clean up the apartment). When, under pressure, he eventually did "sing" the police rushed to carry out a search of the apartment in the Calle Mayor in Gràcia, where they found weapons aplenty. The comrade's brother, on finding out about the arrests, had not dared go there to mop up, in the belief that it was a danger spot. The police tagged the comrade as the quartermaster for the grupos autónomos they described as the OLLA. Unable to tie Llengües in with any armed action, they released him a few weeks later. He was never even hauled in front of the Public Order Tribunal, although they made him wait some years for the return of his national ID card and passport.

3.

TRANSFER OF POWERS

HORSE-TRADING

"And if the street belongs more to us, damn right. And should this entire system
rot and collapse, hell yes."
—PAU MALVIDO, *NOSOTROS LOS MALDITOS*

On December 20, 1973, Admiral Carrero Blanco was blown sky high on a Madrid
street. He was the leader of the government and the dictator's natural successor, but
ETA blew his aspirations to smithereens. The more astute and practical notables
of the Movement clearly saw what their prospects were against this ultraconser-
vative iron-fisted leader. The regime's end was imminent, and the powers-that-be
intended to preserve the powers they had seized in the wake of the Civil War
and side-step any future court proceedings against them. The wheels were set in
motion to plan some horse-trading (horse-trading that entailed the transfer of
powers in return for immunity from prosecution), while also ensuring that they
could retain the bounty from thirty-five years of exploitation of the working class.
That bounty would enable them to cling to power in practical terms, since submission to international capitalism was inevitable. At that point, negotiations for the
drafting of a brand-new social contract got underway—where the body of the text
would change, though not the small print. In public, the supposedly leftist forces
entered into the fray rather timidly, although the horse-trading had been under
way for years behind the scenes. The Catalan bourgeoisie was less timorous, having
raised its head quite some time ago. The murder of Puig Antich quieted all their
voices. This was their way of indicating that all of them—from Pujol through to
the representatives of the PSUC—were the ideal people to douse the flames of
popular uprising licking around significant swathes of the younger generation that
had suffered under the dictatorship.

On October 30, 1973, the Prince took over as temporary head of state. Not
for the first time, since he had done the same thing in the summer of the previous year, but this time there was a widespread feeling that his position was not

going to be temporary. Franco was on his deathbed. The day before, the Assemblea de Catalunya, an umbrella body for most of the Catalan political organizations yearning for a share of power, issued a statement in which it declared that "only by rejecting the return of Juan Carlos I to the throne and by repealing Francoism's underlying laws, along with all of its component agencies and institutions or those bent on perpetuating it, which is to say, only a democratic break can put us on the path that leads to meeting the people's needs." But over time, these words were blown away on the wind. It was very easy to switch from a clean break with the regime to horse-trading with its representatives and those who had helped keep it in place, the markets that represented international capitalism. The United States and Germany were very clear as to what path had to be taken. If the script written by these two powers was followed, the practically unknown PSOE would claw back the ground occupied by the PCE, but neither of these forces was prepared to share its voters. Besides, that script was readily understandable: the US refused to see the Communist Party legalized and Germany had it in mind to capture the social democratic lead.

Since 1968, a section of the younger generation across Europe had been clamoring for structural changes and the pursuit of active policies to open up to anti-imperialist and anticapitalist social dynamics, but the markets that pulled the strings of supranational politics refused to let the Spanish state turn into a source of conflict in the wake of the regime's decapitation by natural causes. Everybody was in a hurry to do a bit of horse-trading. Meanwhile, on November 22, 1975, Juan Carlos as king pledged fealty to the "Principles of the Nationalist Movement" and, within weeks, the deputy premier Manuel Fraga Iribarne was opening discussions with the right-wing Basque Nationalists and representatives of the PSOE.

A broad swathe of the population, however, having nothing to do with this backstage wheeling and dealing, was bringing pressure from below. The labor strikes and the unrest on the university campuses spread right across the country. The CC.OO found itself overwhelmed. The political parties to the left of the PCE lost members, and international capitalism was forced to issue a call to order: "Kissinger, who throughout Gerald Ford's presidency served as Secretary of State, told *US News & World Report*, 'If Spain is left entirely to her own devices, the prospects may be catastrophic and the Western world knows it. It knows that whatever happens over there is vital as far as our political and military bloc is concerned.'"[1]

The political denouement started to become evident by the first half of 1976. The populace took to the streets to press for political change and poured out of the firms to lobby for better pay. The Madrid Metro was not operational on March 5, a strike having brought the service to a complete standstill; this was

---

1. J. Ribas, *Los 70 a destajo: Ajoblanco y libertad* (Barcelona: RBA, 2007), 336.

unprecedented. The army took charge of operating the trains. In Barcelona, on February 1 and 8, tens of thousands demonstrated under the slogan "Freedom, amnesty, home rule," and the political parties were utterly overwhelmed. So were the police. Young people played an active part in these mobilizations and were unmistakable about their differences with the political class, which was even then operating tentatively as a manipulating force in the service of capital: "From a clean break with the dictatorship and a referendum to decide between monarchy or republic, they switched to an 'negotiated break,' implicitly embracing the monarchy imposed by Franco."[2]

Weeks later, in Vitoria, the forces of repression allied themselves with the technocrats who had sketched out the political future. Following days of uncontrolled autonomous, assembly-based workers' strikes, five workers were murdered in the course of a disproportionate display of police strength. The message was clear: either the working class comes around to accepting the leadership of the parties and trade unions, or the unthinking violence for which the far-right fascists were clamoring would return. But the oppressed were clear as to what they wanted and were not deterred: "The events in Vitoria convulsed the country. The workers, aware that the liberalization policy was going to be determined on the streets, switched from moderate slogans and, in their assemblies, opted for combative actions against the high cost of living and the economic failure of Minister Villar Mir."[3]

A couple of months later, on the First of May, police violence returned to the streets of Barcelona following a brief truce marked by popular pressure for instant political and social changes: "On that day, the 'grays' . . . seized back power on the streets of Barcelona from defenseless and startled workers, who were too naïve to know that the majority parties in the Assemblea de Catalunya and "Platajunta" had already agreed on demobilization and compromises on reform (rather than a clean break)."[4]

The Platajunta, as the Democratic Coordinating Platform was popularly known, was a body that grew out of the amalgamation of the two coordinating bodies operating in Spain during the dying days of the dictatorship—the Democratic Junta powered by the PCE and right-wing independents and the Democratic Convergence Platform, promoted by the PSOE and the Christian Democrats. Only two months earlier, the monarchy had been called into question when it gambled on ushering in a phase that would lead "through a consultation of the people, on the basis of universal suffrage, to a decision on the makeup of the

2. J. Ribas, *Los 70 a destajo*, 424.

3. J. Ribas, *Los 70 a destajo*, 390.

4. Malvido, *Nosotros los malditos* (Barcelona, Anagrama, 2004), 82.

ministries and broader state institutions."[5] Repudiation of the people's demands on the part of virtually every political faction was moving ahead at a dizzying rate.

Over that summer, Adolfo Suárez took over as prime minister and automatically talks began with the political parties, which held their first public rallies—though unlawful they were now tolerated. But the PCE was excluded from all these formalities. The script outlined by the Germans and Americans was being followed, point for point. At the same time, the CC.OO was trying to secure exclusive representation of the working class by promoting a single union arrangement as a way of averting any shock and backing legalization of the PCE. That July saw the establishment of the COS (Coordinadora de Organizaciones Sindicales / Trade Union Organizations' Coordinating Body) made up of the CC.OO, UGT, and USO (Unión Sindical Obrera / Workers' Trade Union Unity). A couple of months after that, the parties began to reveal their brand-new narrative, and the demand now was not for a clean break but for a negotiated break. The horse-trading was also going in internally.

The year ended as it had begun. The wildcat strike at the Roca plant in the town of Gavà seemed like an encouragement to the working class to resist the pressure to remain part of the same machine that held it in slavery: "1976 was a spontaneous year in that no party could quite control the revolutionary spirit that was spreading through the streets and factories. Freedom had already taken hold of the people. What was not yet known was how the politicians buzzing around the press were going to handle this wealth of hope."[6]

Early in 1977, the horse-trading reached the courts and the Public Order Tribunal was transformed into the National High Court. The old structures were being recast without any sort of purging and without anyone's heeding the people's demands. One such demand, the insistence on an amnesty, was what lay behind the January 23 demonstration in Madrid, during which the student Arturo Ruiz was murdered by a far-right commando. The following day, the chair of the Supreme Court of Military Justice, General Villaescusa, was kidnapped by GRAPO (Grupos Revolucionarios Antifascistas Primero de Octubre / First of October Revolutionary Antifascist Groups). GRAPO had first surfaced six months before, and from the outset there were misgivings that it might have been infiltrated by the Spanish secret services. Within hours, and again in Madrid, during a demonstration protesting at the previous day's murder, the police killed the student Mari Luz Nakera. Before the day was over another fascist commando raided the offices of some labor lawyers close to the CC.OO and murdered five

---

5. R. Castro, et al., *Diez años sin Franco: Desatado y bien desatado* (Barcelona: El Periódico de Catalunya, 1985), 36.

6. J. Ribas, *Los 70 a destajo*, 364.

lawyers and their assistants. The message appeared to be the same as ten months before, in the wake of the incidents in Vitoria, but no longer just a matter of choosing between a reversion to the past or a future mapped out by international capitalism; now there was the added ingredient that groups to the left of the PCE, as embodied by GRAPO, were involved: "The contention that all these attacks reflected the plans of the same shadowy mastermind was the one most widely believed at the time."[7]

Interior minister Martín Villa put the head of the BPS (Brigada Político Social / Political-Social Brigade), Roberto Conesa, in charge of sorting out the general's abduction. The fact that the BPS had, officially, been done away with, did not mean that it had been dismantled. The horse-trading also extended to the forces of repression. The funeral of the lawyers murdered in Madrid turned into a show of strength and level-headedness on the part of the PCE. A little over a month after the incident, Adolfo Suárez held a secret meeting with Santiago Carrillo. It may have looked as if the Spanish government was straying from the path marked out by international economic and political elites, but this was not the case; in return for legalization of the PCE, Carrillo was ready to "make a public statement accepting the Monarchy and the two-colored flag, as well as plainly proclaiming support for the unity of Spain."[8] The PCE was legalized on April 9. Little by little, all the political parties were accepting the script that had been foisted upon them, but significant segments of the population still dreamed of a return to the Republic against which the mutinous military had risen up in 1936.

June 15 was the date set for the first set of elections, which were won by the UCD (Unión de Centro Democrática / Union of the Democratic Center), a new party formed by the prime minister. Just behind it in second place was the PSOE, and next—with under 10% of the votes—was the PCE, which was beginning to fall apart. At the same time, the CNT was surging ahead. After it was legalized in May 1977, the organization's first three major rallies after thirty-five years underground were massively attended. The San Sebastián de los Reyes and Valencia rallies were followed by one in Barcelona attended by hundreds of thousands. Weeks after that came the Jornadas Libertarias (Libertarian Festival) which again drew in several hundred thousand people. As if that was not enough, the autumn was ushered in by the Barcelona gas station workers' strike, a strike in which the libertarian union provided the backbone and which ended with victory for the workers. The renaissance of the CNT was starting to look scary: "The UCD Government was on the brink of a panic attack. If the CNT succeeded in articulating some of the

7. R. Castro, et al., *Diez años sin Franco*, 94.

8. R. Castro, et al., *Diez años sin Franco*, 97.

people's aspirations, Europe might have a change of mind. The fate of Italy was up in the air, and in Germany the Greens had not yet joined the parliament. Holland, Denmark, Sweden and other countries also had substantial autonomous grass-roots movements."[9]

The response from the establishment was not long in coming and went by the name of the Moncloa Palace Agreements, agreements that "were driven by Suárez and Carrillo."[10] The Suárez Administration was having a hard time of it and was coming under international pressure. Meanwhile Carrillo was worried about his own loss of influence over the workers. They both arrived at the same conclusion, which, as it happened, was the same one advocated by the International Monetary Fund; in the world of work, entrepreneurs needed to be given incentives, and the stability of the working class had to be undermined; in social terms, in return for bearing the costs of a new working pattern, which at the same time was still a form of control over the workers, the workers would enjoy a new welfare state that would strive to emulate that of other European countries like France or Germany, albeit never quite succeeding in this: "The agreements also implied consolidation of democratic reforms, in return for which the workers would bear the costs of the crisis in the economy through a reduction in real wages and a rise in unemployment."[11]

The Agreement was signed on October 25, and in Barcelona, on November 4, there was a united demonstration by all the trade unions under the slogan "For a way out of the crisis that favors the workers." The demonstration was a success; it drew tens of thousands of people and made it plain that the working class was not willing to bear the costs of social and political reforms. But it was an illusion: "Following the umbrella demonstration that successfully mobilized four hundred thousand people in Catalonia the bigwigs in Madrid . . . brought the alliance of the UGT and CC.OO with the CNT to an emphatic end. The possibility of a working class united and putting an end to the Moncloa Agreements terrified them."[12] Just two months after that, right after a demonstration against the Moncloa Agreements convened by the CNT on its own, a fire broke out at the Scala night club when a gang of young anarchists who had taken part in the demonstration hurled Molotov cocktails. Four workers perished in the flames, two of them members of the CNT. In under forty-eight hours, those who had thrown the devices were arrested along with dozens of innocent militants: "It has to be acknowledged

---

9. J. Ribas, *Los 70 a destajo*, 521.

10. R. Castro, et al., *Diez años sin Franco,* 129.

11. G. Wilhelmi, *El movimiento libertario en la transición: Madrid, 1975–1982* (Madrid: Fundación Salvador Seguí, 2012), 178.

12. J. Ribas *Los 70 a destajo*, 538.

that a lynching at the hands of the media was under way and overcoming it was no easy undertaking."[13]

At this point, on January 31, 1978, Interior Minister Rodolfo Martín Villa declared while commenting on the recent attacks (besides the Scala fire, there was the murder of the ex-mayor of Barcelona Joaquín Viola at the hands of a pro-independence group by means of a device attached to his chest, plus the parcel bomb the far right had sent to the editorial offices of the satirical magazine *Papus*, resulting in the death of one employee): "For me, the most worrying of them all is . . . the Scala because it definitely emanated from the libertarian movements. . . . I am especially concerned about such action on the part of anarchist groups in Barcelona." Meaning that, in the wake of the many murders carried out by the far right over the preceding two years, after pro-Catalan independence activists had murdered Joaquín Viola and, months before that, the entrepreneur José María Bultó, after ETA and GRAPO had racked up multiple murders, the minister was especially worried by the Barcelona libertarian groups which, unfathomably, in a harebrained act, had murdered four workers. Seeing is believing. Martín Villa was more worried by the murder of four workers than by the murder of businessmen, former high-ranking Francoists, policemen, and military: "Months later it came to light that an *agent provocateur* had been pulling the strings."[14] It was no coincidence that the *agent provocateur* was under the direct instructions of a subordinate of Commissioner Conesa, the man who had been head of the BPS and under the orders of none other than the minister himself. There was a sense that the two-year dream that had filled the hearts of an entire generation of young people with hope since the dictator's demise had come to an end: "The young see anarchism as the finest encapsulation of many of their aspirations: away with bosses and leaders, away with politicking; total freedom and equality instead."[15]

Nine months later, as murders by the far right as well as by ETA and GRAPO were still continuing, the Spanish Parliament voted through a Constitution on October 31. Only a handful of veteran fascists, members of the PNV (Partido Nacionalista Vasco / Basque Nationalist Party) and left-wing Catalan nationalists voted against it or abstained. The horse-trading was now reaching into the top echelons of the state.

In order to bring the movie to an end in accordance with the script, the PSOE signed up to the horse-trading: Felipe González forced the rest of the PSOE to jettison Marxism and strike it from its by-laws, by means of a hush-hush coup

13. J. Zambrana, *La alternativa libertaria: Catalunya, 1976–1979* (Barcelona: Edicions Fet a Mà, 2000), 167.

14. R. Castro, et al., *Diez años sin Franco,* 143.

15. Malvido, *Nosotros los malditos,* 63.

d'état inside his own party. In May 1979, at the party congress, González put forth a reformist proposition which did not pass. Then, realizing how influential a figure he was, he tendered his resignation, which forced an extraordinary congress to elect a new general secretary while also affording him time to play his hand in the offices, well out of sight of the rank-and-file: "The leader refused to carry on. He refused to be hampered by a line of policy not his own. And he played his trump card."[16] Just five months after that, on September 28, he was re-elected as general secretary and, at the same time, the party formally washed its hands of Marxism. There was now nothing to keep the PSOE from achieving power. But the facts, as signaled by the popular will, departed from the script, and in the home-rule elections in the Basque Country and Catalonia, in March 1980, the socialists gained no ground: in the Basque Country they were pushed into second place behind a brand-new coalition, the HB (Herri Batasuna / Popular Unity), while in Catalonia, contrary to all predictions, the CiU (Convergencia i Unió / Convergence and Union) took the most votes. González had to barge his way into office.

In May 1980, he proposed a motion of censure against Adolfo Suárez. This enabled him to "expose the government's weakness . . . and offer a moderate alternative,"[17] since the parliamentary proceedings were being broadcast on television for the first time. Two months later, during a visit to Lima, Peru, Suárez declared, "I am aware of the PSOE's plan to try to place a military man in the prime ministerial office."[18] On February 23, 1981, all popular misgivings about the monarchy and capitalist democracy evaporated. Civil Guard personnel commanded by the ultrarightist Lieutenant-Colonel Tejero stormed the Congress. In light of the ongoing escalation of armed activities of GRAPO and both wings of ETA, the terrifying prospect of a lurch backward was in the air, but on this occasion the stage management went a step further. Juan Carlos gave the performance of a lifetime and, in a TV appearance, pulled off what he had been trying to pull off for the past five years: getting the population to accept him as its king. The coup d'état was nothing of the sort: "What occurred and how it occurred can be understood only . . . in the context of the king's participation."[19]

A year and a half later, the horse-trading was drawing to an end with Felipe González's appointment as new prime minister. In seven years, those guilty of

---

16. R. Castro, et al., *Diez años sin Franco*, 176.

17. R. Castro, et al., *Diez años sin Franco*, 178.

18. *Zaragoza rebelde: Movimientos sociales y antagonismos, 1975–2000* (Zaragoza: Colectivo Zaragoza Rebelde, 2009), 437.

19. Colonel Pardo Zancada, convicted for his own role in the incidents, in *Zaragoza rebelde*, 437.

numerous offenses had secured immunity, the political parties had switched from clean break to reform, the TOP had become the National High Court, the king had pledged fealty to the Principles of the Nationalist Movement—and, subsequently, to the Constitution—the PCE had abandoned republicanism, the PSOE had done the same with Marxism, the UGT and CC.OO had given their blessing to laws that favored employers over workers, and the people's yearning for freedom had turned into the people's aspiration for the freedom . . . to go shopping.

Capitalism had achieved its purposes.

> "No one believes in revolution anymore, they're off hunting for bargains at the Corte Inglés"
> —ALMEN TNT, "YA NADIE CREE EN LA REVOLUCIÓN"

GERARD

Born into a humble family with a libertarian background in Manlleu, from a very early age Gerard attracted attention on account of his ideas. Among the various family members who had had first-hand experience of Francoist repression, two of his great uncles—both CNT members—stood out. One of them had fled to France and went on to become a survivor of Mauthausen concentration camp. The other was still living in the Osona comarca, broken by the torture he had endured while imprisoned at the end of the Civil War. From time to time, the whole family used to go visit his great uncle in France. From a young age, Gerard used to love listening to his great uncle. He always tried to talk him into retelling the stories of those years of terror and uncertainty.

Manlleu was an industrial town, something like a big company town centered around textile production. With the passing of the years and the arrival of a range of other industries, it expanded to become one of the main industrial centers in the comarca. Gerard's mother, who came from Torelló, and his father, a Manlleu native, were workers, and their precarious finances led Gerard to start working at the age of fourteen when he was not attending school. Back then, his mother had had to work for eighteen hours a day in order to stretch things out until the end of the month.

Born in 1955, Gerard began studying for his *bachillerato* on turning fifteen, at the only high school in the comarca, in Vic. He took part in his first demonstration to protest the Burgos trial. It acted as a starting pistol for the organization of an initial student group that openly claimed to be libertarian. Gerard did not follow the usual evolution of youngsters of his generation whose activism stated off in various Marxist groups; instead, family tradition and his first-hand knowledge of pre-war Catalonia helped ease him into social and political activism. He pored over Mikhail Bakunin, Piotr Kropotkin, Pierre-Joseph Proudhon, and other libertarian classics and dragged other youths along with him. To protest the New General Education Law, a nationwide day of struggle was called on February 14, 1972, and the very first handbills displaying the circle A symbol surfaced in the comarca. That signature scandalized the Francoists, the clergy, and the comarca's authoritarian opposition, triggering several arguments with groups from the authoritarian left, shocked by the appearance of a bunch of anarchist youths in what they had thought was their own stomping ground.

Then contact was established with an anarchist group from the Poble Nou barrio in Barcelona, one of the most active groups in the final years of the dictatorship. In 1973, Gerard capitalized upon this connection to pursue his education in the city and moved into the barrio. In Poble Nou, there was a bookstore in the Calle Pujades, run by a couple living in the same street; it was one of the main meeting places for the clandestine anti-authoritarian movement and a distribution point for clandestine publications. In Poble Nou, as the months slipped by, he came into contact with various Barcelona groups, ranging from the collective that published *CNT-Informa* to some of the members of the grupos autónomos later referred to as the OLLA, and the activists from the GOA (Grupos Obreros Autónomos / Autonomous Workers' Groups) whose activities centered on the neighboring town of Santa Coloma. At the same time, he began to distribute titles from Editorial ZYX. It was at about this point, on the basis of these connections, that he also came into contact with French groups and with the Italian publishers of *La Rivista Anarchica*. It was also at this time that he made his first trip to Paris, where he met up with comrades from both countries.

With the fall of the MIL comrades, a period of great activity was ushered in in the city, and Gerard and his comrades started working alongside the MIL Prisoners' Solidarity Committee. It was a time of wide-ranging radicalization among young Catalans, and that radicalization increased further following the execution of Puig Antich—a feeling of outrage spread through the youth due to the performance of the political-party opposition, which did very little to avert Puig Antich's execution. That spring, Gerard made the acquaintance of the veteran activist Luis Andrés Edo, made another trip to France and went on his first trip to Italy. Finally, in September 1974, after several comrades from the Poble Nou group were arrested (people who had been involved in the clandestine press conference called to claim the Baltasar Suárez kidnapping in Paris, Luis Andrés being one of them) he left for exile in Banyuls-sur-Mer in France where some uncles of his lived.

Shortly after that he moved to Perpignan, where he had links to comrades he had met in Barcelona, comrades like Felip Solé, who introduced him to his cousin Ignasi Solé Sugranyes, whose home became his first address. Once he had settled in, he started hanging out in places frequented by young libertarian exiles. He felt a great ideological kinship with the French people he met hanging out in L'Escletxa, and struck up great friendships, despite the fact that they were his elders. It was at the Librería Española that he met a neighbor from the Osona comarca with whom he started collaborating. This was Eduardo Soler from Vic, and he too was older than Gerard. Together with Eduardo he suffered his first arrest in January 1976, when the house he was sharing was unexpectedly searched and various explosives were uncovered. They both received six-month prison terms and served a couple of months in Perpignan's tiny, medieval prison. On his release, the comrades from L'Escletxa cautioned Gerard that, in their estimation, Eduardo was bad company and that there was more to his dark personality. But at the time, when they had spotted the Spanish police keeping Felip Solé's apartment under surveillance as well as other places were activists mingled, it never occurred to him that infiltration might be yet another weapon in the armory of the police.

After he left prison, Gerard met Agustín Rueda, newly arrived in Perpignan, and they quickly became friends, partly because of the closeness of their hometowns, partly because of their social background and ideological evolution. Agustín too had come to the libertarian movement without ever having been active previously in any Marxist group. It was during these years—1975 and 1976—that Gerard stated specializing in crisscrossing the Pyrenean border, helping numerous comrades enter and leave France.

Months after that, he got involved in an international operation passing counterfeit checks, an operation planned in Italy but implemented simultaneously in several countries in Europe. The passing was done sporadically and helped raise funds for several European groups and collectives as well as for ordinary criminals partnered with them. It was Gerard's fate to be sent to Holland with a female comrade. He was carrying several phony ID papers to be employed in cashing a succession of French money orders without arousing suspicions; in each of the offices targeted, Gerard would walk in using a different identity, passing himself off as a tourist or businessman. The repeated recourse to this type of action necessitated changes to the whole French postal money order system. The postal bank noted the brazen repetitions by those behind this international campaign, so much so that that part of the financial sector was brought to the brink of collapse. In the course of this operation, Gerard was arrested in Amsterdam in December 1976.

He was interrogated by police from several countries before they managed to identify him. Once they had done so, he was shipped off to prison where he was held in complete isolation for a month and then moved on to the dangerous prisoners' ward. That prison experience was the toughest of the several he was to have during his life: restricted association time, the feeling of isolation caused by the language barrier, missing family and comrades, and the fact that he had to spend his days in the company of murderers and dangerous, unscrupulous inmates made his prison time was hellish. A year later, in December 1977, he was expelled from the country, banned from returning and bundled onto a plane bound for Barcelona. Just days earlier, Michel, a comrade arrested in the course of the same operation but in Sweden, had also been expelled, and when the plane carrying him landed in

Barajas, several members of the forces of order were waiting for him; they placed him in Carabanchel Prison in preventive detention, with no charges pending. To avoid the same thing happening to Gerard, lawyer Mateo Seguí, the member of parliament Rodolfo Guerra, and senator Lluís María Xirinacs were waiting to greet him when his plane landed at El Prat airport. This gambit worked; Gerard arrived back on Spanish soil without a problem and went underground again.

More than three years had passed since he left Barcelona, but he had no problems upon his return in linking up with some of the comrades who had been part of his support network prior to Franco's death. These were the comrades that welcomed him back, people like Luis Andrés Edo, who was like a mentor to the young libertarian activists. At around this time, Edo introduced him to Irma.

In Perpignan in 1976, he had met El Rubio a non-political criminal from Almería who had embraced anarchist ideas. This was pretty commonplace back then, due to the fact that subversive activity inside the prisons was partly the product of the encounter between libertarian inmates and ordinary inmates. Both groups lobbied for amnesty, given that their being in prison was a byproduct of a fascist regime based on social inequalities. A month and a half after his arrival in Barcelona, El Rubio made contact with him, and they arranged to meet up in the first week in February. A few days earlier some French friends Gerard had met in L'Ecletxa two years earlier, including Bernard and his French partner, Isabelle, had come down from Perpignan to take part in a range of actions. The rendezvous was in the Plaza Vila de Madrid, but a number of circumstances made the activists miss it. So it was fate that brought about Gerard's fall, since El Rubio was an informer, and several Civil Guards had been waiting for him at the rendezvous site. That day, the Civil Guard personnel charged with arresting him, seeing that the activists had not shown up, headed for Sant Adrià del Besòs to arrest a shepherd who from time to time would help libertarian activists get across the border, in the hope that he might offer them some sort of lead on the French militants. As they were moving the shepherd by undercover police vehicle to the barracks in the Calle Sant Pau, as fate had it, they crossed paths with Gerard and Isabelle in El Moll de la Fusta. The two policemen stopped the vehicle, and after one of them snuck up on Gerard from behind, they pointed their submachineguns and proceeded to arrest them. The two guards called for assistance from the provincial office of the Ministry of Defense, which was just across the way from where the arrest had taken place, and after reinforcements had been requested from the Sant Pau barracks the prisoners were removed to the police station. There they were subjected to a very rough interrogation, especially the French comrades, in whose case it included a range of torture methods such as the *bolsa*, in which a bag was placed over their faces, along with brutal beatings. At the same time, the Civil Guard raided a farmhouse in Maçanet de Cabrenys in the Alt Empordà. This farmhouse belonged to some young French people and was used by activists as a staging post for crossing the border. In all, ten people were arrested during the operation, including Ignasi Solé Sugranyes, one of Gerard's friends and regular collaborators.

On February 17, within a few days of Gerard's arrival in the Modelo Prison, a prison riot erupted. Among the many libertarian prisoners there at the time were the ones charged with the arson attack on the Scala, "Boni" and El Moro (who had also been arrested on the basis of information provided by El Rubio a few days earlier), plus Gerard and his co-arrestees, but whereas the Scala accused stayed in the Second Ward, all the others had been in the First where the riot had erupted. When the riot squad entered to subdue the uprising they headed straight for the First Ward, firing rubber bullets and clubbing all the inmates, especially the libertarians, some of whom they accused of having detonated a device at the Modelo's gates on January 23. Gerard still carries a memento of that experience in the shape of a gash in his head. Days later, they found out about the murder of their friend Agustín Rueda in Carabanchel Prison, and on learning that the comrades being held in Madrid had launched a hunger strike, some of them joined it. Further detainees arrive at around this time, among them some comrades accused of having raked the Cornellà police barracks with gunfire as a response to Agustín's murder, and just before he was released that April, the members of the ERAT had been admitted. Like the comrades in the Scala affair, they had been caught due to informing by Gambín.

On his release, Gerard moved to Osona, where he had not been living for the past five years. He had previously gone there to set up an important libertarian network, but the situation now was very different: aside from the CNT, which was beginning to gain a strong foothold with locals in Vic, Torelló, Seva, Manlleu, and Roda de Ter, an ateneo libertario had been opened in Vic. Despite that presence, he was progressively distancing himself from action (a result of his being worn out and disillusioned). Even so he remained part of the cultural agitation network of the CNT and the Ateneo Libertario. It was active pressure brought to bear by that network—which called demonstrations, lock-ins, and other actions— that forced the dismissal of the charges against him, although, officially, he was never brought to trial for lack of evidence. Furthermore, a few months later, the Osona Committee for Solidarity with Libertarian Prisoners organized a Festival of Solidarity on July 22–25, which drew a large attendance. Neither Gerard nor his friends had forgotten about the comrades languishing behind bars.

After that summer he secured his diploma as a teacher of Catalan and quickly found a job at a school where he exploited his knowledge of French. Meanwhile he also worked on setting up the Café Rossinyol in Manlleu, a local replica of the El Pla de la Garsa restaurant that Ignasi Solé had opened in the Calle Assaonadors. The curious thing about the Café Rossinyol was that it occupied the premises of the former Civil Guard barracks, and members of that corps took that as a personal affront. This led to unrelenting harassment over the three years that Gerard was the proprietor. Not that his return to the area where he had been born and raised was spared other conflicts. The members of the craven left that had buried its head in the sand at the time of the murder of Puig Antich or during the revolt by the non-political prisoners demonstrated their ideological impoverishment by also harassing his nearest and dearest.

In 1982, he returned to Barcelona where he settled for the next seven years, working at El Pla de la Garsa restaurant, and severed all connections with activism, assuming that the battle had been lost.

NO BORDERS

"I haven't the strength to light the fuse anymore, but my conscience is undiminished. There are others around and rightly they revel in the stuff that sustains my hopes. A better world rather than the best of worlds."

—MARÍA MOMBIOLA

France was the chief exit from the Spanish state and the place where the largest network supporting the militants operating in the Spanish interior were concentrated. But she was not the only one: Portugal, Switzerland, Holland, Belgium, and Italy also boasted relatively large groups that were part of the support network. Amsterdam, Lisbon, Brussels, Zurich, or Milan were cities where the activists might spend an interval resting up or attempting to create, maintain or expand aid networks and secure safehouses and provisions. In many of these cities, activists from Spain worked hand in glove with local groups that also indulged in armed action.

As far as Mediterranean activists we concerned, Perpignan was a must-visit, but Toulouse was referred to as the Spanish Colony due to the sheer numbers of exiles living there. On reaching France, if the plan was to stay there, what was needed was a Political Refugee Certificate, initially a permit valid for three months and later valid for an indefinite period. To secure such a certificate, one had to be living on French soil, generally in some comrade's home, and fill out a form that was then sent off to the National Refugee Bureau in Paris. It was actually a pretty straightforward process, but at the same time it did require a modicum of support from the comrade who had taken one in.

In Toulouse, there were a number of stopping points for newly arriving libertarians seeking refuge on political grounds. The most significant public space was the CNT premises on Rue Belfort, but equally important were the Amorós bookstore run by Jaume Amorós Vidal, a libertarian militant from Vilafranca del Penedès who had been in exile since the 1940s, and the second-hand bookstalls in the Sunday flea-market. That Sunday market was a weekly rendezvous point for the entire libertarian community, a natural communications center where the elderly exiles, and by extension, their ,families, could hear news, especially if some new comrades had arrived, how many of them and who they were, what they needed and where they were lodging. It was their special window on the country that they had been forced to leave behind.

Other rendezvous points, equally important, were private homes such as the home of María Mombiola, who harbored dozens of young activists coming up from the south, or Hortensia Torres's home. María Mombiola, born in Zaragoza on March 3, 1914, as María Lozano Molina, took the name of her partner Ángel Mombiola who was shot in France by German troops in 1944. As to Hortensia *madre* (so called to differentiate her from her daughter), she, along with her partner Mario Inés, kept up her activism in Barcelona until well into the 1950s. This was one factor that allowed her to keep in touch with some of the Spanish networks into the 1970s, and her apartment was regularly used to crash in. Hortensia, the matriarch of an entire family of activists was a public figure who worked for the SIA (Solidaridad Internacional Antifascista/International Antifascist Solidarity). She was a strong woman due to the times she lived in, including a war and a no less cruel post-war period; for a time, around May '68, they called her *Mama Che* since one of her sons, aged fourteen, used to wear an army jacket and a black beret displaying a red star in the center, and beneath it his locks fell to just above shoulder-height. He was "Little Che" and "used to make a really heart-warming effort to play up his resemblance to Che."[1] On more than one occasion, Spanish police officers showed up to Hortensia's home uninvited, but even when she had her suspicions, Hortensia would offer them a cup of coffee and bombard them with questions, trying to find out if the really were police. After the 1970s, and especially after Franco's death, Spanish libertarians living in France were obliged to be on their guard. There was a huge upsurge in the numbers of informers and Spanish spies.

In the Perpignan of the early 1970s, the CNT local was no longer the chief destination of young anti-authoritarians. Whenever somebody arrived from Spain, the exiles who ran the place still asked to see their union cards, but these youngsters had no credentials, as the CNT had gone underground and had all but evaporated inside Spain. In Perpignan, the first port of call from 1974 onward was the Librería Española bookstore run by Enric Melich. Melich had been a member of the French Resistance, the maquis, which had been active until the sixties. The following decade, he began harboring and providing logistical support to all the youngsters determine to fight, first of all the dictatorship, and, later, against the

---

1. J. M. Rouillan, *De memoria (I): Otoño de 1970 en Toulouse* (Barcelona: Virus, 2009), 22.

return of the Bourbons. Such was importance of his bookstore that sometimes, when a new arrival dropped in at the Perpignan police headquarters for information about how to go about getting temporary papers, they were referred to the Librería Española.

The other popular port of call was Mariano Puzo's kiosk outside Perpignan's movie theater. Those were the days of *Last Tango in Paris* and *Emmanuelle*, movies banned in Spain, for which reason there was a steady flow of movie-loving tourists from the south. Among the many fans of the seventh art lurked youngsters who, once they had crossed the border, had no intention of going back. El Garfio, [Meat Hook] which was what some people called him, stood at his stand where he sold sweets and dried fruit and gave them directions to where he thought they might find a welcome. Aragón-born Mariano Puzo had been an important partner of the libertarian guerrillas in the 1940s and 1950s. In November 1947, while they were making preparations in the Mas Tartàs base in Ossejà for José Luis Facerías and his group to make their crossing of the border, a hand grenade exploded which caused Mariano to lose his left forearm.

In Perpignan in the dying days of Francoism, another important point of contact for young people was a set of premises known as L'Escletxa, located on Rue de la Lanterne; it was the local of the FAF (Fédération Anarchiste Française / French Anarchist Federation) to which young French activists belonged. Some of them later went on to operate south of the Pyrenees.

Ten minutes apart, both sets of premises, the Librería Española and L'Escletxa were blown up on the night of July 14, 1976. Both bombings were ascribed a few years later to Eduardo Soler, an informer who worked for the Spanish security forces as well as their French counterparts. Within months, Eduardo Soler, who had wangled his way into libertarian activist circles in the city a couple of years earlier, bought the bookstore off Enric Melich and, as we shall see, caused some irreparable damage.

Initially the crossing of the border was done in one direction only, south to north. Activists south of the Pyrenees would cross over into France either on the run after their involvement in the anti-Franco resistance had been uncovered, in which case they applied for political asylum, or to collect gear (raging from books to weapons) with a view to continuing their activities within Spain, in which case they had no need to apply for asylum as their stay would be brief. There was a third group, though, and over time it too would provide a significant cohort of activists. This was the group made up of draft dodgers and deserters, young folk who refused to perform or to complete their military service for the fascist Franco regime.

Moreover, over time, this one-directional crossing of the border was undergoing changes due to the activism of upcoming generations of European youngsters who had grown up in the shadow of May '68. The first instances of borders crossing "in the inverse direction," from north to south (in the form of young activists from countries in the north coming down to operate inside Spain) was that of the MIL's French activists, who decided in 1971 to go into action south of the Pyrenees. They were followed by libertarian comrades from Zurich, the ones who, as we have seen, took part in the odd OLLA operation in Barcelona. After a hiatus of a couple of years, French activists taking part in operations mounted inside Spain became pretty commonplace (as was the presence of the children of exiles, who had been born or at any rate raised in their neighboring country).

In the last week of January 1978, El Moro was arrested in Barcelona. El Moro was the son of a former militiaman, José Mira, who, during the Civil War, had served as the delegate of one of the ten *Agrupaciones* making up the Durruti Column. José Mira had had five hundred men under his command. When the war ended, he crossed over to Algeria and settled in Kabylia, where El Moro was born. As a military trainer, his father backed the armed rebels seeking independence for their country, but later, once independence had been won, the pressures applied to Europeans forced the family to move to France. Like many a son of Spaniards, El Moro carried out his very first armed actions in support of the MIL prisoners in the city of Montpellier where he was living.

A few days after that, during the first week in February, and again in Barcelona, Bernard Pensiot and Isabelle Dominique Loeb were arrested. Meanwhile Víctor Simal and Oscar Magro were arrested in a farmhouse in Maçanet de Cabrenys used as a support base for border crossings: all four were French. Victor's parents were Catalans, and Bernard belonged to a group of youngsters who had used L'Escletxa in Perpignan as the nerve center for their activism. Both were brutally tortured in the Civil Guard barracks on Calle Sant Pau in Barcelona. They served sixteen months in Spanish prisons before being placed on conditional release but, since they failed to show up for their trial when it did go ahead, Victor was rearrested on August 15, 1989, in Santiago de Compostela while working for French public television. He spent two months in prison in Galicia but was eventually acquitted on all counts.

On May 24, 1978, while entering Spain via La Jonquera in a car carrying several firearms, Jacques André Garcin was arrested; he was a member of the Montpellier group and was placed in the Girona Prison.

All these young activists belonged to French autonomous or libertarian groups, and they had crossed the Pyrenean border in pursuit of an internationalism that was an inseparable and intrinsic part of their activism, reckoning that their efforts were needed inside Spain perhaps more so than in their own country.

On September 7, during a demonstration in support of the gas station workers' strike, the Italian activist Pasquale Vaira was arrested; he was jailed in the

Modelo for a few days. Before the month was out, on the night of September 27, Jean Claude Torres, a former member of the MIL, was arrested in Badalona. He was wearing a blood-stained shirt and seemed to have drunk too much, but they could not connect him with any armed action. The forces of order had had no word about a tunnel that a group of comrades were trying to dig in the Girona Prison, using the sewer network in an effort to free Jacques André Garcin and three comrades arrested the month before in the course of the holdups of two bank branches in Lloret. On the same night just a few hours earlier, five comrades, having worked on an escape plan, approached a concert being given by Al Di Meola and Música Urbana for the inauguration of the Youth Pavilion in Badalona, and had a few more drinks. On returning to Barcelona in a stolen car, they had an accident in which one of the comrades sustained some superficial injuries; after wiping their fingerprints from the car, they decided to split up. It was at this point, after they had split up, that Jean Claude was arrested along with one of the Valencian comrades. Incredibly, despite his record, Jean Claude was released on the French border a few days later. He had been expelled from Spain on account of his past, but no attention had been paid to his present.

A few months after that, on February 23, 1979, Patricia Bouwer, the niece of El Moro, was arrested in Barcelona along with another twelve comrades. Internationalist action had become a fact as far as these youngsters from both sides of the Pyrenees were concerned. Before the year was out, a tunnel was discovered in the vicinity of the Modelo Prison in Barcelona. At first, no arrests were made, but once they picked up the first Valencian comrades involved in the digging, Jean Claude was implicated as well. Also involved in the tunnel was the brother of El Moro, one of the inmates who would have reaped the benefit had the operation been pulled off.

A year later, on October 12, 1980, Alain Drogou, a French activist who had been engaged in the fight in Spain for several years, was arrested in Valencia in the presence of several autónomo comrades. He had been arrested on a number of occasions and was later linked to the FIGA. And on May 20, 1981, in Bilbao, the Portuguese activist Francisco José Oliverio was picked up in the course of a crackdown that also hit Vitoria, Errenteria and Valladolid and resulted in the arrests of ten comrades.

Throughout these years, and especially during the 1970s, the situation was pretty much the same in France and elsewhere in Europe. Young Spanish militants suffered repression at the hands of the various national security forces. Oriol Solé had already sampled French prisons as a member of the MIL. The same goes for his sister, Mariona, in Switzerland after she helped smuggle antitank mines meant for the OLLA into France, and which reached Barcelona inside a suitcase left on the TALGO train service. Also in 1974, several members of the GARI, Spanish nationals, were arrested in France—people such as Ángel Moreno Patiño, who served ten months in Paris, or Josep María Condom Bofill, who served several months in Fresnes Prison. Mario Inés Torres served nearly three years in Paris for his GARI connections, from September 1974 to May 1977. In Portugal, Madrid resident Paco was arrested in mid-1975 while preparing to raid a quarry with other comrades. On returning to France, he was arrested again in Perpignan on January 8, 1976, following a search of the apartment where he was living. Josep Palau fell along with the sinister Eduardo Soler. Both received six-month prison sentences for possession of explosives. Toward the end of the year Michel and Gerard were arrested in a collective drive to cash counterfeit money orders. Michel was picked up in Gothenburg, Sweden, and Gerard in Amsterdam. The same thing happened to Sabata who was imprisoned in Stockholm during a similar operation.

French subject Robert Touati and the Madrid activist Jaime Diego Ruiz Donales perished in Toulouse on March 8, 1976. The explosives they were about to plant, symbolically, at the door of the police barracks due to be visited the following day by the French Interior Minister Michel Poniatowski, went off inside their vehicle. Their partners, Paloti and Sylvie, who were nearby, called the emergency services before taking to their heels. The action had been intended to press for the release of the three GARI members still behind bars. Diego had obtained the explosives in Perpignan, where they knew him as "El Madriles." Luckily for the Madrid-based grupos autónomos, the Spanish police did not probe too deeply, since a proper investigation might have led to a series of falls in the Spanish capital. Before turning up in France, Diego had been living in Lisbon for a little over a year. Portugal was the territory that the Madrid comrades used as their base outside of Spain, especially after the April 1974 revolution there.

The earliest groups of young Madrid autónomos fleeing to Portugal crossed the border as part of an action in solidarity with Puig Antich or right after his murder. At more or less the same time the Carnation Revolution was under way. They were made welcome there by elderly Portuguese libertarian activists like Modesto or Custodio, activists who had defied the dictatorship and who, from the house they had in the Graça barrio's Rua Angelina Vidal, were publishing *A Batalha*, the emblematic newspaper of the Portuguese libertarian movement. Right from the outset, these premises were the center of operations for the Madrid autónomos. It was also where they met with the activist who had had a hand in organizing an attempt on Franco's life, an attack called off due to the presence of two children at the very moment and location when the dictatorship should have been blown up by an explosive device. That activist, who died while the Madrid comrades were in Lisbon, was a man of few words: during one period in detention he had bitten right through his own togue to avoid betraying his comrades. With a revolution in progress, the youngsters decided to play their part, and over time, some of them moved south, where they came into contact with the LUAR (Liga de Unidade e Ação Revolucionaria / Revolutionary Unity and Action League), a revolutionary left-wing armed group with which they developed close links.

In Italy in 1977, the activist Guillem de Pallejà was arrested and charged with membership in Azione Rivoluzionaria. Guillem had fled the Iberian peninsula and reached Italy with the support of Mario Inés Torres, who was starting to become a bit of an expert at crossing borders. Two years later, in 1979, Miguel, on the run from the Basque Country for the previous two years, was picked up on the French border, coming from Belgium. He served six months in Valenciennes Prison and was later deported to Switzerland.

There were various ways of crossing borders. One of the most commonplace, as long as one had support from comrades on both sides, was to cross on foot, while covering most of the distance by car. A car would drop the activist wanting to cross over at a safe distance from the border and another car, on the other side, would be waiting for him at a specified location not far away. The activist needed to hike for a few kilometers which was the most ticklish part of the journey of course, but it was a quite straightforward operation and the risks were limited.

When gear had to move across the border, this was very often done with vehicles that had been prepared in advance: the gas tanks might be divided in two, one half being a hiding place for weapons; that was very commonplace. In such instances, the vehicle would be manned by a single activist. Over the years, several comrades using this method were caught.

For a number of years, there was also a very small network of safehouses on both sides of the border, very close to it. This meant that the crossing cold be made in a single day and travelers could rest before pressing on. However, old-style crossings continued, the way the former maquis had done them. When he had to smuggle gear across, Petit Loup preferred to do it solo and on foot since he was familiar with the mountains and had no doubts about his own physical strength. It was the same with Agustín Rueda. Others, as long as they were not too overburdened, and when the goal was simply to relocate themselves elsewhere, preferred to use public transportation services between the small towns on either side, services mainly used by the townspeople and only moderately monitored.

The time of day chosen for crossing the border also had to be taken into consideration. At certain hours it was easier due to the strict timetables by which the border agencies operated. The safest times were in the early hours of the morning before the change of shift when the guards would be asleep, at mealtimes or during the afternoon siesta. There were also more daring comrades who trusted to their ability to circumvent the methodical monitoring methods of the police on both sides. Between the two customs posts, the French and the Spanish, there was usually a line of police in position. Customs agents monitored the people crossing over whereas the police made it their business to check goods passing over. On more than one occasion, Enric Melich smuggled folk south-to-north in a very straightforward manner; in order to get past the initial check by customs agents, he would hide the fugitive in the trunk; the agents would ask to see Enric's papers and would wave him through. Then, before they came to the police checkpoint, the runaway would move to the front passenger seat. When they came to the police line, the police would search the vehicle and find nothing out of the ordinary. Once this second check was over, the passenger would climb back into the trunk and enter French territory without a hitch.

However, the safest procedure was still to rely on the historical network that had been in use since the Second World War, one that relied on the experience of smugglers from the southern side of the Pyrenees and the collaboration of Civil Guards who had been recruited, either because they were ideologically opposed to the regime or in need of supplementary income. These were policemen who would knowingly look the other way when it came to letting a particular vehicle over the border at an agreed hour. This procedure, though, was used mainly to assist the escapes of activists who enjoyed the backing of long-established organizations. The autónomo activists found it hard to avail themselves of it.

JOSÉ

His involvement in clandestine actions dated back to when he was fifteen or sixteen. Those were very innocuous propaganda actions, but the regime's inflexibility turned them into criminal offenses. Born in 1953 in Ribes de Fresser, he grew up in Elgoibar until his family eventually settled once and for all in Barcelona's Sants barrio where, before the end of the 1960s, he and two of his brothers came to join a cellular structure of small grupos autónomos scattered right across the peninsula: Murcia, Madrid, Vitoria, Zaragoza, Barcelona. Their actions consisted mainly of daubing graffiti and group distribution of leaflets, but as they got to know one another and developed a group consciousness, they also started mounting pickets, setting up self-defense squads and clandestine student demonstrations. These were very small groups: in Barcelona they would have no more than ten or twelve members, but they had access to a network of letter drops that meant that they could publicize their actions and proposals safely to groups in other places. The first expropriation, the next step in the active expansion of the group, was carried out at the Universidad Autónoma in Bellaterra. They needed a photocopier to print the subversive propaganda they would then go on to distribute.

José was drawn into grupo autónomo membership in the most casual way, impelled by his youth. Things were about to explode, and the physical, cultural, and educational repression left only one path open to many restless young people witnessing the dying days of the regime. It's not just that their education was limited, history had been misrepresented, and they were just waking up to that fact. Catalan culture and working-class culture were harshly repressed, and even the most progressive sectors of the Church were suffering the fall-out. Aggression was ever-present, and they had to defend themselves. Their consciousness was firming up; even though they had never been involved in big political debates, everyone read the same books and headed off into the hills to share the conclusions at which they arrived individually; not only were they educating themselves politically, they were getting stronger as a group.

In the dying days of Francoist rule, around 1973 and 1974, they began carrying out urban guerrilla activity. They didn't use firearms, though, and mainly threw

Molotov cocktails and did propaganda actions. This was the point at which they came into contact with the Estudiants Llibertaris and continued on their ideological rapprochement with anarchism, an ideology with which they were discovering common ground. On weekends, in a quarry in Molins de Rei in the Sierra de Collserola, they began experimenting with incendiary devices. They also trained as a group in how to withstand torture in the event of their being arrested.

From their vantage point in Barcelona, they came to realize that the propaganda potential they possessed was nonexistent elsewhere in places such as Murcia or Málaga, and they made up their minds to rectify that. José started making trips up to Perpignan to pick up propaganda materials for shipment to southern Spain. The group's members were specializing, and José took charge of vehicle procurement. However, the group's sphere of influence was broadening, and its cellular and radial format meant that, even though the core was still only ten or twelve people, anything up to a hundred people might be involved on occasion. Each group member had an autonomous network of his own. Thus, José could call on a backup network if need be, a network made up of teachers free of all suspicion but who would, for the sake of friendship and loyalty, harbor him if needed. At the same time, as the person in charge of the procurement and preparation of vehicles, he set up a structure with some libertarian comrades who had a mechanic's workshop. There he readied the false bottoms in the fuel tanks, the hiding place in which all sorts of clandestine gear was ferried over the border.

And then came 1975, at which point they came to the conclusion that the situation had altered irreversibly. On the one hand, they needed to brave legality, leave clandestinity behind and operate openly. On the other, they needed to insert themselves into a broader movement, since the revolution could not be imposed on people but had to be the outcome of considered thought and mass action. That year they held a congress in Málaga: this was the first time that all the groups had come together, and they decided to make contact with the organized libertarian movement. In Barcelona, that was easy: in January 1976, José and other members of his group took part in the CNT reconstruction meeting held in the Sant Medir church in his barrio. These days, he believes this was a serious tactical error because in the short term, integration into the CNT meant the breakup of the network and therefore the loss of their biggest strength, which had consisted precisely of their being autonomous: they were able to function as a network, and break apart as needed.

It was in the year that they joined the CNT that José took part in setting up the Syndicate of Love. After nightfall downtown city dwellers in need of greater freedom came together to mingle. After finishing his work for the union, José would go partying. His roommate had repeatedly argued that he needed to get out and about at night: if all they did was work and handle union business, they would end up becoming a couple of SOBs that would demand the same sort of uptight righteousness from the others as well. In his roommate's opinion, the alternative consisted of going out every night and learning from the wide variety of interconnected nightlife. As they were young and full of energy, this became their normal practice. From job to union, from union to the Ramblas, and from the Ramblas to bed.

Around the Ramblas and the Plaza Real, which were teeming with life back then, movie directors, musicians, writers, cartoonists mingled with prostitutes. On many a night, once the fashionable music bars closed down, young unpretentious libertarians would grab one last drink in the dimly lit bars playing sexy music in the backstreets of the Barrio Chino where the prostitutes plied their trade. It was during such nocturnal mingling that some young sex-workers raised their own issues. They wanted liberation too. The girls were dependent on the pimps who exploited them because they had no outside support to rely upon. The young people did not give it a lot of thought. Despite the reluctance of the Entertainment Workers' Union, but under its auspices, they launched the Syndicate of Love for the girls to join. For some months, José and other comrades, before going to work, made it their business to gather the girls together around the doors of the bars just as their shift was ending. They went armed in case they had to deal with any pimps who tried to reclaim what they regarded as their workforce.

The Librería Español in Perpignan was José's starting point. He was personally handed his first shipments of propaganda materials by Enric Melich, and José took them over the border himself. Later, he made the acquaintance of Eduardo Soler who introduced him to a truck driver who might facilitate the work. On the one hand, José might be spared the risk of arrest; on the other, every shipment would be much larger, given the truck's capacity. The first time the truck driver crossed the Pyrenees carrying the propaganda, when José approached the pick-up point in Sants train station to pick up the material, he had a feeling he was being tailed. Having taken the usual security measures, and finding his suspicions confirmed, he managed to shake off his pursuers, alerted his comrades and hightailed it to Murcia. The truck driver was an informer belonging to Eduardo's network, although they had yet to make the connection between Eduardo and betrayal. They merely tipped off their contacts in Perpignan so that they could sever all contacts with the driver.

In Murcia, he was welcomed with open arms, having come from a hive of activity like Barcelona. A very active group was starting to take shape at the campuses, and he quickly joined it. They printed and distributed propaganda, held joint workshops with autonomous groups of workers, and participated individually in political projects that the CNT refused to get involved in as a union. When groups of workers already organized on the basis of assemblies proposed joining a union, he would pay them a visit to tell them that their best option would be to affiliate as a federated structure. That way, if the union failed to live up to expectations, they could easily un-affiliate and try their luck with some other union. As far as they were concerned the CNT was still just a means to an end. The purpose of their struggle was to encourage the growth of the movement, drawing in more and more people: their tools were the CNT, propaganda, and their own individual commitment. In Murcia as in Barcelona before it, their first action was to steal a photocopier so that they could churn out their own propaganda. They walked into a national school in the town of Ceutí and snatched it.

It was in Murcia that the issue of guns was raised. After a lot of discussion, they decided to use weapons as yet another tool in their struggle. They took it for granted that if their struggle gained mass support and clashed with the interests of the authorities, it would sooner or later be outlawed. Given that prospect, they decided to hold on to a clandestine structure. That took cash, and in order to get hold of some they might need guns; but they never regarded themselves as an armed-struggle group and their preferred means of raising funds was counterfeiting. They made contact with a comrade working in a bank who primarily sold apartments on the Mediterranean coast to foreign investors. Together, they devised a strategy that allowed them to get hold of the money they needed through sales of nonexistent apartments, and this lasted quite a while. Besides, this sort of fraud was low risk. When the police stumbled upon it, the banker comrade was not even jailed since the management chose to start over rather than have customers discover how untrustworthy its financial practice was. The news never reached the public.

On January 30, 1977, on one of his trips up to Perpignan, there was a crackdown in Barcelona that resulted in forty-six arrests in connection with a peninsular conference of the FAI. On his return to the city, José was arrested. Not that he had any connection to the Federation, but down in Murcia there was a comrade who was a member of it, and he had involved other libertarian activists in Murcia as well as in Málaga. This was the first time the name of Joaquín Gambín had cropped up. José believes that at that point Gambín had not yet turned informer, but others believe there was a direct connection between him and the dismantling of the Murcian group. It looks as if Gambín was the source of an arms shipment received by the militant belonging to the Murcian FAI. The rest of the people arrested, who were CNT members, had no knowledge of this, but the police, in order to make the announcement more juicy, lumped them all together, from the theft of the copy machine carried out on June 20 of the previous year to the weapons found on the FAI militant, not forgetting a bank holdup in a Murcian town on December 11.

The police station on Via Laietana was filled to overflowing. The anarchists rounded up a couple of weeks earlier filled every cell, and José was cuffed to a radiator in the middle of the corridor. Following the GRAPO murder of one of their colleagues in the Barcelona Metro, the police were seething, and since he was right in their path, José took a blow every time a police officer passed him by. Seventeen days later he was behind bars in the Modelo.

He arrived there just a week after the COPEL had announced its existence with a riot in Carabanchel Prison and, even though José was in a cell with some comrades, he was drawn to the ordinary prisoners. In any event, this was a time during which the political prisoners enjoyed special treatment. The warders could not be sure where the political situation was headed and as a precaution, they treated them with respect for a time. On October 28, there was a riot and, like many of other inmates, José found himself in isolation. Within days, while he was in solitary, the amnesty was announced. He was among the second to last group of libertarians to get out—a group that was fourteen strong—but nearly a dozen comrades were left inside; they came mostly from the Sants barrio.

On his release, he again took charge of organizational and propaganda matters, supporting and helping to set up Radio Libertina and the Ateneo Libertario in Sants, but eight months later, in June 1978, the amnesty was revoked, for him as well as for another sixteen comrades. Officially, it was being rescinded because clemency had been granted to those who had fought for democracy, and he did not fit the description. The fact of the matter is that the seventeen comrades affected by this revocation stood out as combative CNT militants who had been agitating for a clean break, which is to say, they rejected the compacts that certain sections of the union were working toward as a means of bringing peace to society.

At the same time, along with his comrades, he carried on prioritizing counterfeiting activity as a means of raising funds. This was the point at which they contacted a doctor who was working for the Diputación in Barcelona, and they successfully defrauded that institution of some millions of pesetas. A Christmas bonus was paid to all doctors working in Diputación-run hospitals in the same way, on a specific date, by means of a coded check. For weeks they had been readying ID cards and professional credentials from the College of Physicians, all of them phony, as well as the bank checks to be used. Once everything was ready, they waited until the night before payments were due, and the comrade told them what the code was that would appear on all the checks to be handed out the following day. Dozens of young libertarians ensured that, early the next morning before the genuine doctors could cash their checks, they showed up instead at the various bank premises to cash the phony checks made out the night before. Ten percent of the overall figure raised finished up in the coffers of the group so that it could carry on preparing actions, with the remainder being kept by each of the participants to be spent however they saw fit.

José was arrested again on May 21, 1979, this time, though, while crossing the border via La Jonquera. Civil Guards discovered, hidden under a false bottom in the trunk of the Seat 1430 he was driving, two submachineguns, a revolver and a selection of ammunition. Under questioning, he stated that he had gone to pick the car up in Perpignan and that he was supposed to leave it in a street in the Sants barrio with the keys in the exhaust pipe. The police knew rightly that he had not come from Perpignan, although they were none too clear as to where he had come from. Everything appeared to suggest that one of the two comrades in the know about the operation had sold him out. One of them was highly trusted. Three days after that, José was sent to Figueres Prison. Just three months later, on August 29, the media picked up on the discovery of a tunnel on the premises of the prison. José had been working on it along with a couple of non-political inmates, a young Colombian who was actively helping him and a French inmate who acted as lookout. All three were transferred. They passed through the Modelo, the Huesca Prison, and served three days in Carabanchel Prison before the French guy and José finished up in Segovia Prison. On arrival in Segovia, José asked to be taken to the political prisoners' ward, even though he was not acknowledged as being one at the time. Having been arrested on his own and as they were unable to pin any other armed actions on him or membership of any armed group, his offense was categorized as smuggling arms with no political motivation.

By then, the situation in the prisons was not what it had been two years earlier. In the wake of COPEL actions, heroin had flooded the state prison system, and José opted to be locked up with his libertarian and autónomo comrades from Madrid, Valladolid, Valencia, and Barcelona then serving time in Segovia. In concert with a few of them, he had another go at tunneling out, but luck was not on their side. He remained in Segovia for about a year until his lawyer, Mateo Seguí, finally secured him a provisional release.

Once back on the outside, he felt alone. The situation had changed. The repression and social changes had devastated the libertarian movement. He was in despair, disoriented, and had lost trust in his comrades. He decided to move away. But first he stood trial in Figueres on a tax matter. He had failed to pay the VAT on the guns he had been trying to smuggle into the country. With Mateo Seguí's help, he was acquitted. In the end, he crossed the border via Andorra and fled to Perpignan. A few months later, he moved up to Paris to secure the phony papers that would enable him to move around safely. Once he had his new papers, off he went to Italy, to Livorno where he had contacts in free radio circles, but the situation there was pretty much the same as in Spain: after years of struggle, the battle had been lost. He made up his mind to try his luck in Amsterdam.

In Amsterdam he was welcomed by an old girlfriend who was his introduction to the *kraker* movement. The *kraker* movement drew youngsters from all over

Europe, ranging from petty criminals to activists, intermingling with Dutch students as well as Latin American refugees on the run from dictatorships at home. It was a broad-based, maverick movement, and he quickly realized that he could spend some time there without having to go into hiding or live under the radar. He was conversant with how squatting worked, and he squatted first in an apartment in a building scheduled for demolition, but where one tenant was still refusing to move out. He knew that he could live there without being bothered by law enforcement. At the end of that period, he moved to another squat. Little by little, he was accepted into the movement and secured a degree of stability. He began sharing with two Italian and two French comrades, plus one Catalan and one Luxembourger. While the Italians came from a workers' autonomy background, the background of the French guys was Trotskyist. They had no language in common, but they held assemblies. Gradually he started adapting to this new reality. In the district where he was living, near Albert Cuyp Street, the *kraker* movement had a strong foothold.

He found work cleaning at an abortion clinic . After he had been working at the clinic for some months and had earned the trust of his colleagues, he suggested carrying out abortions on girls from Spain where abortion was still banned. His proposal was accepted, and he set up a network through two siblings of his who were teachers back in Catalonia; they helped many of their students and friends of their students to get to Amsterdam, where José helped them through these difficult moments. Like his Dutch colleagues, he also helped out by working without pay two days a week for a press that produced a range of alternative publications and, with other comrades from Spain, he produced radio programs covering the Spanish political transition. International solidarity groups took an interest in his position and offered him legal advice. An Amsterdam lawyer contacted Mateo Seguí and together they settled on the tactics to be adopted in the event that he was arrested. Once it became safe to be open about his involvement in the movement, after helping set up the Café Molly, one of the nerve centers of the *kraker* movement, he took part in a TV program about the young democracy in Spain; this was shortly after the Spanish Parliament was stormed by Lieutenant-Colonel Tejero.

In 1985, along with his Dutch girlfriend, he moved to Nicaragua, seeking to support the Sandinista revolution. They spent two and a half years there, during which time their first child was born, and then returned to Holland. Once back, they settled in Den Bosch, but in 1991, after they had a second child, they decided to move back to Spain. The offense for which José had never been tried (the business of the gun-smuggling that took place twelve years earlier) had passed the statute of limitations. First his partner settled in Catalonia with the children, and they started school. Meanwhile he remained temporarily in Perpignan. But since his legal standing lacked clarity, they decided to put the law to the test.

One day in 1992, the four of them, traveling in a car with Dutch plates and driven by his Dutch partner, with two golden-haired children plainly visible on board, crossed the border without a hitch. Within days, and with Seguí accompanying him, José reported to a police station to request a brand-new ID document after reporting the loss of his previous one. They took his fingerprints to verify his details and asked him for an address to which they should forward the new documents. He gave them his father's address. Three days after that, members of the Policía Nacional went there looking for him, but of course he was not there. Things were starting to move, and his lawyer had to deal with the courts and the police to have José's record expunged. In next to no time, his legal status had been regularized and, after thirteen years, he had his new ID card.

CULTURE OF CHANGE

Now don't go thinking I am an oddball
I know a lot of others who think the same way
You make me sick with your worthiness
Long live parties and frivolity.
—CUCHARADA, "NO SOY FORMAL"

Toward the late 1960s, young people in Spain began to experience first-hand what turned out to be a revolutionary change in the dying days of Francoist rule and the years right after the demise of the dictator. The new culture, chiefly emanating from the United States, but also from the United Kingdom and the experiences of May '68 in France, was beginning to embed itself in a significant sector of the youth dissatisfied with the backward culture of nationalist Catholic Francoism. The earliest rock groups to depart from the commercial models and the first hallucinogenic trips were accompanied by experiments in communal living and, very shortly thereafter, publications that tried to give a voice to this new generation. The main aim was, starting on an individual level, to break with the rigidity of day-to-day living under the regime: "We have our work cut out for us sorting matters out for ourselves, and between ourselves we can try to be freer, shrug off our complexes, and put up more of a fight against those who would keep us cowed and quiet and uncommunicative."[1]

During the first half of the 1970s, young people dreamt of a life that was free in every possible sense and direction. For a start, they needed to shrug off a neutering education that thwarted all natural contact between people and restricted sex to Holy Spirit-blessed reproduction, exclusively between a man and a woman, and only after a previous visit to church. They wanted to break free of the lifetime of serial productivity that was the lot of every person born in countries dominated by

---

1. Malvido, *Nosotros los malditos*, 61.

the guiding lights of the Crusades: school, military service, work, marriage, reproduction, and death. They had an intuitive sense that there might be other forms of amusement beyond the alternatives on offer from the OJE (Organización Juvenil Española / Spanish Youth Organization) and, finally, they dreamt of a life where everyone was free to determine their part through everyday life, without any sort of impositions foisted upon them by their surroundings: the family, the mainstay of Francoist society, a society that revolved around the laws laid down by the Movimiento Nacional.

To begin with, one of the major nerve centers of the countercultural movement in the late 1960s and early 1970s was Seville. American servicemen from the bases in Morón and Rota, when out on leave, mingled with Seville youngsters in the clubs and *bodegas* where hitherto the only music had been flamenco. Young Andalusians were tuning in to American radio stations on those bases and stumbling across the new electric music. The emergence of the band Smash was groundbreaking. Nothing like it had ever been heard before; the flamenco idiom translated into the language of rock and the rhythm of rock with the addition of flamenco depths. As the band itself declared in its *Manifiesto de lo borde*: "It is not a matter of indulging in 'flamenco-pop' or 'blues-style flamenco' but of going for all-out mongrelization." A few years after that, artists like Lole y Manuel or Triana reaped the fruits of this, or were themselves the fruits, of those first risky ventures into fusion between roots and brand-new musical trends. At the same time, the new independent popular theater came surging through under the aegis of groups like the Teatro Estudio Lebrijano, Esperpento, or La Cuadra, the latter of which took its name from one of the new premises where such rebellious new approaches were welcomed: La Cuadra de Paco Liria. The two areas, music and theater, came together on several occasions as when Esperpento staged Bertolt Brecht's *Antigone* with a live Smash soundtrack at the University of Seville.

That was the Seville that the illustrator Nazario left behind in order to relocate to Barcelona, where the constant arrival of U.S. Sixth Fleet ships in the city harbor brought musical styles—which were not only unfamiliar but also banned—to some of the young people hanging out in the bars nearest the port. In the Barrio Chino's discotheques and seedy bars there came the very first cultural exchange. At the same, time well-to-do youngsters were traveling to far-off lands, either in pursuit of education or pleasure, and meeting young Londoners, Parisians or Californians (such trips were the main conduits for Situationist texts, underground comics, or folk and progressive rock singers and groups reaching Spain).

In Barcelona, Pau Riba, Sisa, and Oriol Tramvia, all three of them veterans of the Grup de Folk that performed in the late 1960s were a few of the artists who best reflected in music the libertarian mindset of these young people. Each in his or her own way, with no preconceived musical ideas and without any specific label attached to the music. They themselves mirrored the self-education of a generation. But they were not alone, not by a long shot. The explosion of these new approaches to music, hushed up or sneered at by media wedded to the cultural policies of the government, came on July 26 and 27, 1975, in Canet, with the very first Canet Rock Festival, attended by around forty thousand young people greedy for new liberating experiences. Between 7:00 p.m. and 7:00 a.m., a dozen groups performed, including Pau Riba. It had also been advertised that Sisa, who had just released *Qualsevol nit pot sortir el sol*, would be making an appearance, but his performance was banned by government order. This prompted the festival organizers to play the title song of the album over their sound system, chorused by the entire audience, turning those few minutes into the most moving moments of the entire night. But there was more to it than the music. There were loads of artists who stood at their stalls trying to interest the youngsters in their creative ventures: there were comic illustrators, underground and fringe magazines, etc. The July 31 edition of *La Vanguardia* recounted how at one such stall, *duros* (five-peseta coins) were on sale for four pesetas. The person behind this unusual offer was Picarol, a driving force of the counterculture and future dynamo behind Radio PICA.

The festival went ahead the following year, but by then the situation had altered. The dictator was dead and the youth were looking forward to other real possibilities: "As is customary now, political displays took place at the El Canet Rock Festival, but anarchist groups and their black flags predominated, and anarchist 'slogans' were chanted in between the performances of the singers or by stalls at the festival."[2] That year, to be sure, the three singers Pau Riba, Sisa, and Oriol Tramvia were able to perform without a hitch on the main stage. The festival was held for another two years, and the last time, in 1978, there was involvement by new bands that stood out for their aggressive, wholly urban approach, a so-called punk approach; at the Canet festival, the new music style was represented by Blondie from the United States, and by upcoming local performers like Els Masturbadors Mongòlics or La Banda Trapera del Río.

A few weeks later on June 23, there was a twenty-four-hour festival devoted almost entirely to such new groups held at a campsite in Castelldefels. Organized by the Cuc Sonat group—which revolved around Xavi Cot, the real driving force behind the punk movement in Barcelona—and the two Catalan groups that had performed at the Canet Rock Festival, Kaka de Luxe, and Basura o Mortimer, among others. The attendance was estimated at upward of twenty thousand people. These youngsters "have moved on from poetic-mystical-alchemical music . . . to urban rock. From acid to alcohol and what have you. From family to urban bands, parties, and orgies. From alternative lifestyles to practical action and group

---

2. *La Vanguardia*, August 10, 1976.

organization. What has absolutely not altered is their personal provocative stance, spectacularly out of step with political fashion."[3]

As for the publishing world, *Star* and *Ajoblanco* were the major reference points for this new youth culture, but not the only ones: over time other more specialist publications emerged, such as *Alfalfa* (focusing on ecology) or *Globo* (focused on psychotropic substances). *Star*, built around the energy of Juanjo Fernández, was an all-around mischievous magazine (comics, literature, music, movies, and much more) that released its first edition in June 1974, and it was a constant target of the cultural oligarchs. Issue no. 13 was impounded by the government because of a comic strip by Miracle, who went on to become a singer with Els Masturbadors Mongòlics. Shortly after that, before issue no. 16 was released, the magazine was banned for a year, and its relaunch edition in July 1976 was again confiscated. And with good reason, as its pages caricatured a society in decline and boldly offered provocation to the law- and established-order-compliant. One of the main ingredients was the comic strips with explicit references to sex and drugs, but there were also important articles about the new music as well as sociocultural articles that dealt with things such as the counterculture abroad, new connections being made in the Iberian Peninsula, or alternative living experiments (communes, banned substances, diverse sexual options, etc.). Its final edition came out in 1980.

Ajoblanco covered the same time period: launched in 1974, it was wound up in 1980. This magazine pursued clearer social aims as part of the burgeoning libertarian movement in social terms, and it introduced the young to ideas such as ecology or antipsychiatry, without neglecting what were at the time more mundane matters such as sex, communes, and drugs. It grew up around the figure of Pepe Ribas and was well known for having its readers contribute content and assist in its distribution. Some editions had print runs in the order of a hundred thousand copies. It also had a temporary ban slapped on it, but since its graphics were not as explicit or daring as those of sister publication *Star*, it had better luck with the regime's censors.

As a countercultural capital, Barcelona was a magnet drawing in creatives from all the country, especially illustrators. In dribs and drabs, many of those who had started out publishing their output independently and illegally in their respective hometowns began to move into the city. A fresh surge of cultural energy was delivered by communes like the one on Calle Comerç, where some of the most outstandingly provocative illustrators like Nazario, Mariscal, or Max lived, permanently or temporarily. All three were recent arrivals in the city and, together with other illustrators, they made up the El Rrollo Enmascarado collective, which published a banned comic of the same name.

3. Malvido, *Nosotros los malditos*, 54–55.

None of the creative arts were left out of the countercultural explosion. Drama groups like Els Joglars or Comediants were renowned throughout the country, and after Franco's death many actors, technicians, and theater and movie directors decided to form a union together with musicians. They set up the Assemblea de Treballadors de l'Espectacle (Entertainment Workers' Assembly), a markedly libertarian outfit that announced its public debut with a spectacular staging of *Don Juan Tenorio* in the former El Born market on November 19 and 20, 1976, barely a year after the demise of the dictator. The show was watched by around twenty thousand spectators, and the mounting of it involved some of the most outstanding countercultural artists from every sector. It was a sort of trial run for the self-organizational capacities of the city's artists. Months after that, along with the CNT and the libertarian movement organized in its ateneos, the Jornadas Libertarias Internacionales (International Libertarian Days) were staged, during which *Ajoblanco* printed the *Barcelona Libertaria* newspaper. The Jornadas offered, free of charge, dozens of theatrical and musical works as well as numerous debates and talks on political and social issues. It was the first occasion when these two formally opposing countercultural communities came together—*layetano* rock, which was on its last legs after a ten-year existence, and the strident new punk rock that was forcing its way through. It is estimated that upward of five hundred thousand people passed through the Parc Güell (where the shows were staged) and the Salón Diana (which hosted the debates and talks) between July 22 and 25, 1977.

In Madrid, things were moving in a different direction. The fact that it was the nation's capital meant that the pressures and the repression there was more intense, and this had an impact on the creative sector also. In terms of music, whereas Barcelona had its *layetano* prog- rock, Madrid spawned groups such as Burning ("incendiary energy" as Oriol Llopis said of them in issue no. 21 of *Star* magazine), Indiana, and Moon which, along with a few others, headlined the compilation disc *Viva el rollo* in 1975. Launched in 1974, Burning were not punks, far from it, but their wildness and aggression were light years ahead of the music coming out of Barcelona and its surroundings, which would not give birth to La Banda Trapera el Río for another two years.

On the comics scene, 1975 saw the opening of the Cascorro Factory, a collective of illustrators that became known for the publication of *El Carajillo* and for their stall on El Rastro on Sundays. Among its members were Ceesepe, El Hortelano, and El Zurdo, and over the ensuing years they churned out publications by the dozens. And, as in the field of music, the differences with Barcelona were striking: "Cascorro Factory members were less indifferent to social issues than those from El Rrollo, and more political, as well as more outrageous in the way they dressed. The pace set in Madrid was breathtaking."[4] In places like as La Vaquería or La Bobia, these illustrators and scriptwriters mingled with members of independent theater troupes like Los Goliardos or TEI (Teatro Escuela Independiente), followers of alternative cinema like Pedro Almodóvar, and young painters and photographers itching to break new ground. La Vaquería opened in February 1975, at no. 8 Calle Libertad, at the instigation of some young poets (Antonio López Luna, Emilio Sola, etc.) and was utterly destroyed on June 8, 1976, when it came under a bomb attack mounted by the Guerrillas of Christ the King. In the commune that some of its founders set up in an apartment on the same street, the CNT's very first local in the city opened for business some months later.

Nineteen seventy-six also saw publication of the very first edition of the magazine *Bazofia,* and shortly after that came *MMM–Órgano official de la locura* (*MMM–Official Organ of Craziness*). Another significant distribution center for brand-new countercultural ideas was the LACOCHU center (Laboratorios Colectivos Chueca / Chueca Collective Workshops), where members of the PREMAMA (Prensa Marginal Madrileña / Madrid Fringe Press) could be found: this was a coordinating body that attempted to churn out the huge contingent of fanzines (illegal publications) that were beginning to circulate in various parts of the city. Through LACOCHU, a number of music groups also made their name: they included Cucharada which, heavily influenced by the new independent interactive theater of the Living Theater troupe, would occasionally work alongside companies like Tábano or TEI. Cucharada members often performed on the streets and on a number of occasions fell afoul of the Social Menace Law, to which they dedicated one famous, provocative song. There was a generational and stylistic change in 1977, when publications like *Bazofia* and the PREMAMA coordinating agency faded away, and the fanzine *La livianidad del imperdible* (*The Fickleness of the Safety Pin*—from around which the group Kaka de Luxe emerged) was published. All of it triggering the subsequent eruption of what became known as La Movida.

The countercultural explosion was pretty much the same in all parts of the country. Thus, all these music and drama groups passed through Studio, a hall opened in Valencia in the late 1960s. In May 1974, the rock opera *L'home de cotó-en-pèl* was staged there, giving rise to the prog-rock group Cotó-en-pèl. A couple of years after that the comic *El Gat Pelat* was published, and the El Tebeus del Congle illustrators' group was formed.

In Zaragoza, meanwhile, among other things the Bohemios bar was opened, which later changed its name to El Golem. The El Grifo drama group was also formed, and some of its members published the magazine *El Pollo urbano* in 1977.

---

4. J. Ribas, *Los 70 a destajo,* 386.

When the Colectivo Zeta was launched some months later as an umbrella for a number of illustrators, including Carlos Azagra, the *El Pollo urbano* publishers provided them with legal cover for their magazine, which came under a significant attack from the official courts for "scandalizing the Catholic faith."

In the Basque Country, the Gerrhaundi collective in Azpeitia made its mark. A social experiment by youngsters with close ties to the workers' autonomy sector, it evaporated following police harassment prompted by the armed actions of the CAA.

> "Transvestite willing to sell or trade penis and three testicles, brand-new, hardly used, in return for one female sex organ, rather on the tight side if possible."
> —AD APPEARING IN THE CONTACTS SECTION OF
> THE MAGAZINE *STAR*, NO. 22

DANI

Rotten city brings us night and fear
Her streets full of fire while she sleeps
—LA BANDA TRAPERA DEL RÍO, "CIUTAT PODRIDA"

Born in Barcelona's Poble Nou barrio, Dani grew up to the noise of heavy machinery from its factories. This historic working-class barrio was like one big community within the city. His father was a taxi driver, his mother a seamstress; years later the family relocated to Vallcarca because his mother was stricken with asthma due to the pollution in the working-class quarter. But by then the lad had already acquired a class consciousness, and the oppressive, bland surroundings of his childhood days never left his memory. In July 1974, just ten days after he had turned fourteen, he started work in a bank as an errand boy. His main occupation there was ferrying documents from one office to another, his briefcase constantly laden with papers and cash.

Dani wrote and enjoyed writing poetry, but he was still just a kid, and this made it impossible for anybody to take him seriously. In a community of workers that was starting to see light at the end of the tunnel after thirty-five years of dictatorship, the teenager came up with a way of getting some of his efforts into print: among the offices regularly on his route were some belonging to media outlets. With each visit he gained the trust of some of the journalists he knew and suggested that they trade. He would act as propaganda link between firms in return for being able to have his writings published in newspapers such as *Mundo Diario* or *Tele-Expres*. Agreed. He would drop in on offices, and comrades from the CC.OO or the USO slipped into their professional correspondence some trade union propaganda that needed to be brought to another workplace. And so he began to come into contact with the realities of trade unionism. Once, after the PCE's clandestine printing network in Madrid had been dismantled, he even traveled to the capital by train lugging two suitcases filled with underground propaganda. He was escorted as far as the train station by his father, who of course was clueless as to what was inside the suitcases.

He was evolving ideologically in this labor context, and met a libertarian comrade in the bank where he worked. Not that he was the only one. There had also been libertarians inside the commissions just as there were workers in the USO who advocated self-management. In addition, Dani was stating to take part in activities as spokesman for local youths.

The youth groups came from the neighborhood associations, and the group from his barrio in the Calle Tirso had a sizable library used mainly by young people in need of education. Then Dani found out first hand what it was to run the police gauntlet. In September 1975, he tried to take part in a protest against the dictatorship's most recent executions and headed up to Cerdanyola by train. Right at the exit from the station, they ran into lines of Civil Guards who forced them to run the gauntlet between the lines while they doled out truncheon blows, kicks, trip-ups, punches. The important thing was to keep one's balance, try to get through quickly, and not fall down because, if one fell, the violence escalated.

After he had been working for eighteen months, in January 1976, he took part in a clandestine meeting held in the Sant Medir Church in the Sants barrio. At fifteen years of age, he was not the youngest one there. On the other hand, he was startled to find that the entire turn-out for the meeting was made up of youngsters and over fifties; its purpose was to rebuild the CNT. This was followed by a period of frantic social and political activity which took up all his time. He finally joined the Vallcarca Youth Forum, which some months later amalgamated with a youth group from El Carmel and was rebranded as the Ateneo Libertario. Barcelona youngsters, eager to break down taboos and everything that was forbidden, flooded en masse into libertarian organizations and bodies the way their grandfathers had fifty years before them. And where no such organizations or bodies existed, they set them up.

Those were the years of the pharaoh-like works on the construction of the La Rovira tunnel connecting the barrio and the city center. Entire streets and building disappeared, and the residents were rehoused in other areas with some homes left to stand, vacant, for months on end. So, swayed by a few movies and documentaries arriving from Germany, they began squatting in these or at any rate using them for parties. There was a proliferation of communes across the city. Hundreds of them announced their presence in the contact pages of magazines such as *Ajoblanco* or *Star*. Hallucinogenic drugs, tripping to a Jethro Tull, Genesis, Hendrix, or The Doors soundtrack, feminism, the new ecology movement—there was a blend of them all in these shared spaces. In some instances, the wages of all the comrades were pooled to make up a common fund and the money then doled out. Nothing belonged to anyone in particular. A shared existence was much more fun.

Dani divided up his day between lending a hand with the many libertarian publications, demonstrations, new leisure activities, and work. Among the many publications on which he worked, since he had never given up on his writing, were *Debates*, *Fuera de Banda*, and the last few editions of *La Cloaca*; many of these were printed at Gràfiques Tordera in the Gràcia barrio, a press shop belonging to Jordi Solé Sugranyes and Pilar García, who never pressed for payment when a bill was occasionally overlooked. Both of them still had their links to the struggle. As for demonstrations, those were some particularly tough years. Activists who were ready for urban guerrilla warfare took part in them, and sometimes pistols even put in an appearance; Molotov cocktails were packed with shrapnel; there were extraordinarily powerful catapults, and when the time came for physical confrontation, no one shied away. One time, they tried to reach the underground cells at police headquarters, the station on the Via Laietana. They used cars as shields; and after releasing the handbrake, they inched forward, dreaming of an impossible assault on the police stronghold. Little by little, but relentlessly, they saw the insides of all the police stations, but their young age helped them get out again, pretty much unscathed. And then, at one such violent demonstration while a gas station workers' strike was on, one of his roommates fell. That comrade, an Italian not really familiar with the city, paid the price for his inexperience and even served a few days in jail. Meanwhile, Dani was working away. Time and again, he lost his job as a result of being arrested, but the comrades quickly made it their business to find him a new one. Even comrades from other unions searched on his behalf. Back in those days, solidarity was still a thing.

He applied to the university and, after several years away, he resumed his studies. The campuses were in ferment. Politically organized students capitalized on every opportunity in an attempt to bring classes to a standstill. The assemblies were in constant session. The libertarians were calling for rationalist courses and the abolition of examinations.

In late 1978 or early 1979, Dani found himself in the Modelo for the first time. A pistol had been produced during a demonstration and everyone stood accused of it. He spent ten days there, but the fact that several comrades were with him made his stay more bearable and not particularly severe. In situations like these, there was safety in numbers and back then there was still a climate of solidarity, what with the prison revolts over the previous months. But once back on the streets, he carried on where he had left off and was rearrested within months. Oddly enough and strange though it might seem, once he arrived at the gates of the Modelo, they turned him away.

The demonstration at which Dani had been arrested was every bit as violent as the ones over the preceding weeks and the ones that were to follow, no more and no less. They had made their way right down the Paralelo attacking bank branches and keeping the police at bay until, on reaching the Drassanes barracks, they found themselves pinned against a wall. This was a tactic known as *la bolsa* (the bag): completely cornered, the kettled-in demonstrators were slaughtered from a distance as the noose tightened until eventually, with nowhere to go, the demonstrators gave up. It was not the first time he had seen the tactic applied; on an earlier occasion he had been arrested in just such circumstances. On that earlier occasion, the demonstration had started off from Las Cotxeres de Sants. They had made it as far as La Bordeta where they had decided to turn around and press on as far as the Plaza España; once there, they ran right down the Gran Vía until they were cornered at the corner of the Calle Bruc. After they were arrested, they were taken to the police station at the High Court on Calle de Lauria; the prisoners were brought in via two different doors. One was reserved for the exclusive use of the policemen who had infiltrated the ranks of the demonstrators and who had, with the activists, withstood the relentless hail of rubber bullets; there were a lot more of the "undercover boys" than he would have thought, had he not witnessed it for himself. On the second occasion, in Las Drassanes all of the demonstrators were bundled into several police buses and driven straight to the Modelo. The activists had been at it for several straight days and the police stations were full. Fear turned to expectation when they were refused entry to the Modelo because there were too many prisoners there to admit in one go. These being the circumstances, the police chiefs decided to remove them to the court cells, but being guarded there by just two or three Civil Guards, the latter also refused to take responsibility for such a large batch of activists. In the end, after touring Barcelona in police vehicles for several hours on end, they were all released.

It was during one such demonstration that Dani met Irma who stood out for her constant goading of the forces of order and because she was one of the few women taking part in the ongoing revolt.

That year he made a radical decision in his quest for revolution. Along with another comrade, he boarded a ship at anchor in the port of Barcelona and stowed away as far as the Mexican coast, from where he moved on to Nicaragua, hoping to fight in the ranks of the Sandinista revolution. Sympathy for that anti-imperialist movement was spreading. He was disappointed, however, and within months returned, using the same means, to Barcelona. The leading revolutionary Edén Pastora was beginning to distance himself from the Sandinistas. The bureaucrats and Communist Party hacks who had hijacked the FSLN (Frente Sandinista de Liberación Nacional / Sandinista National Liberation Front) were dividing up the appointments and the power among themselves.

Gradually but inexorably, things back in the city were changing. Always attracted to the counterculture, Dani felt more drawn to the aggressive stance of the new punk movement emanating from the English-speaking countries. La

Banda Trapera had previously performed at the Canet Rock Festival and had also taken part in the Jornadas Libertarias during the summer of 1977. Lou Reed had defied the regime with a legendary, and condemned, concert in 1975. An entire generation of young people cut its hair and traded its brightly colored, loose, baggy clothes for tight trousers and black leather jackets. They opted for La Orquídea in the Calle Bruniquer, or the Orfeo Negro, which Xavier Sabater opened in the Calle Sant Domènec del Call, rather than the Zeleste. Of late, they had been drifting away from the influence of orchestras such as La Platería or Mirasol Colores, and away from the psychedelic rock of Pink Floyd, turning on to Lou Reed or Iggy Pop instead. Unwittingly, they were coming to realize that the battle had been lost, and that they had no future. Doors records gave way to those of The Clash, and the latter's first big hit, *London's Burning*, was construed as a death cry: *Let's burn down Barcelona!*

The libertarian bubble was continuing to deflate. Some ex-comrades were busily making money; others were still at their nocturnal activities, mostly for appearances sake; the battles for control of the CNT were getting uglier with every passing day and materialistic capitalism was stymying every form of collective or liberating lifestyle.

The trial for the arson attack on the Scala nightclub was the swan song as far as Dani and many other young people were concerned. The fate of the comrades charged with that outrage could as easily have been his own. In December 1980, during one of the demonstrations organized to denounce the police frame-up and show solidarity with the comrades, Dani was arrested. In the Plaza Urquinaona, a huge staircase with scaffolding had been set alight and it had collapsed onto the Maryland Cinema. The pitched battle had been impressive. When the mass of demonstrators was split by a police charge, Dani's group attempted to move directly ahead via the Ronda Sant Pere. But the police had occupied the El Corte Inglés building, and so they decided to retrace their steps and head down the Via Laietana. As they neared the police station, all available personnel poured out of it, and the entire group was arrested.

The judge ordered pretrial detention without bail for all of them, and Dani was sent straight to the First Ward of the Modelo, which back then was the ward used for minors. The Modelo was no longer the prison he had known a couple of years earlier, back when the libertarian inmates commanded respect; toward the end of 1980 the Modelo became hellish. Heroin had taken a hold and was in every nook and cranny. The inmates, the bulk of them addicts, had lost their dignity entirely. The warders, knowing that they had the upper hand now, had lost all fear of (meaning respect for) political prisoners. Judges aligned to the old regime, never having been purged, realized that control of the prisons was back in their hands, and they turned a deaf ear to inmates' complaints about ill-treatment and irregularities. The worst thing, though, was the filth, the unhygienic conditions. Prisoners were required to line up half-naked and were showered with a dust that was supposed to be a preventative against a wide range of illnesses. All one could do in there was try to survive. There were no educational facilities available. No diversion. All one could do was watch one's back and survive. At that point Dani really did wake up to the fact that all was lost. Without the support of the organization (beyond the provision of lawyers) and with no solidarity on the streets, with no pressures being brought to bear to lobby for their release, his comrades and he suffered quietly, over the victims of that time and space. His time and space.

Some months later, the judge set a bail that the CNT could not afford. Dani was left alone and isolated from reality, except for visits from his sister. When he was suddenly informed that the judge handling his case had been changed and that his replacement had ordered him provisionally released, he could not believe it. Once back on the outside he realized that he had to stand down, as a further setback might prove irreversible. Luckily, he found support from the cultural bodies and pursued his literary predilections. These were concentrated on the Ateneo Enciclopédico, a range of poetry publications, and the punk movement, and step by step, he dropped out of activism.

Within months the PSOE took power, and the CNT pulled some strings, although Dani always thought that it could have done more on behalf of many comrades. In his particular case, he was never brought before the courts, although he was never pardoned either; his file was merely *misfiled* in some box at the courthouse—to this very day.

4.

REPRESSION

OPPRESSION

Repression was a constant presence at every level: physical repression, judicial and media repression, and, finally, there came a brand-new, hitherto untried repressive formula—repression through dependency.

Physical repression was the first sort that these young people experienced. The dictatorship's rule was based upon force and members of the security forces used violence as a matter of course. There were none of the sophisticated checks and balances we know today, and they reckoned that none were needed. Physical force was all the armory they needed, and hatred fueled every arrest. The execution of Puig Antich was a vengeful act that they tried to disguise with the support of the military judges (the really odd thing is that they had not finished him off at the time of arrest).

The change in the regime wrought no thoroughgoing change in the machinery of repression, and even though physical force was not their only tool, murders were constantly happening, both inside the police stations as well as in the prisons and on the streets, where the police and the far-right groups did not hesitate to use guns in order to break up demonstrations. Time and again, deaths led to further deaths. In the wake of the murder of five workers in Vitoria in March 1976, several more workers perished during protest demonstrations in Tarragona and in Basauri. On September 27, 1976, in Madrid, during a demonstration to commemorate the Francoists' most recent shootings, Carlos González Martínez was murdered by a fascist gang. On January 23, 1977, again in Madrid, and again at the hands of a far-right gang, student Arturo Ruiz was killed. The very next day, during a protest demonstration over that, the police murdered Mari Luz Nájera, another student. In Barcelona, on November 11, 1978, Gustau Muñoz Bustillo, a member of the PCE(i), was killed. In Valencia on June 29, 1979, in the course of a strike, a worker belonging to the CNT, Valentín González Ramírez, was killed. The list of those murdered during demonstrations and other acts of protest throughout Spain between 1976 and 1979 is never-ending.

As for arrests, these were as violent as ever. Directly responsible for such violence, and someone who can never be forgotten by those who sampled his methods first hand, was Francisco Álvarez Sánchez, head of the Anti-Anarchist Squad in Barcelona in the years after Franco's death, a man known by the nickname of El Técnico. In 1982, his work in Barcelona complete, he was transferred to Bilbao where he took charge of the Intelligence Squad. At the time when the GAL was set up, a year or so later, he was appointed director of the Intelligence and Special Operations Bureau of the Interior Ministry. In 1994, he was jailed for a number of months for his links to the GAL.

In the police stations, torture methods referred to by such names as *la barra* (the bar), *la sauna, la bañera* (the bathtub), or *la bolsa* (the bag), were an everyday occurrence when dealing with those arrested for political activities, especially those that could be linked to armed actions as a response to state aggression. This was the case with the young people arrested in January and February 1977 during the FAI conference in Barcelona, or the days thereafter. Miquel Didac Piñero, who spent seventeen days in custody, publicly exposed—once released—the tortures inflicted upon him during his lengthy stay in the police station in the Via Laietana. He also spelled them out in full detail to reporters from *Cuadernos para el Diálogo*:

> He was subjected to "the sauna" which consists of slow asphyxiation that sets the entire body sweating while taking a beating, tightly wrapped in three blankets. The person sits with his head down and resting on the two feet of an officer, leading to asphyxia and panic. Piñeiro [sic] was subjected to "the bar" on February 12. His testimony is as follows: "This consisted of being cuffed, after my wrists had first been bandaged so no marks would be left...then I was forced to squat down with my hands under my knees. Once in position, and after having first received a flurry of punches and kicks, two detectives slotted a long metal bar with a curve in the center between my arms and legs (under my elbows and knees), and I was left dangling in the air for something like three hours, head down, between two tall tables that ensured that I could not rest my head on the floor."[1]

In all likelihood, this form of treatment was prompted by the fact that back in April 1974 when Didac had gone on the run they had printed his photograph in the media during the operation to dismantle the OLLA. Activists making fools out of them was not something that they could permit.

A month after publication of the magazine detailing his torture, Didac was rearrested in his home in La Escala. Visually impaired and possessing no driver's license, he was nevertheless charged with having been the getaway driver in a holdup at the Agroman firm in Barcelona. During this second detention he

---

1. *Cuadernos para el Diálogo*, September 17, 1977.

was not subjected to torture, other than psychological torture. During interrogation, they brought him over to the second-floor window of the police station and threatened to throw him out. They also tried to trick him using the stratagem often used in police stations: before interrogations concluded, a policeman entered the room and carelessly left his gun on the table, within sight of the detainee; they all decided then to allow him some time to think things over and stepped out of the room, hoping the suspect would pick up the weapon, which was, of course, not loaded, so that they would have a pretext to go on beating him. That very same strategy was used with the comrades from the Scala case: "They all stepped out and left me lying on the floor for I do not know how long. They had left one of their guns, unloaded for sure, on the table. All of a sudden, they burst back into the room. 'Sonofabitch! You were just about to pick up that pistol and kill us, right?' I was still slumped on the floor and the kicks and punches started up again."[2]

In Didac's case, the backstory to this charge came to light over time. The Agroman workers who had identified him from photographs shown by the police in the wake of the holdup, retracted, claiming that the police had threatened them that unless they identified Didac as one of the guilty parties, they themselves would be charged with making a false report of armed robbery so as to hold on to the money themselves. This was but another ploy used by the police, concocting phony charges and false evidence, or straightforwardly using their hired *provocateurs*.

During the January–February 1977 crackdown, about seventy people were arrested. It is hard to believe that, by sheer fluke, the only armed group dismantled—which a dozen people were tied to, although some of them obviously had had nothing to do with anything—had Gambín as one of its activists. Most of the arrests were made on January 30 at a Barcelona bar during the FAI Peninsular Conference. No weapons were found. The arrests spread right across the peninsula but despite intensive interrogation no weapons could be unearthed. And then the Murcian group fell; in theory, it was made up of FAI members. The fact of the matter is that most of those arrested had no connection with the anarchist federation but were involved in libertarian propaganda actions. Guns were found in relation to this group; to be precise, Joaquín Gambín was found with them when arrested. We will probably never know whether he triggered the arrests, but it is hard to believe that it was a fluke.

According to the books *La CNT en la encrucijada* and *Los servicios secretos en España*, Gambín, a non-political criminal, had worked with the state forces before to thwart a prison escape bid back in 1959. Despite this background, Gambín, known as El Grillo, remained active in libertarian circles for a further year and had

2. X. Cañadas Gascón, *Entremuros: las prisiones en la transición democrática* (Bilbao: Muturreko Burutazioak, 2000), 39.

an active hand in the Scala affair, which dealt the Spanish libertarian movement a blow from which it never recovered: that was in January 1978.

With Spain in turmoil, agents of Inspector Roberto Conesa learned their lesson: they planted arms in the greatest hotbeds of rebellion, which suspicion had previously been cast upon, hunted down the most ferocious opponents and, once their work was done, the bourgeois press would add the finishing touches by portraying "all" the antiestablishment groups as dangerous terrorists who might further destabilize the precarious political and economic situation. Thereby costing them the support of the citizenry. A script painstakingly written by law enforcement in cahoots with the international secret services to ensure that the populace lost any sympathy it had for what had become by then a significant movement.[3]

Also in 1977, collusion between the police and another person with ties to libertarian activists came to light: that person was Eduardo Soler. A native of Vic, the son of the owners of the Casa Soler restaurant in the center of that town, he had been living in Perpignan since late 1973. On arrival in the city, he bragged of having been behind the arson that destroyed the central headquarters of the telephone company in Barcelona on June 8, 1973. In *La CNT en la encrucijada*, it states that this act resulted in the failure of the workforce in their dispute against the introduction of modern worksite monitoring technology, but the city's mayor declared on June 12, 1973: "We have the full reports from the Company and from the firefighters, stating that it was accidental. It started in a given spot and for some unknown reason, spread."[4]

On January 8, 1976, Eduardo, who used a range of names (Fernando, Rafael, Antonio, etc.) and was about forty years old, was arrested in Perpignan along with Gerard when the explosives that the latter was storing in his home were uncovered. They were the only two people to have any knowledge of them. Gerard had been in town for about two months and had met Eduardo at the Librería Española. Initially he thought it just a coincidence: nowadays he has no doubts as to the reason why he was arrested. The arrest bought Eduardo the prestige he needed if he was to engage deeply with the teams of activists moving through the city: besides, under threat of being expelled from the country, he ensured that a campaign of solidarity was mounted in his support. From then on, his back was covered, and he had tales of victimhood to relate. But the members of the FAF in Perpignan began to have their suspicions, and they passed those suspicions on to

---

3. J. Ribas, *Los 70 a destajo: Ajoblanco y libertad* (Barcelona: RBA, 2007), 521.

4. *La Vanguardia*, June 13, 1973.

Gerard. Shortly after that, Eduardo blew up the dais from which Santiago Carrillo was supposed to have addressed a rally at a campsite that the PCE had in Argelès-sur-Mer and recounted the attack to some of his comrades. At the beginning of that summer, on July 14, two attacks were mounted on the two most significant centers for libertarian activism in Perpignan, L'Escletxa (the FAF's local) and the Librería Española. The upshot of these explosions was that both premises were closed down, but, months later, Eduardo reopened the Librería, which he had bought from Enric Melich, in what was his last roll of the dice. Everybody knew that the bookstore was an implicitly trustworthy libertarian center, and from that privileged vantage point, Soler was able to monitor almost every move of the libertarian activists passing through the town.

A few comrades had their suspicions, but Eduardo carried on with his activities. Eduardo introduced a truck driver to José, and right from the very first trip the driver made smuggling arms, when José turned up to take delivery of them, once in Barcelona, he realized that the police were tailing him. Some comrades of Sabata's paid him a visit in Perpignan and availed of their visit to pop into the bookstore to buy books not available back in Spain. On their return to Girona, the police were waiting for them at the border. But all these young people were too innocent and naive to dare raise the alarm. Until it was too late.

One year later, Felipe, one of the young activists who had crossed the border to seek shelter, started to raid quarries to procure explosives. Eduardo acted as his driver. When Felipe and Agustín Rueda crossed the border illegally in October 1977, bringing all the explosives with them, they were arrested. It was Eduardo that had dropped them off right at the border in his car. The Spanish police hastened to cover for Eduardo by putting out a story that bore little resemblance to the facts: "In the late evening of last Saturday, the 15th, Civil Guard personnel on duty in Figueras traded gunshots with three individuals in the vicinity of the French border. . . . At 6 o'clock the following day, three individuals carrying several packages entered Spanish soil. . . . Two of them were successfully arrested, and the third fled in the direction of France despite shots fired after him."[5] No such gunshots were traded since the arrested duo were not armed. Nor did the one that got away, Eduardo Soler, ever set foot on Spanish soil, let alone had the Civil Guards fired shots at their collaborator. The activist duo, who by then had their doubts about their driver, tipped off their comrades back in Perpignan. From Sallent, a friend of Agustín's made a trip up to Perpignan to clear up any doubts, but, unbelievably, Soler, having dropped out of sight for a few days, turned up again and carried on unmolested with his work. Four months later, he was definitively unmasked, but by then it was too late.

---

5. *Los Sitios de Gerona*, October 18, 1977.

In February 1978, Gerard, living under the radar in Barcelona, had a rendezvous in the Plaza Vila de Madrid with Bernard, who had just arrived from Perpignan. The meeting had been arranged by El Rubio, who was working with the Spanish police at the time. Gerard missed the rendezvous and could not be arrested, but Eduardo, confident in the efficiency of the police and knowing that the whole thing had been a trap, tipped Enric Melich's wife off about his having been arrested, even though Gerard had not been arrested This was definitive proof, and Eduardo Soler was finally forced to distance himself from the libertarian movement.

El Rubio, the nickname of José Juan Martínez Gómez, was a horse of a different color. Born in Almería in 1956, he came from the same generation as the young libertarian activists and was yet another of the non-political criminals who was drawn to the libertarian movement on account of his kindred anti-authoritarian urges and for social support, should he be arrested. El Rubio turned up in Perpignan in the late Francoist period and it seems that, like many another young person, he was dodging his military service. In Perpignan, he associated with the libertarian movement and at the Librería Española he met the woman who would become his partner: she was working in the sex shop right beside the Librería, and Gerard worked there too.

As explained in the book *Atracadores*, El Rubio was arrested by the Civil Guard in January 1978 in Sant Sadurní, and following the usual violent interrogation session he asked to speak to the Civil Guard Intelligence Service.[6] Once in the Calle Sant Pau barracks in Barcelona, he provided information that led to the arrest of El Moro and three other comrades in Madrid a few days later. Then, again according to the book, El Rubio relocated to Perpignan and persuaded the FAF comrades to pop down to Barcelona in an attempt to free the arrested autónomos. When he got back, he set up the rendezvous with Gerard in the Plaza Vila de Madrid and, even though Gerard failed to keep the appointment, he was arrested in the city within hours. It was also El Rubio who provided the tip-off regarding the Puig farmhouse in Maçanet de Cabrenys, where other comrades fell, also in the first week of February 1978. El Rubio called Víctor Simal, a guide at the Maçanet border crossing, and asked him to go to the farmhouse to pick up some comrades who needed to get out to France after having escaped the police crackdown. By the time Víctor showed up at the place, its inhabitants had already been arrested, and there were Civil Guards there waiting for him. One agent from their Intelligence Service acknowledged: "After the services he had rendered us, we rewarded Juan José and smuggled him into France. From that point on, our collaboration was sporadic." In Perpignan, the arrest victims' comrades had only to put two and two together to see that if Eduardo Soler had had wind of the plan to arrest Gerard

---

6. C. Quílez, *Atracadores* (Barcelona: Cossetània, 2002), 61.

during the rendezvous organized by El Rubio, this meant that he too was working on behalf of the Civil Guard Intelligence Service.

At the time, there was fierce rivalry between the Policía Nacional and the Civil Guard as they wrestled for control of the antiterrorist fight. Six months later, El Rubio himself was in the very same prison as all the young people on whom he had informed. On August 28, 1978, he was arrested in Barcelona with two youths after shots were traded with officers from the Policía. One of those arrested, Manuel Cruz, admitted to his involvement in several actions carried out by the ERAT and that he had fled to France after the dismantling of the group. The three of them were charged with having held up a bank on August 21. When the case came to trial in the National High Court in April 1980, El Rubio was acquitted, even though he had been identified by one of the bank employees. But there was no way that could shake off the response from some COPEL inmates housed in the Modelo. When they got wind of his arrival there, they tipped off the libertarian activists whom he had betrayed. One day, those inmates asked the libertarians to ensure that at a given time they were clearly visible to the warders; that way, they could avert any chance that they might be accused of having been behind the beating he was to receive from the other prisoners.

In the end, El Rubio was splashed all over the front pages of Spanish newspapers three years later when, in May 1981, he led the raid on the Banco Central in Barcelona, taking a number of hostages for a couple of days. It seems that some of the weapons he used in that operation had been supplied to him by Eduardo Soler. It was a rather unusual holdup since, at one point in the negotiations, El Rubio was demanding the release of the far-right military personnel and Civil Guards jailed for the raid on the Congress of Deputies on February 23 that year. However, after all the raiders had been arrested and the identity of the bank robbers' leader came out, the media made great play in their headlines of his ties to the anarchist movement, without mentioning his links to the Civil Guard Intelligence Service.

We shall never know just how many young people lost heart after brutal interrogation by the Civil Guard or Policía Armada, to begin with and then the Policía Nacional, but the fact is that the vast majority of those arrested for armed actions during those years were told they might recover their freedom, and their files might be mislaid, if they would trade intelligence about their comrades.

Another ploy used by the state forces in their attempts to get to the active groups that the police could not infiltrate, the ones that they sometimes were not even able to locate, was to set up ghost groups replicating the actions and dynamics of the grupos autónomos. The object was to conjure up a degree of kinship that would facilitate a rapprochement with and subsequently a dismantling of the latter.

Or at the very least, sow confusion in the populace and earn themselves medals whenever they thought the time was right for dismantling them. The GAR

(Grupo Anarquista Revolucionario / Revolutionary Anarchist Group) was one instance of this.

The GAR surfaced in Valencia in the summer of 1977. The grupos autónomos in the city had been operating for the previous couple of years, and the police had no leads on who belonged to it. Over that summer the GAR raided several banks and even a UGT local. At the start of September 1977, it was broken up, and five people were arrested, among them a UGT member and a member of the JS (Juventudes Socialistas / Socialist Youth), denounced by their organizations as *provocateurs* in the hire of the state. Some months after that, on January 3, 1978, the GAR claimed responsibility for an attack carried out on a Valencia discotheque that that had been left entirely destroyed, a discotheque whose owner was known for his ties to FN members who frequented the place. Whoever it was that made the telephone call burst out: "We don't want those fascist pigs partying anymore."[7] Oddly enough, the premises and the entire contents had been placed under receivership and no longer belonged to the fascist Luis Gabin. Besides, some neighbors stated that they had seen several individuals removing some furniture and other stuff from the premises in the early hours prior to the explosion.

Another constant factor with which those activists had to contend was repression by court. Thus, whereas the young libertarians charged with carrying out holdups and possession of weapons were sentenced to twenty-four years in prison (as in the case of Juan Manuel Fernández Asensio, arrested in March 1981 following a holdup of a bingo hall), the fascists implicated in the murder of the young libertarian Jorge Caballero, who was stabbed in the heart in Madrid on April 14, 1980, were only fined 50,000 pesetas (about 300 euros) and served no prison time following their arrest.

Other telling cases included those of the Frenchmen Bernard Pensiot and Víctor Simal who, even though there was no evidence to connect them to any armed action, spent sixteen months in Spanish prisons. Or the case of Francisco Cuero who, having been charged with involvement in the digging of tunnels in an effort to break out some jailed comrades, spent upward of three years in pretrial detention, before later being merely fined. Although the dismal record-holder has to be Guillermo Marín, sentenced on January 10, 1985, to thirty-three years in prison for several holdups and for planting three explosive devices that had harmed no one. It is worth highlighting that the heaviest sentences were handed down once the PSOE had taken over the premiership. Such sentences bore no resemblance to those handed down under the so-called "Transition," which rarely went as high as twenty years.

---

7. *El País*, January 5, 1978.

As for repression of the media, the most outlandish instance concerned José Miguel Maluquer, who was arrested in January 1977 during that FAI conference; he was one of the many young libertarians rearrested following the Scala fire, and, like many more, having had no hand, act or part in the incident, was freed a couple of days later. Two weeks after that, a married couple, the Violas, were killed when a bomb strapped to the body of the former city mayor went off, and somebody placed a phone call claiming responsibility. Which would amount to no more than a malicious canard, except that the following day the media carried the photograph of the young activist who, plainly, had had nothing to do with the incident.

A couple of days before, faced with the intense campaign of support for the prisoners that was mounted by those groups who had mounted simultaneous attacks on the Modelo, the Durán Home in Barcelona, and the courthouse in Granollers on the night of January 22–23, *La Vanguardia* stated apropos of the two actions in Barcelona: "All these two latest attacks have done is add to fear among the citizenry, which feels defenseless in the face of this rash of criminal acts, which merely trouble the peace of mind of the residents of Barcelona. Yesterday... due to a stroke of luck, and no thanks to the intentions of the perpetrators, there were no casualties, although many people were greatly distraught at one or the other of the explosions."[8]

That was the same month that Martín Villa made his notorious announcement acknowledging that the young Barcelona libertarians were more of a concern to him than ETA or GRAPO and, on that assumption, he was even so bold as to ban the carnival in Barcelona, just as Franco had done before him:

> Anyone not belonging to a party or trade union and who is even slightly active can be regarded as a libertarian, and the current blight is libertarian. The Minister has said as such. And if the Minister says so, the civil governors, police chiefs, commissioners, sergeants, corporals and (allowing for differences) the lower ranks will say the same. Everything falling under the heading of "libertarian"—the COPEL, criminality, drug addicts—they are all thrown into the mix and make up the undesirable scum that is to blame for so many misfortunes. And from the authorities we have a climate of fear and anti-criminality paranoia being fostered in order to get people to crave peace and order. And peace and order are what the powers-that-be are offering.[9]

Reporting the dismantling of one Barcelona grupo autónomo, bridging the

---

8. *La Vanguardia*, January 24, 1978.

9. Grupo de Carnavaleros Cabreados, "El Grucaca Manifesto," in Malvido, *Nosotros los malditos* (Barcelona, Anagrama, 2004), 113.

months of January and February, the media emphasized: "Similarly, a quantity of 'hashish' that, according to their own admissions, those detainees used prior to going out to carry out their holdups and terrorist acts, has been intercepted."[10]

On the other hand, in order to conjure up the desired atmosphere of social panic, the media did not shrink from publishing police communiqués in full detail, communiqués that brazenly pointed to the guilt of all those arrested for those very actions. Thus, whereas *La Vanguardia* of February 7, 1978, pinned the blame on a dismantled grupo autónomo for the holdup at the Barcelona Central Fish Market on October 13 of the previous year, that same holdup was ascribed on February 28, 1979—again by *La Vanguardia*—to a different group more recently dismantled. And on the same basis, the proceeds from that holdup were wildly inflated. On February 7, 1978, it was reported as 1,700,000 pesetas (about 10,000 euros), whereas a year later, on February 28, 1979, this figure had soared to as many as ten million pesetas (around 60,000 euros), according to *La Vanguardia*.

Confusion was another weapon in the armory used to misrepresent the activists. Following the arrest of the members of one group in July and August 1979, the August 4 edition of *La Vanguardia* reported that "they were part of a group that appears to have been part of a breakaway from the MIL, what would later become the OLLA, which is these days hiding behind a sort of independent anarchist group." And *El País* the following day reported "alleged direct links with the OLA [sic] (an armed grouplet, radical nationalist in character, broken up years ago) as well as with ETA."

Although it succeeded in gradually isolating the activists, this three-pronged repression made up of the security forces, the courts, and the media, fell short of putting an end to those groups. For that, nameless youngsters would need to leave the struggles, and direct repression did not seem to be reducing either their intensity or their numbers. The only way of ensuring that was by means of a change of priorities. It was a matter of curtailing their ability to resist and distancing them from their social surroundings, the very things that had driven them into activism. The only way to pull this off was to lash out indiscriminately and employ an indirect strategy vis-à-vis those quarters of society from which they came. That strategy, already tried in the USA in the wake of the unrest of the late 1960s, was introduced in Barcelona in mid-1977: "Somebody from the ateneo in Sants mentioned that, back at the time of the Jornadas Libertarias, the Red Cross had reported that someone was circulating low-grade heroin, but not much was made of the matter. Nine months later, there was a massive, orchestrated epidemic of it."[11]

---

10. *Los Sitios de Gerona*, February 3, 1978.

11. J. Ribas, *Los 70 a destajo*, 549–550.

It was heroin that really managed to break the back of that generation of young people, most especially the ones who were using direct action from inside the prisons to lobby for changes inside the prison walls and a general amnesty that would also cover social and ordinary prisoners. It crept in quietly but suddenly, in the jails and on the streets alike. In the city, where the COPEL was causing the system headaches, the need to escape an oppressive reality was a guarantor of success; on the streets, it took the involvement of the "undercover boys," who "reappeared following the restoration of the Generalitat in late 1977, in places like El Paraigua, El London, and the Rivolta pizzeria on the Calle Hospital with little bags of heroin given to pushers as gifts."[12] Too many young libertarians fell into that alluring trap. A lot of them became hooked during their stays in prison; others simply during those wild nights where nothing was off-limits and experimenting with banned substances was commonplace.

The stupidity of those youths, incapable of realizing the vicious cycle into which they were being drawn, was also matched by witless countercultural magazines mirroring the generation in which they had grown up, with their glib talk of such substances and their short-term effects, with no ability to gauge their long-term impact: "The dénouement was not long in coming. There came a point at which the young militant libertarians who set the second half of the 1970s ablaze with their ideas and their energy, were forced to choose between the syringe and the necktie."[13] In the Basque Country, this tactic came a little later on, once it was found that the new political system left no room for the demands of the populace. This occurred roughly, be it by coincidence or otherwise, a year after Francisco Álvarez, the head of the Barcelona Anti-Anarchist Squad, arrived in Bilbao. There, there was proof of the state's involvement in heroin distribution: "Albeit that at the time it was an open secret that there was a connection between the state security corps and their involvement in drug trafficking, it was to be authenticated in 1989 when that conspiracy was publicly exposed in the so-called "Navajas Report." That report clearly spelled out the date when the conspiracy had begun: in 1983, the very point at which the ZEN (Zona Especial Norte / Special Zone North) plan had been launched."[14]

---

12. J. Ribas, *Los 70 a destajo*, 69.

13. D. Castillo, *Barcelona: Fragments de la* contracultura (Barcelona, Ajuntament de Barcelona, 2010), 12.

14. *Emboscada en Pasaia: Un crimen de estado* (Barcelona: Virus, 2008), 210.

DENÍS

Since I was born under a bad sign
I can hold my tongue no longer
About what I suffered as a child
Or what may befall me.
And in this land I find myself
Reaping the whirlwind
With the truth in my mouth
Smelling dead flesh.
—MANUEL GERENA, "AUTORRETRATO"

Denís's parents had moved up to Catalonia from the province of Granada and they finished up in La Botjosa, a mining district in Sallent in the El Bages comarca. The textile and mining settlements of the Berga district and El Bages reflected the need of entrepreneurs, first, to boost their profits and, secondly, to keep a close check on the working class. To put it another way, they were spawned by the union of modern notions of capitalism and older, more feudal notions. Thus, the entire lives of working-class families who arrived in the settlements, driven by necessity, revolved around work, and all the profits from their upkeep went straight to the company owner, who ran the company store and what few public facilities there were, ranging from the social center to the schools. The difference being that the textile towns belonged to Catalan bourgeois families, whereas the mining towns were owned by Spanish corporations. In the case of La Botjosa, the owners were the Potasas Ibéricas S.A. company, a subsidiary of Explosivos Río Tinto. The workers and their families lived right beside the mines, in barrios or settlements created for their exclusive use and which took care of their basic needs. The goal was to create settlements that were closed off from the outside world, where there was no social intrusion and the will of the employer was law. Out-and-out ghettoes inhabited mostly by Andalusian and Extremaduran immigrants with not much contact with the native-born locals.

Denís was born in a shack in La Botjosa on November 14, 1952. Although they had no home of their own, that shack housed Denís, his parents and his uncle. Not for another four years would the company grant them their first half-way decent accommodation. Denís grew up in the midst of extreme poverty and brutal oppression. There was a cultural and a physical oppressiveness that also sought to deny these families' children any escape, thwarting any betterment of their social circumstances. The children of the exploited of today would become the parents of tomorrow's exploited, just as the children of today's bosses would be parents to the bosses of the future. The adolescent Denís caught on that the purpose of such a wretched existence was to avert any interruption to the continuity of production, and from a very early age he tried to climb out that dark pit, the potash mine that oh-so-*disinterestedly* provided them with a home, sustenance, education, etc. Denís was eleven or twelve when the schoolmaster asked the pupils to write an essay about their barrio. He penned a critical text in which he complained of the alcoholism among the menfolk, the women's submission to their violence, and the lack of expectations. Within days, his parents received a visit from the schoolmaster to ask them to call their son to order. The teacher, Don José Fresno, was another player in the social pantomime and, as Denís was to write years later, even as he was teaching his pupils to sing [the Falangist anthem] "Cara al sol" in such a hopeless setting, his own daughters were enjoying a university education that was off-limits to them: "In the barrio, the schoolteachers and the priests were symbols of an education geared toward the benefit of the strong."[1]

Any attempt to break out of this cycle was forever being dynamited, and the only option was self-education. Besides football, Denís, from a very early age, stood out because of another of his passions: reading.

In 1966, he finished his primary education, and like every other youngster from the settlement, on turning fourteen he had to find himself a job to help support the family financially. On April 24 the following year, he began work as an apprentice at the auto parts plant Matricerías Riudor in the neighboring town of Santpedor. Since, under that social arrangement, the miners—most of them illiterate—had no way of providing their children with a decent education, they at least wanted to see them learning a trade, but Denís was not interested. However, so as not to upset his father, he agreed to go through a trade apprenticeship and let himself be ruled by the stifling economic reality. One year later and he had company in the shape of Manel Tirado, his boyhood pal, alongside whom he spent another three years working in Santpedor. They were years of shared learning in every sense, and during trips from one town to another, always together—sometime cycling,

---

1. Denís's handwritten text.

on other occasions by bus, walking half of the route, sometimes, with pals who had a car and might give them a ride—they analyzed the settlement's educational plight and planned ways of breaking the chain of oppression that was holding the working class population back from getting ahead.

He spent the summer of 1969 with some other comrades setting up a youth club in the hope of getting the youngsters from the settlement to engage with self-organization and start to break through the vicious cycle foisted upon them from without. He pulled this off in September that year when the articles of association of the youth club were approved by the parish, once it had imposed limits on its autonomy. From then on, his main purpose was to inject some social and cultural impetus into the mining settlement. Over time, the youth club persuaded the company to let it have the use of some premises, and this made the youth club truly autonomous. These premises were used for recreational activities such as dances, slide shows, or sports tournaments alongside activities unrelated to youth activity, things like meetings to lobby for job security or reductions in the prices of goods in the mining settlement's bar. Through the youth club, a music festival was organized in the settlement in 1971.

At the same time, ever since he was very young Denís had been heavily into playing football. He was an outstanding center forward and idolized the Scottish player Denis Law, which is where his nickname came from. As a youngster, he started playing for the club in Sallent, and from Sallent moved on to a club in Manresa. Later, he was scouted for the Moià club, where, for the very first time, he was paid for playing. Also there at his side was his inseparable friend Manel, but even that was not enough for them. After a lot of hesitation, they decided to go a step further by trying to widen the extent of the organization among the settlement's residents. It was at this point that they launched a sports club, Dynamo ERT, which even had a groundbreaking female section. They launched the club with an eye to promoting popular, socially conscious sport: "We had two aims: one was to expose football as an ideology and expose its structures, offering an alternative to both; secondly, to turn Dynamo into an effective weapon of struggle, capable of reaching out into other aspects of the barrio's issues."[2] The club's name was directly connected to the influence of the socialist countries. Those were the years of the Cold War, and the Communist Bloc was the only politically tangible alternative for the young rebels-in-the-making. Instead of a hammer and sickle, their badge consisted of a pick and a spade laid across each other—typically mining tools. They agreed to tack on the company name (ERT: Explosivos Río Tinto) in order to make it clear that this was the town team, and in return the company agreed to cover the costs of the gear (shirts, boots, balls).

---

2. Letter from Denís to a comrade from the settlement.

On January 3, 1972, a dispute broke out between the company and workers in the potash mines in Sallent. The employers' response to the initial demands for better pay was to sack eight miners. Whereupon the workers took over the mines for twenty-three hours, backing down only after mass sackings were threatened and a promise was made that the eight miners sacked would be rehired. Three weeks after that the company broke its promise. On February 10, a comrade from the mine in Balsareny, owned by the same firm, was dismissed. Spontaneously, the workers' response spread to both mines, which within hours were brought to a standstill, except for the office staff. The workforce from the Balsareny offices joined the strike on February 12, while the workers in Sallent carried on working as they were on separate contract. On February 12, the two mines were besieged by Civil Guard personnel who stopped food getting through to the locked-in workers. The reaction to this was that the miners' wives, including a few very bold types like Pepa Gómez, after holding a few meetings, decided to lock themselves inside the church in Sallent. The following day, a Sunday, found upward of three hundred women locked inside the parish church in Sallent, and a significant segment of the population backed their struggle. The bakeries, cake-shops and bars, the only establishments open for business on Sundays, looked after feeding them. Young people collected provisions and delivered them to the sit-in, while a few women looked after the children of the women locked inside. That night, the company let the workers know that it was prepared to rehire seven of the eight men dismissed. The workers' reply was emphatic: all eight comrades were to be rehired and wages were to go up by 1,500 pesetas a month (about nine euros).

Denís was up to his neck in this dispute. There was no sort of trade union backing, there was no structure taking the miners under its wing, and there was no experience of this sort of a dispute. Solidarity and steadfastness on an individual level was the only chance of a good outcome.

That Monday, a sympathy strike spread across the comarca. The only places open were a few food stores, because the citizens had decided that this should be so. In the early hours of the morning, the Civil Governor had ordered the Civil Guard to withdraw from the two mines. The company again urged the workers to come out, but they only restated their demands. The next day, workers not locked inside the mines mustered at the gates of the companies but did not return to work. On Wednesday, February 16, after six days locked inside the mines and a four-day lock-in at the parish church in Sallent, the company agreed to every one of the workers' demands.

During this time, by now with somewhat of an education, Denís was enjoying all of the argument and counterargument: whether with other comrades, with the miners, with the people who made up an underground cell of the PSUC, and even with the priest in Sallent, he enjoyed arguing about society and life in general, the future and the past, dropping in phrases from philosophers such as Wilhelm Reich, his favorite. When he spoke, a hubbub of voices grew up spontaneously around him, but in the long run all his opponents, especially the priest, kept out of his way. His gift of gab, his ability to get into minute details, made him unbeatable. His libertarian outlook (ideologically he was not yet a proper libertarian, or at any rate did not realize that he was) became a bit of a drawback when the end of the regime was in sight.

Six months after that, Denís publicly denounced the business strategy of the factory in which he was working; it was popularly known as the "glove factory" in Sallent. The glove factory was a recent addition, but it got plenty of work, and it used fiberglass with no thought for safety nor for proper gear for handling it. He started by exposing these issues, but he also discovered the reality of the factory. Every six months, its owners would dismantle it and move on to a different town, the aim being to avoid having a fixed workforce. Several meetings were held at his home, but he had a hard time getting the comrades to mobilize to demand their rights. In the end, he was sacked from his job, but not before he had achieved his purpose: that the factory should stay in town. His involvement in these two struggles, the mine strike and the complaint against the factory, together with his gifts of oratory, give him a higher profile than others, and that was to have dire consequences.

That summer, after the miners' strike turned into a moment of unforgettable solidarity between the residents of the settlement and the inhabitants of Sallent, a group of youngsters from the settlement and a group of youngsters from the town, among them Dolors Capdevila and Jordi Fàbregas, decided to organize a music festival together, with the aim of further encouraging cultural activity plus deepening their class consciousness. Advertised as "Six hours of progressive music," the festival took place on September 24 on the trail between the schools in Sallent and witnessed performances by groups such as Toti Soler's Om and Jaume Sisa.

On November 19, 1972, Denís took part in a demonstration in the course of which traffic was blocked on the highway through the settlement. The demonstration was called for the purpose of lobbying for an underpass, or, failing that, a set of traffic lights, after a resident had been knocked down and killed; she was the mother of a friend of his. After traffic was blocked on the road linking the towns of Manresa and Berga, Civil Guard personnel from the barracks in Manresa were sent in. These Civil Guards did not stand on ceremony and started firing their submachineguns in the air at the first opportunity. The demonstration was quickly dispersed. The demonstrators had not been looking for a confrontation; they were simply asking for additional safety measures for the local inhabitants. However, Denís took a hefty blow on the back from the butt of a Civil Guard's rifle when he confronted the officer. When the shooting began, he had been trying to help his uncle, who was suffering from Parkinson's disease.

On the afternoon of the following day, he was with some friends at the entrance to the local bar. The sergeant from the Sallent barracks walked up to him, and after summoning him, but without a word of explanation, dealt him an almighty punch in the stomach, taking his breath away. Helplessly, his friends merely picked him up and helped him back on to his feet. That same night, he was arrested in his home. At the same time a couple from the settlement, Pepa Gómez and her husband Rafael Camacho, who had both been to the fore in orchestrating the demonstration, were also arrested. All three were jailed: Denís and Rafael were sent to the Modelo in Barcelona.

On arrival at the Modelo, Denís was sent to the Sixth Ward, the one used for minors (the age of majority at the time being twenty-one). His cellmates were a couple of youngsters: one of them had only been admitted a week earlier, and Denís and he became firm friends. His name was Andrés Grima.

Andrés, another twenty-year-old, was an anarchist militant from Madrid's Autogestión Obrera (Workers' Self-management) group. Months earlier in Madrid, on arriving back home from a clandestine meeting in the El Pilar barrio, he found a carload of police parked at his door; imagining the worst, he decided to make himself scarce. He later found out that his suspicions had been correct and that, unable to find him, they had arrested his two brothers. He also found out that his fellow members of the group had been rounded up that same evening in their respective homes, so he decided to head to Barcelona. In Barcelona, he was initially harbored by people from the Negro y Rojo group, who put him up in a garret at the intersection of the Calle Aribau and the Gran Vía, where they had their propaganda gear and a bed. But when he found out the risks involved in staying in the safehouse of an active group, he made up his mind to move on. Living under the radar also led to his sharing an apartment with a Galician militant, also clandestine, a member of the PCE(i). On November 12, after meeting some comrades from Perpignan in the Ciutadella park, with an eye to organizing the escape of a Valencian activist to France, Andrés realized that he was being tailed. He managed to shake off his pursuers, but on showing up that afternoon for a safety rendezvous on the corner of the Calle Aribau and the Calle Mallorca, he was placed under arrest, as was the Valencian activist, his roommate, and his roommate's girlfriend. In the Modelo, Andrés helped with Denís's anarchist education, while in return he learned about the ability to fight for one's own dignity. Together, they resolved not to let their surroundings brutalize them and to fall back upon their humanity in such unfavorable circumstances.

When Denís was freed on March 20, 1973, after payment of a 10,000 peseta fine (about sixty euros), he told Manel that he would have liked to spend a little more time there in order to complete his social and political education. Living alongside Andrés had been an unforgettable learning experience for him. On April 8, 1974, he had been acquitted of disturbing the peace, but by then the damage was already done. Four months behind bars for asking for an underpass so that his neighbors might cross the road in safety. His time in prison during the turbulent years of the late dictatorship left an indelible mark on the social evolution of this young twenty-year-old. As if that was not enough, on leaving the Modelo, Denís realized that he was now a marked man to the local political bosses in the comarca, who were not about to forgive him for his connection with self-organizing in the working-class settlement.

On May 9, 1974, he received his call-up papers and reported to the Naval Military Command. During his time in military barracks, initially in Cartagena and later in El Ferrol, his father died and, within months, he was followed by his mother. Their deaths secured him the only furlough he enjoyed during his entire stay in the barracks, but there was no end to his restlessness. Along with another comrade, he set up a clandestine library in the lockers in his barracks. On his return to Sallent in November 1975, he found that nothing was the same. His friends were now grown-ups, and the group that had been the driving force behind the youth club had scattered. Some of them had married, others had left the settlement. Having no job, he felt like a burden on his sister and began to withdraw into himself. Pondering the possible ways to force social change he spent many a long hour poring over books. On the odd day, he made a trip down to Barcelona where a comrade he had met during his military service was living.

In April 1976, he crossed into France for the first time, on his own (a neighbor who was to have gone with him dropped out at the last minute). His immediate intention was to find a job, but at the same time he had a plan for the medium term, to build a bridge between the restless youths in El Bages and the libertarian organizations established in the south of France. He settled in the town of Cornellà de la Ribera, where he found work as a casual worker, picking fruit.On July 10, in an effort to regularize his life, he joined the French Football Federation as a player for SMOC Perpignan, a club that, with his help, managed to move up a division during that time. At the same time, he started hanging out with libertarian refugee circles in Perpignan, places such as La Belle Taverne and the Librería Española. He was put up overnight by various comrades, sometimes in the home of Bernard Pensiot, or Gerard or Felip Solé. That October he sneaked back into Spain bringing libertarian propaganda supplied to him by Enric Melich. It was then that he kept a rendezvous on the Ramblas in Barcelona with Andrés Grima who, having served out his sentence and being freed from prison, had settled in Barcelona for good. Denís turned up wearing a jersey that Andrés had made him a present of three years before in the Modelo and he positively radiated clandestinity. Andrés thought that he had been hiding out in the hills. He told Enric Melich, who bumped into Denís on the same avenue in Barcelona, that he had walked it all the way from France carrying a heavy knapsack.

He turned up in Sallent again that November and tried to slip back into his social and sporting dynamic: on December 4, 1976, he organized a performance by the flamenco singer Manuel Gerena and the Trotamons band at the town's social club, but at the last minute this was suspended for reasons out of his control. At the same time, he took an interest in organizing a local CNT federation in the town. He was homeless, but some musicians let him stay at their rehearsal room. Once the mining company (which owned the premises) got wind of this, it decided to close it down rather than let Denís carry on sleeping there. Denís then moved into an abandoned farmhouse on the outskirts of Sallent. By that point, the local oligarchs knew him by sight, and thwarted in his search for work in the comarca where he had grown up, he was forced to head back to France in February 1977. He felt let down by the locals in the town and, more broadly, in Sallent and the comarca, for which he had tried to do so much. He was at a dead end: "The questions . . . have always come from you. . . . Questions that . . . prompted me to become a leader and, of necessity, a martyr . . . I am an ordinary person, a regular guy and I turned a blind eye to death (to say the least) in order to look life in the face (assuming that there is such a thing as life where I am concerned, as I am starting to have enduring doubts there): at least I gave it a go."[3]

That second trip to France was made surreptitiously. Two comrades from the same comarca, from the town of Balsareny, were keen to wriggle out of their military service. He had a word with Manel, and Manel volunteered to drive them across in his Seat 600. They would meet up in Barcelona. Galera, a deserter, turned up in his army uniform, which he tossed into the port of Barcelona along with his bedroll, before they set off; the other comrade, Juan Felipe, had yet to report to the barracks but had made up his mind that he was not going to do so; all four of them, along with Juan Felipe's wife, climbed into the car. Manel drove, passing through La Collada de Toses, a village near Puigcerdà where Denís pointed out the route they were to take to bring them to the foot of a mountain, where Manel dropped them off. They now had only to get to the summit, and they would be across the border.

In Perpignan he found himself in dire straits ("if you were considering coming up this summer, I couldn't recommend it, because if only you knew the dismal conditions I find myself in, sleeping on the floor, living here and there, living in tents."[4]), but, dissatisfied as he was, he was trying to stay in touch with reality on

---

3. Letter from Denís in Perpignan to a comrade from the settlement.

4. Letter from Denís in Perpignan to a comrade from the settlement.

the other side of the Pyrenees. His countercultural inclinations even prompted him to attend the third annual Canet Rock Festival on July30 and 31. That year, he was forever crossing backward and forward over the border, and in the late summer found himself back in Barcelona with a comrade whose acquaintance he had made in Perpignan; he was due to hand him a number of copies of Anton Pannekoek's *The Workers' Councils in Germany*, a book that had been published by Mayo del 37 some years before. At the same time, he joined the libertarian movement once and for all: the city was one of the operations centers of the grupos autónomos. Along with Felipe, Seisdedos, and El Cordobés, he started planning actions. However, one fine day El Cordobés went missing, and the first suspicions of infiltration surfaced. Also camouflaged among the dozens of activists there were individuals suspected of working hand in glove with the police on both sides of the border. And then those suspicions shifted to another of these questionable individuals. He went by a number of names, but his real name was Eduardo Soler and at that point he was running the Librería Española which he had bought off Enric Melich in the wake of the bomb attack a year earlier. The youngsters made up their minds to take a gamble in order to confirm or dispel their suspicions.

On October 15, 1977, Denís was arrested with Felipe just after they had slipped across the border, at Coll de Banyuls in the Empordà. They had with them a 150-kilo load of explosives. The Coll de Banyuls pass had been an important crossing point for post-war smugglers, and it was one of the few places where one could drive right up to the borderline on the French side. The promoter of the action, who accompanied the two youngsters as far as the border but who headed back to Perpignan without a hitch, was Eduardo. In his red car he drove them as far as the inhospitable, treeless location covered in low scrub; there was no escape route from it and no hiding place. Lights from the seaside town of Banyuls-sur-Mer were flickering a few kilometers behind them; ahead of them was nothing but darkness. The borderline ran right across the crest of the mountain range. Once they had reached the peak and crossed the invisible line, there was nothing for them to do but head downhill, and once a start had been made on that, there was no turning back. Burdened as they were, turning back and heading back up the slopes would be quite impossible. Before starting out on the trip, Eduardo had tried to talk them into carrying guns so that they could defend themselves against any possible brush with the Spanish security forces, but the young men, who did not trust the man, ignored him. Their aim, as they strove to minimize the risks, was to enter Spanish territory and hide their cargo in an abandoned farmhouse a few hundred meters from the border. As they crossed the borderline and started to head downhill along the narrow trail, they heard a gunshot. This was in the early morning, and they knew that there was no turning back now. It was then that they realized that there was a string of Civil Guards barring their path. They knew that it they were to try to flee uphill, they would be killed. They were arrested.

They were taken to the very same farmhouse where they had planned to stash the explosives, and there, waiting for them, were officers from the Policía Nacional's Anti-Anarchist Squad based in the Via Laietana in Barcelona. It got them then and there that Eduardo Soler was indeed a "plant." In the farmhouse they were repeatedly questioned about where they stashed their guns, the belief being that Eduardo had convinced them to going armed. During a brutal interrogation, one of the members of the squad even used a leather whip on the youngsters, like some sort of a medieval punishment, or as if they were slaves in the United States a hundred years ago. They were then driven in separate vehicles as far as the Via Laietana station in Barcelona, where the rough treatment continued. Some days after that they were hauled before a judge in Figueras to make their statements, and the young men met up again there following torture sessions that left Denís with several broken ribs. In the end, Denís and Felipe were jailed, initially in Figueras and later in Girona.

In Girona, Denís ran into a Balsareny resident, José Simón Cazorla, who was serving time for petty robbery. Social inequality had filled the state's prisons, and there were other youngsters from El Bages scattered through a range of prisons. Quico Roqueta came from Artès and was in jail in Valencia; Antonio Oller from the settlement was in Barcelona, etc. Once behind bars they carried on with their self-organizing efforts: in January 1978, following the arrival of some members of the COPEL, who had been moved out of Carabanchel Prison following rioting there, the inmates decided to mount a hunger strike. It lasted several days but at the same time it gave them strength: "Even here, there is breath and life; we want changes and we are going to have them."[5] As a result of their activism within the prison, and because they were helping with the expansion of the COPEL in Girona Prison, the two young men, Denís and Felipe, were switched to Carabanchel, arriving there on February 2 after a night spent in the Modelo in Barcelona and another night spent in Zaragoza.

On the very day they arrived in Carabanchel, a libertarian grupo autónomo in Madrid was broken up; its members arrived in the prison a few days later. Joining forces, they all started working on a tunnel, intending to escape. Denís, who had some technical expertise in mining, was the pacemaker, but on March 13, after the tunnel was discovered—most likely due to treachery by another inmate—the warders were hellbent on finding out the name of the diggers, resorting to their usual interrogation methods. Within hours, that same night, on March 14, Denís

---

5. Letter from Denís written from Girona prison to his sister in January 1978.

was murdered in a brutal beating involving prison officers, acting with the connivance of the prison's governor, doctors, and chaplain.

Months later, José Simón Cazorla wrote in a letter to Manel: "My letters are meant to accomplish a task to which I have committed myself. That mission is to carry on with the fight begun by a fine comrade who, once in Girona Prison, I promised to fight for ideals akin to the ones for which he was fighting . . . and for which he gave his life."

THE MURDER OF AGUSTÍN RUEDA

They know how to silence mouths with one pass of the scythe
Slowly and mercilessly.
No one will ever know the worry of the hours
Before one catches the last carriage.
—BARRICADA, "EL ÚLTIMO VAGÓN"

At around 9:30 a.m. on March 13, 1973, warders in Carabanchel Prison uncovered a tunnel in Ward Seven. It was instantly reported to the governor, and questioning sessions began automatically, conducted by the chief warder in the presence of the governor himself, Eduardo José Cantos Rueda. Almost a dozen inmates who had come to prominence for their support for COPEL demands and their prisoner self-organizing, were sent for and beaten by the chief warder and seven or eight other officers. Since the results proved unsatisfactory, the governor decided that the interrogations should continue in the underground cells of the prison under the supervision of Deputy Governor Antonio Rubio Vázquez. In the course of these initial interrogation sessions, even the prison chaplain was on hand; at no point did he voice any objection to what the warders were doing. The chief warder already had two outstanding allegations of torture hanging over his head from the previous year.

At around 11:00 a.m., having endured a brutal beating, Agustín Rueda was placed in one of the so-called "death-penalty cells" He was in a pitiful condition and unable to stand upright. In the cell his condition worsened and, at the insistence of other inmates who had suffered the same treatment, he was visited, twice, by the prison doctors, José Luis Casas García and José María Barrigow Pérez, who confirmed his dire physical condition but did nothing beyond giving him some suppositories. Twelve hours later, Agustín was removed to the prison infirmary where he passed away in the early hours of March 14. The two doctors had left the prison premises when their shift ended without as much as drafting the appropriate report; that report was drawn up the following day, by which time the prisoner was already deceased. They falsified the date in order to avoid subsequent disciplinary measures. When Agustín was removed to the Carabanchel Prison hospital, all the prison doctors could do was sign his death certificate.

Warders spent the morning of March 14 preparing their respective alibis. A false and far-fetched version of events designed to preempt a judicial investigation. Finally, shortly before noon, by which time Agustín had been dead for about ten hours, the governor informed the Police Court.

News of Agustín Rueda's murder spread through the Carabanchel inmates, who quickly realized that the prison administration was out to hush it up. Prisoners receiving visits from their lawyers that day were given the task of getting the awful news out past the prison walls. Within hours, those inmates who had received beatings had a visit from the director-general of prisons, Jesús Miguel Haddad Blanco, who ordered them removed from the isolation cells and taken back to their respective cells. Agustín's sister learned the news from the television on the night of March 14.

On March 15, a panel of senators visited the prison to look into what had occurred for themselves. One of the warders explained to them that a hollow had been found, in which Agustín Rueda, whom they described as proficient in the handling of explosives, had been planning to place a device to blow the prison up. Two of the warders then locked themselves inside a cell with eight of the inmates to question them further. Some reporters were told that it was at this point that Agustín had attacked the two officers with a knife. Others were told that he had fallen down some stairs. Another version had it that he had been lynched by other inmates.

In Madrid on March 16, once an autopsy had been performed, libertarian sympathizers expressed outrage and, unsolicited, a delegation walked the coffin carrying the comrade's body through the city center before handing it over to the family for onward transfer to Sallent. That afternoon, thousands took part the many mini-demonstrations held one after another around the city. At the same time, the police raided premises in the Calle Moratín where the Prisoners and Ex-Prisoners' Families and Friends Association (AFAPE) was holding a press briefing. Everyone there, reporters and lawyers included, was arrested. But by then the news had gone public, and there was no stopping the many reactions to the murder. That same afternoon, an officer from Carabanchel Prison was assaulted and injured in Madrid city center. Also in Madrid, four CNT members were arrested for putting up posters reporting the killing. In a gesture of solidarity with the family and to denounce what had happened, other comrades from Wad-Ras Prison—women jailed in connection with the Scala affair, for involvement in the grupos autónomos, and militants of the PCE(i)—declared a hunger strike. The strike was subsequently joined by the Els Joglars theater troupe. Members of Els Joglars had been jailed over the play *La Torna*, based on the murder of Heinz Chez (real name Georg Michael Wetzel), the prisoner murdered on the very same day as Puig Antich was executed. They stayed on hunger strike for a week—except for the PCE(i) women who, on direct instructions from the party leadership, were required to keep up the strike. Later one of them was expelled from the organization for disobeying orders. On the same day, the governor, deputy governor, and chief warder from Carabanchel Prison were dismissed.

On Friday March 17, Sallent ground to a standstill. As the hours ticked by, every business, every company pulled down the shutters and locked its gates. That afternoon a huge demonstration toured the town, while down in Madrid there were repeated *saltos*, attempts to demonstrate, and clashes with the armed forces. In the early hours of March 18, the coffined body of Agustín Rueda arrived in Sallent. The strike was total that day: that afternoon, Agustín was buried in his hometown cemetery. The first tense moments came when the body arrived. The forces of order prevented the coffin from resting in the family home as had been agreed when the journey from Madrid had begun, and they forced its removal to the funeral home at Sallent cemetery. Later, in an attempt to thwart any demonstration of solidarity, the security forces obliged the same funeral home to give the family just thirty minutes' notice of the actual burial. Hundreds drawn from all over Catalonia lingered in the vicinity of the family home. When Agustín's sister emerged to make her way to the cemetery she was followed by a cortège of upward of five thousand people. The route to the cemetery had been taken over by riot personnel from the Policía Nacional, who monitored the public mourning ceremony from a cautious, though provocative distance, especially from the hills overlooking the cemetery. The police provocation even went to the extent of posting officers on top of headstones near the space set aside for Agustín's corpse. The populace kept calm, the most notable frictions being between the family and CNT General Secretary Enric Marco, who addressed the mourners without asking permission from the family and, during the subsequent press conference, named himself chair of the news conference.

On March 19, the Policía Armada barracks in Cornellà was raked by gunfire in an action later claimed by a libertarian *grupo autónomo*. On March 21, a demonstration was held in Barcelona to denounce the murder. Some *saltos* followed, and there were clashes with the police throughout the city center.

The following day, the director-general of prisons, Jesús Haddad, was gunned down in an attack outside his home in Madrid in an assassination ascribed to GRAPO but claimed by another two organizations. The statement issued by GRAPO claimed the action as its response to Agustín's murder, but some of those interrogated along with Agustín expressed doubts about that. Later, even the media were talking about the possibility of the murder's having been the work of some far-right group.

Just before midnight on March 22, a device planted behind the Civil Guard barracks in Hospitalet was defused and within hours, on March 23, another device planted in CNT premises in Madrid was also disarmed.

On March 26, there was a news report that a device had exploded at the police station in Montpellier, and that action was claimed in the name of the "Grupo Autónomo Libertario Agustín Rueda." The day after that, two SMOC Perpignan teams played wearing a black armband as a sign of mourning, after releasing a statement in reference to Agustín: "[We wish] the world would be as kindly as you were."

On March 30, four people were arrested, accused of having been behind the machine-gunning of the police barracks in Cornellà.

On April 8, another hunger strike erupted among the libertarian prisoners. Initially these were nine comrades in Carabanchel, who were joined on April 12 by the twelve libertarian comrades from Wad-Ras women's prison, who had already been on a week's hunger strike that March. Half a dozen inmates in the Modelo and other comrades held in Valencia and Alcalá also took part in the strike. The French newspaper *Sud-Ouest* estimated the number of libertarian prisoners on hunger strike was twenty-six.

On April 21, the trial was held for the action that had led to the imprisonment of Agustín Rueda. His codefendant received a two-year prison term in the first terrorist trial held during the new era of democracy.

Months after that, the prisoners who had undergone that brutal interrogation with Agustín were dispersed around several prisons around Spain. Pedro García Peña and Alfredo Casal Ortega were removed to the top-security prison in Herrera de la Mancha, where they came under ferocious pressure from warders. Finally, in 1979, on August 13 and November 21 respectively, they sent lengthy submissions to the judge retracting their earlier statements which had named those responsible for the killing. The judge was startled by these submissions, though. He intuited that something odd was going on and summoned both prisoners to testify before him: they acknowledged that their retractions had been sent as a result of mistreatment they had been undergoing since arrival in Herrera de la Mancha: Alfredo Casal, on the very day he arrived there, after undergoing a further brutal beating and prior to his going into solitary for forty-two days, had been forced to eat his thirteen-page statement.

The killers served less than a year in prison. In February 1979, the judge in charge of the First Section of the Madrid Provincial High Court, Luis Pérez de Lemaur, ordered their release.

On March 14, 1979, first anniversary of the killing of Agustín, the Palace of Justice in Barcelona was evacuated after someone had placed a suspicious package there.

The case arising out of the killing of Agustín opened in Madrid on December 9, 1987. Almost ten years after the events and shortly after the judge in charge, Alberto Gutiérrez, who had always done his best to obstruct court action, was due to retire. The defendants were the governor, deputy governor, nine warders directly responsible for the killing, and the two prison doctors.

On February 9, 1988, the sentences were revealed: from six to eight years in prison for those responsible for the murder for their "reckless endangerment" and "injury," as well as four years for the two doctors for "negligence." During the trial, the scandalous details of the murder came to light. The autopsy report explained that it had found "an exceptionally vast picture of injury, indicative of undue cruelty, in the form of multiple contusions covering almost the entire surface of the body, displaying unmistakable signs of having been thrashed to the point of such pain that the subject was unable to revert to physical normality," and expressing the view that "given the victim's strong build . . . and the aforementioned fact that he was not bound and restricted, it must necessarily be concluded that the injuries were produced by multiple assailants." And it went on to argue: "The fact that there was no discernible fracture, of either the ribs or the skull, and that still intense contusions had been caused to the lungs and meninges, this indicates that the beating was delivered with expertise. It can be stated that so many external injuries sparing the underlying bony structures cannot have been produced by anything other than special dexterity." It declared that death was the result "of the combination of injuries and the absence of appropriate treatment." In short, the report made it clear that the warders were professional torturers out to inflict pain, but at the same time it held that Agustín need not have died, had the doctors done their job properly.

Those violent torturers were chief warder Luis Lirión de Roble and prison officers Julián Marcos Mínguez, Hermenegildo Pérez Bolaños, Nemesio López Tapia, Alberto Ricardo Cucufate de Lara, José Luis Rufo Salamanca, José Luis Esteban Carcedo, Andrés Benítez Ortiz, José Javier Flores Ramos, and Alfredo Luis Mayo Díaz.

FELIPE

"The history I have lived through is an authoritarian history in which folks are not supposed to educate themselves. They force you to make decisions that no one would, left to their own natural devices."

—FELIPE

Back in 1970, Alcoy had about sixty thousand inhabitants, and there were few signs of what Alcoy had been during the Civil War. In 1936, the CNT was the majority presence among the workers of the textile plants that abounded in the town. The entire productive and commercial set-up was collectivized after the troops in the city's army barracks refused to support the fascist uprising and went over to the side of the people. Things stayed that way up until the Nationalist forces emerged victorious. Felipe arrived in Alicante Province in 1970.

His parents, peasants from Almería Province, had been forced by necessity to give up on farming and to seek work in some of the many mammoth construction sites the regime was rolling out across the country; in 1955, while they were working on the construction of the La Engaña tunnel in Burgos Province, Felipe was born. At the time, the La Engaña tunnel was the longest ever planned in Spain. The work was begun by several companies of republican prisoners and was later supplemented by wage laborers. When the project was complete, the family moved on to the Madrid airport site in Cuatro Vientos, after which they made their way back to Almería, intending to revert to farming for a livelihood.

Felipe lived there until he was eight or nine years old, at which point the Home-Schooling scheme, whereby the regime and the Catholic Church sought to provide a way out for children from small farming communities with no schools. Priests would sweep through these villages, arranging propaganda meetings, screening films showing idyllic scenes of children receiving high quality education, thereby encouraging the most gullible to send their children off to the cities for an education. Felipe spent a couple of years in Almería, then Vélez Rubio, and finally he arrived in Ogíjares, in the fertile plains of Granada, where he spent three years in the care of the Marist Brothers. During those six or seven years as a boarder, he had more than enough time to have his eyes opened to the fraud of the priests managing the Home Schools planned by the Education Ministry. When his parents were forced by the economy yet again to move to Alcoy, he decided to pay them a visit and never went back to boarding.

In 1971, he started work in the plant where his brother, Seisdedos [Six Fingers], had worked before him. It was through him that he met a group of young people with whom he formed an anarcho-syndicalist workers' collective and set about mounting propaganda activity with an eye to reorganizing the CNT, although he had no contact of any sort with it. In late 1973, having just turned eighteen, he managed to secure the post of trade union liaison, to sort of cover his back and ensure that his activities did not attract attention. At that time, some afternoons he would approach a riverbank where he met the teacher Rodrigo. Maestro Rodrigo was an older man, an anarchist who had been a teacher under the Republic and who had been barred from the profession following the Franco victory. He had spelled out the hard facts about the 1936 revolution to Felipe at some length, trying not to add fuel to the fire in his heart, which craved immediate change. In addition to Felipe and his brother, the trade union group also included El Alcoyano They were active between 1972 and 1974 when, following the campaign that strove to avert the execution of Puig Antich, a mistake led to Seisdedos and El Alcoyano having to go on the run, via Valencia, to Perpignan. The group was broken up. The apartment where the *vietnamitas* used to print up their propaganda were stored was uncovered, and those members who had stayed on in Alcoy were arrested. Up until that point, all Felipe's activity had consisted of was an attempt to organize the working class, but after fifteen days in the Policía Armada barracks and the brutal treatment at the hand of its members, the eighteen-year-old started to think that maybe he needed to work on self-defense as well.

After he was put on provisional release, Felipe returned to his activities, promoting strikes and demanding better pay and working conditions, going so far that the owners of the textile plant urged him to return to work only on Friday to pick up has wages and to forget about working Saturday to Thursday. Despite his activity, the owners of the small family firm never turned him in. It was in the late summer of 1975 that he fell for a second time, while daubing graffiti with the brother of El Alcoyano in solidarity with FRAP and ETA members, who were shot a few days later. Again, it was members of the Alcoy Policía Armada that arrested and beat him, but this time the judge ordered him imprisoned, and they were taken to Alicante Prison, where they were held in solitary for fifteen days. These were bold young men, however, and their outlook on life was impassioned and in the moment. To them, solitary was a double punishment, and after several eruptions of never-ending rioting they succeeded in getting access to the news on television. Two weeks after that, they were transferred to Murcia Prison, where they were at the same time as political prisoners from other organizations such as the ORT (Oganización Revolucionaria de Trabajadores/Workers' Revolutionary Organization) or the PCE. After two months in prison and having paid a fine, Felipe was freed on November 19. The dictator died hours later. In Alcoy, he returned to work, but at twenty years of age, with two charges pending before the TOP and with Policía Armada personnel dogging his every move, he made up his mind to cross the border. One day in early 1976, he turned up at his brother's Perpignan home.

The situation there in the capital of Roussillon was very different from how things had been in Alcoy. He became a CNT member, but there was no bridging the generation gap. Many youngsters who had crossed the border to get away from the regime had already moved beyond trade unionism and needed a more emphatic answer to the harassment visited upon the population during the dictatorship years. Arming themselves was now on the agenda. On March 6, just a couple of weeks after arriving, he found out that El Alcoyano had been picked up in Valencia with two Valencian comrades. He stayed on in the home of Seisdedos for about a year and then moved into the home of a young man known to them as El Cordobés. He later found a job as a gardener, rented his own apartment in the old city and moved out. In Perpignan, he met up with other activists and started making plans with them. One was Agustín Rueda, whom they dubbed "El Secretario" and who signed letters he sent home as Denís; they would meet up after work in La Belle Taverne where Bombetes ("Light Bulbs" in Catalan) was working. He was a libertarian militant who had fled Barcelona in April 1974 after they linked him with the OLLA on account of his involvement in the MIL Prisoners' Solidarity Committee. One day, El Cordobés and his wife went missing. Gradually, two and two were put together, and they came to the conclusion that he was most probably a Civil Guard. It was at about the same time that he became acquainted with Eduardo Soler. Eduardo was about twenty years their senior and was the new owner of the Librería Española. They assumed that if he had persuaded Melich into handing the bookstore over to him, he must have been trustworthy, and they allowed him to dabble in taking part in their activities. He was the only one among them who had a car and he volunteered to act as their driver.

In early 1977, Felipe was sacked and found a new job in a furniture factory beside the train station. Shortly after that, with Eduardo doing the driving, he began raiding quarries around Perpignan and stashing the proceeds (Goma 2 explosives, dynamite, detonating wire and percussion caps) at home and in the bookstore. This was the point at which they and El Secretario started planning how to get these explosives into Spain. Around this time, they made contact with some former GARI activists. The latter gave them the run-down on their suspicions about Eduardo, but in the light of their joint activities of the past few months, they refused to pay this any heed. At the beginning of that summer, both El Secretario and Felipe slipped over the border, although they did so separately and with different destinations. They arranged to meet up at the end of the summer in Perpignan to make their way back over the Pyrenees together and smuggle the explosives back at his house into Spain.

The met up in the late summer and weighed up their options, now that they had been alerted to Eduardo's questionable reliability, but in the end, they decided to risk it and cross the border carrying the explosives and relying on Eduardo's help. Their only purpose was to stash their cargo on the far side and try to see if their colleague was an informer. They would cross over via Coll de Banyuls, a location unfamiliar to Felipe and would stash the explosives in an abandoned farmhouse. Over the days leading up to the operation, Eduardo did his best to talk them into going armed; he kept on and on about it, but they refused; they were clear that if he was an informer, guns would only make their predicament worse. And if he was not, they would have no call to defend themselves.

On the agreed date, October 15, 1977, Eduardo drove them as far as the border in his car. It was early morning. The road across the border was in a dip between two mountains. They slung their knapsacks over their shoulders and set off downhill. Within minutes they both heard a gunshot and realized that their suspicions were correct. It must have been a signal. They mentioned it, but now that they had loaded up, there was no turning back. There was a small valley on their right with a mountain on their left and beyond. Shortly after that they were just about to cross the valley when they heard the call to halt. In front of them, atop the mountainous crest on the far side some Civil Guards loomed with guns trained on them, edgy and convinced that they too were armed. Right then, they were in fear for their lives.

Slowly, they dropped the knapsacks to the ground. The guards approached them and, discovering that they were not offering any resistance, they calmed down. They handcuffed them, asked them where their guns were and, after checking that they were not carrying any, forced them to walk on, keeping them apart, unable even to see each other and moving directly ahead. The violence started en route. Shortly after that, they forced Felipe to veer off slightly while Civil Guard personnel lined up a few meters away and loaded their weapons, feigning a firing squad. Their journey ended when they came to the farmhouse where they had been intending to stash their cargo and there some members of the Barcelona-based Policía Nacional Anti-Anarchist Squad were waiting for them. They called "El Secre" by his name. The needless violence continued.

Amidst punches and threats, they were driven in two separate cars to the Via Laietana station in Barcelona, where they were held in isolation for three or four days, over which time the beatings continued. They were then driven up to Figueres, where there was a judge waiting for them. The two friends were reunited after their hellish detention and the days thereafter. They had both taken quite a beating. The judge committed them both to prison, and they were removed to the city jail. They stayed there for about two weeks until they were taken to Girona, where they were held for around three months. Their arrival in Girona roughly coincided with the arrival of some prisoners who had been transferred from Carabanchel because of their involvement with COPEL activities. The government was out to undermine the organization's unity. Together, they embarked on a hunger strike to press for better conditions, a strike in which half the prison got involved. The warders forced them all to go to the canteen at mealtimes, and half of the prisoners ate while the other half looked on. They gave up the strike after a few days, but the prison authorities realized the implications of having two young libertarians at a small prison like the one in Girona. They were both then relocated to Carabanchel, arriving there on February 2, 1978, after spending a night in the Modelo in Barcelona, followed by another night in Zaragoza.

In early 1978, Carabanchel was a powder keg. Overcrowding, lack of expectations and vexatious treatment by the warders meant that the place might blow up at any moment. On arrival, the young men had set about planning their escape. They made contact with COPEL members and with a group of GRAPO militants who had recently been sent there in the wake of the abduction of General Villaescusa and the businessman Oriol. They set about work on a tunnel that would leave them outside the walls. Days after that, some comrades from the Madrid grupo autónomo arrived in the prison and took turns at the excavations. Felipe and his comrade ensured that, for safety reasons, they would never both be working in the same place. One would dig while the other kept a lookout and vice versa. After everything they had been through together, they trusted each other implicitly. One mid-March day, Felipe was due to come and dig as they carried on working toward a path to freedom, while El Secre was to keep a lookout in case the warders turned up unexpectedly. But neither of them were able to operate according to plan.

After going to the bathroom prior to slipping into the tunnel, Felipe spotted that the warders had uncovered the tunnel. There was every indication that one of the inmates familiar with the escape plan had run out of patience and decided to give away his comrades in return for some prison advantages. That inmate must have drawn up a list of all those involved, and the warders summoned the first inmates named on the list. The aim would have been to question them and throw a scare into them all, but the warders' brutality as they spent the first interrogation brutally beating El Secre, leaving him in such a state that he died hours afterward, ensured that none of the rest of those implicated were ever interrogated. Felipe was told by the trusty in charge of the prison infirmary what had befallen his comrade. Within days, someone told him that that trusty was the very person who had betrayed them, but he was never able to confirm this information.

A month or so after the murder of his comrade, Felipe was brought to court. He received a two-year prison term for possession of explosives. By then, he had already served more than six months behind bars, so he would be back on the streets again within months. After the murder of his predecessor, García Valdés was the new director of prisons, and he gave the go-ahead for periods of leave and sentence reduction by means of work. Felipe started work in the miniature boats workshop alongside one of the Madrid comrades, and from there they devised and planned a fresh escape attempt. Felipe's role would be to stand by the doors. He was the one who closed the door of the van that, loaded up with inmate-manufactured boats, would also carry seven prisoners hidden under a false bottom; one of the seven would be Juanjo. But it was not long before his opportunity arrived. One of the warders, having learned that periods of leave outside the prison were now standard practice, suggested to him that he should apply for one. His belief was that, with less than six months left to serve and his comrade having been murdered right there in that prison, the prison review judge would grant it to him without any sort of a hitch. Weeks later, in June 1978, Felipe left Carabanchel on leave, his mind made up never to come back.

He passed through Valencia, but the grupos autónomos there had broken up, and the most active members had moved away to Barcelona. He decided to follow suit. In the wake of the continuous falls at the beginning of 1978, activists were flooding into that city and returning to action in brand-new grupos made up of youngsters from both France and Valencia or Madrid. Shortly after arrival, three comrades from one of these brand-new groups fell—Paco from Valencia, Michel from France, and El Kilos from Madrid. A holdup at the Banco de Madrid branch in Lloret de Mar did not go according to plan. Felipe's first move was to start planning for the escape of these comrades.

His first go was an attempt to get Michel out of Girona Hospital, where he was recuperating after having been shot twice. The thinking was that helping to get him out of the hospital would be easier than breaking him out of prison. They came up with a plan whereby they would smuggle a nun's habit through to him. They put the disguise together, and Felipe held it in his home, but in the end, they could not get it to Michel since he was under very strict surveillance. Michel was then moved to the prison where his comrades were. So, they set about looking into the chances of breaking them all out of jail, and expeditions to Girona began.

They decided to mount an escape bid through the sewers, after locating, close to the prison, a sewer fed into by a pipe of around sixty centimeters. It looked like an easy undertaking. The gap between the sewer and the prison walls would have been around a little over ten meters, although there was a considerable incline. Outside the walls there was a strip of land about six to eight meters wide, after which the ground fell away and there was a bank with shrubbery. The pipe was at the next slope, and then the sewer into which it fed. The youngsters boarded the train in Barcelona, armed and carrying the required tools to venture into that underground realm, but the situation was extremely delicate. On one side, the exit was too close to the prison premises. When the comrades entered the pipe one of them stayed outside as a lookout but from that position not only could he see the Civil Guards in the sentry boxes surrounding the prison but he could even eavesdrop on their conversation. Keeping watch in those conditions could ruin the nerves of even the most laid-back person. On the other hand, once inside the sewer things were more complicated as there were several offshoots which narrowed and there were also some virtually insurmountable inclines. And as if that was not enough, there was the additional issue of the overpowering stench that accompanied them the whole way back to Barcelona. Doubts as to which offshoot they should follow were resolved by arranging with inmate comrades to flush detergent down at a prearranged time. Initially they sorted out the first few narrow pipes by ensuring that the comrades entrusted with entering the sewer network were the two most lightly built comrades, himself and Nano; they bought diving suits in an effort to circumvent the problems of the stink, but of course they failed in the attempt. They did end up under the prison, but the piping had become so narrow that they could not budge, much less dig upward. After a month of trying, they had to give up. Besides, in order to ease the tension that had built up over some days working in Girona, they decide to give themselves a night off and the partying was such that two of the comrades—Cri Cri and El Morito—wound up getting themselves arrested. El Morito, a Valencian comrade with an unblemished record, was released the next day, but Cri Cri, even though they could not tie him in with any criminal offense, was escorted as far as the border and expelled from Spain, due to his being a former member of the MIL.

Some months after that, in 1979, Vigo provided them with plans of the sewers in the Modelo; Joan had obtained these from the School of Architecture. The escape plans were switched to the Barcelona prison where several French and Catalan comrades were being held. While they set about planning the best way of getting inside the walls, Vigo and Juanjo were arrested with another nine comrades. A copy of the escape plan came into the possession of the police, who broke the story to the public, in the belief that it had been aborted: "Likewise, they were found in possession of a highly detailed plan of the Modelo Prison in Barcelona, the purpose being to dig tunnel from the outside in, in order to prepare the escape of several prisoners, to which end they planned to rent some premises in the vicinity of that prison."[1] But this hurdle simply led to a change of plan: rather than rent some premises, Felipe used some phony papers to rent a van. Next, they bought some industrial blowtorches with which to cut through any grille they might run into and make a hole in the van's floor. The idea was to position the van on a manhole above a drain, yank it up from inside the van and slide into the underground system. On the night of the operation, they loaded up the van with the blowtorches, guns and other necessary equipment and parked it above the manhole. They were just getting ready to enter the sewers when they spotted a Policía Nacional van hovering around. After a few minutes of great hesitancy, they decided to call the operation off, dumping the van and the all the gear, except for the guns. Then they went for a second option, which was a lot more wearisome but at the same time, safer.

Using phony papers, Felipe leased a tiny flat on the ground floor of an apartment building in the Calle Vilamarí. During the 50s and 60s, some of the broad inner courtyards of these buildings had been parceled out, and two or three small flats had been built there; usually, these were occupied by the porters. They passed themselves off as agronomists carrying out some research and, over some months, they removed tons of dirt into bags that they carefully stacked in one of the rooms, trying to make sure that they were not stacked up against the walls. First, they dug a vertical two-meter shaft, and then they worked at an angle for a further 1.70 meters until they had gone seven meters deep, the depth at which they had been told they would run into the sewer that would bring them up inside the prison premises. They carried out the requisite electrical and ventilation work for digging at that depth. They divided up the work; those not at work would rest up in a couple of apartments they had leased in the city. But the information given to them regarding the pipework in the sewer system proved incorrect. Instead of being seven meters underground, the sewer they were after was actually only two meters down. They started searching for it by digging right and left, but there was no sign of the pipe, so they decided to come up, but eventually, after a lot of effort, they found it; just as well, as they were not able to pump oxygen into the new shaft. They wasted precious time searching for the pipe, and the additional excavated soil caused a wall to crack, alarming the neighbor lady living on the other side of it. When days after they had found their way, Felipe took a phone call telling him that the landlord would be coming to inspect the flat the next day, he assumed that the game was up. That night, several young people scrubbed the place of fingerprints before making themselves scarce.

Felipe then traveled down to Valencia to support a comrade, Joan, who had

---

1. *La Vanguardia*, February 28, 1979.

devised an escape plan to break out a social prisoner with whom he had become acquainted during his time inside. The prisoner would ensure that he was transferred to Valencia Hospital a day ahead of an agreed date, and his escort would be jumped by armed men in the hospital corridors. It would be up to Felipe and Joan to jump the two police officers while, outside, other comrades would cover their retreat from a separate vehicle. This action was a disaster. On the appointed date, November 17, Joan and Felipe kept watch at the hospital entrance, and once they saw the policemen coming with Ramón (as Joan's friend was called), they hurried to intercept them in one of the hospital corridors. Within minutes it was all proceeding according to plan: the two young men were walking down a corridor in the opposite direction to Ramón's police escort and as they passed one another they grabbed the two officers by the shoulders, giving them no time to react. All of a sudden, Ramón took to his heels. Felipe, startled, turned to see where he was going, and the police officer capitalized upon his bewilderment to wriggle free. Then Felipe made to draw the revolver from his pocket, but unfortunately the catch on the chamber snagged on his trousers, resulting in the chamber's rolling along the floor; he stooped quickly to retrieve it but when he straightened up, he could see that the policeman was already drawing his regulation weapon. Felipe replaced the chamber but, seeing that all the shells were now scattered on the floor, all he could do was hurl the revolver at the policeman and take off at a run. Before he knew it, he had taken two bullets. Same as Joan. By some miracle they both survived, but one of Joan's wounds looked pretty gruesome: one of the shots had entered, grazing his eye and exiting through the back of his head, without touching his brain.

They were held in the hospital, cuffed to their beds, no better treated than on previous occasions. Initially, the police stood on ceremony as his paper identified him as Swiss. When he came to after two days' unconsciousness, he asked to see the Swiss consul. But within days, instead of the Swiss consul, it was members of the Barcelona Anti-Anarchist Squad that showed up, and his hospital stay turned into a nightmare. In spite of his serious condition, the policemen carried on with their short-cut methods. One day, one of them gave him a kick that sent him sprawling off the bed, and his tubes were ripped out, causing him unbearable pain. The next day, he underwent an urgent operation for pancreatitis triggered by that violent fall. He then decided to ask for a voluntary discharge: the sooner he got out of hospital and into prison, the better and safer it would be for him. This rush led to his being moved back into the hospital fifteen days later, but at least he managed to avoid being manhandled over that two-week stay. Once he had recuperated, he was taken to Mislata again, although the policemen guarding him took him, quite unlawfully, to the police station once the doctor had discharged him. Luckily, the judge got wind of this and alerted his lawyer, García Esteve, who made sure that they brought him back to the prison. He spent only a day or two in Mislata, after which he was sent to the cellular prison in Burgos, a punishment prison where the warders could do pretty much as they pleased and without supervision. There an attempt was made to implicate him in a sham escape attempt, and one night he was abducted for a number of hours before he was returned to his cell. He spent about a year there before he was transferred to Carabanchel.

And then came his trial; although his Valencian lawyer, García Esteve, and Carmen Pertejo, a young lawyer from the same chambers, had attended him throughout the whole preparation of the charge, his defense counsel was Marc Palmés from Barcelona, who ensured that he received a sentence of about four years, three for assaulting the authorities during the attempted hospital escape, a year for unlawful possession of weapons, and three months for attempted escape after they linked him to the Calle Vilamarí tunnel. In another trial for breach of sentence after he failed to return to Carabanchel after his approved period of leave in the summer of 1978, he was given a further three months.

After he was released, he was feeling low. A social outcast with no support, with his entire family affected, getting back into real life was complicated. Knowing that mere association with him might create problems, he decided to distance himself from the anti-authoritarian networks. Although, at the same time, he was one of the people who helped keep alive the flame of friendship between all the now not-so-young people fighting against the system of oppression under which he had suffered.

Despite this distancing, he was arrested again a year later. They came looking for him at his home on some utterly bureaucratic pretext, something along the lines of his not having served his sentences in the proper order, as if prisoners have any choice as to the order in which they serve their time. Carmen Pertejo quickly submitted a habeas corpus claim, a newly introduced court procedure, and even though it was granted, Felipe was not able to avoid serving another two weeks behind bars.

THE PRISONS

I'm going to burn down the high nobility
I'm going to steal away their cash
To buy more gasoline
and carry on setting fires.
—LA BANDA TRAPERA DEL RÍO, "CURRIQUI DE BARRIO"

The state prisons were an honest mirror held up to Spanish society and during those years went through the same evolution and turmoil as the outside world: initial demands were repressed through brute force (during the latter years of the dictatorship); then came a point where it was believed that social change might be possible (the years directly after Franco's death); only to finish in the same political disappointment experienced on the outside (following the signing of the Moncloa Agreements and, later, the Constitution).

Franco's prisons were utterly third-world prisons. Warders not only allowed, but positively encouraged the inmates to fight with and betray one another, ensuring that, as on the outside, relations would be founded upon the law of the jungle. The young, foreigners, gay people, and those without support from their families represented the weakest link in the chain. At the other extreme were the prisoners who enjoyed favors from the warders; the trusties who ran the prisons on the basis of informing and force, things that made the bulk of the inmates their enemies. However, political prisoners, who "were acutely conscious of their status as victims of the dictatorship's repression, a consciousness grounded in theory and bolstered by a record of clandestine activism"[1] were basically excluded from this set-up. Such prisoners banded together to secure differential day-to-day treatment, the sort of treatment that might make it possible for them to serve out their obligatory

---

1. C. Lorenzo Rubio, *La revuelta de los comunes: El movimiento de presos sociales durante la transición* (Valencia: Desorden Distro, n.d.), 3.

stay with rather more dignity than the ordinary or social prisoners enjoyed. As on the outside, from 1973 onward, there was an upsurge in the demands for changes, and rioting spread from prison to prison, albeit in a disconnected way. Of all these prison riots (Burgos, Seville, and Teruel in 1973; San Sebastián and Valencia in 1974; and Ocaña, Burgos, and Barcelona the year after that) the one with the greatest media reverberation was the riot in the Modelo Prison, precisely because the Modelo was packed with political prisoners who ensured that public opinion got to hear about the reasons behind the riots and their outcomes. The trigger for it was the death of a social prisoner known as El Habichuela following a beating received from some warders, prominent among them Juan Guisado, "El Matagatos." But there was nothing exceptional in that. Mistreatment, beatings and torture was commonplace in every prison. "One needs to know and be in touch with the inmate population, the repeat offenders, to properly know the extent of the crimes of the machinery of exploitation and subjugation in this fascist system."[2]

Following Franco's death, rumors about a potential amnesty, and the demand for one from the civilian population on the outside, triggered a high level of anxiety in the inmate population, which slowly began to organize itself: "If it is to be understood, the prisoners' struggle should be seen in the context of the downfall of Francoism and a practical criticism of existing institutions. Prison was unmistakably one of the most characteristic symbols of the Franco era. Almost everybody had spent some length of time in prison or had some friend or relation behind bars. So many crimes had been committed within those walls that the people had built up a boundless hatred of prison as an institution."[3] But even as they were getting themselves organized, the social prisoners were beginning to appreciate that any amnesty would not be applied to them, that they were not about to enjoy any of the opportunities on offer to their neighbors in the same ward, and the situation began to become unsustainable. Added to which there was the aggravating factor that a goodly number of those political prisoner assumed that they were morally superior due to their political grounding, for which reason they clung to their privileges and supported the ordinary prisoners' being left out of the amnesty. There were some exceptions to this notion that ordinary prisoners were socially inferior to political prisoners, and these were to be found mostly in the ranks of the ETApm, Trotskyist, and libertarian prisoners. Take the anarchist prisoner Fernando Carballo, the longest serving political prisoner in Spain; when he was released after twenty-six years inside, he called for an amnesty for *all* prisoners.

---

2. Letter from Felipe written from Carabanchel Prison to his brother on April 9, 1978.

3. Grupo Autónomo Libertario, "Report from the Modelo," in *Comunicados de la prisión de Segovia y otros llamamientos a la guerra social* (Bilbao: Muturreko Bututazoiak, 2005), 54

Or the ETA member Wilson, whose message was the same. But they were not the only ones and some of them, upon their release, involved themselves in the campaign calling for a comprehensive amnesty. Finally, in July 1976 an amnesty was granted, but thousands of prisoners in Carabanchel, who had either been found guilty or were in pretrial detention for common criminal offenses, found that the political reasons behind their imprisonment (forty years of social injustice) had not been acknowledged. They went into action and rioted on July 30.

On that day the roof of one of the prison wings was occupied: "We could stand it no longer. And as if that was not enough, things were further inflamed by the contempt that the political prisoners displayed toward us, especially, oddly enough, the ones due for release under the amnesty. In the end, we came to blows on several occasions."[4] Over the ensuing days some of the prison officers brutally targeted some of the inmates (prominent among them Ricardo Pérez Rabanal, a member of the FN, as were many other warders—he was later transferred to the Modelo in Barcelona and in 1978 was still noted for his violence—or Julio, aka "El Legionario," who made his name years later in the new prison in Herrera de la Mancha). This excessive repression planted the seeds of the COPEL.

The driving force behind the COPEL (Coordinadora de Presos en Lucha / Prisoners-in-Struggle Coordinating Body) was a group of Carabanchel Prison inmates. Beginning in the autumn of 1976, after a few months of hush-hush efforts, it produced a list of demands that included, in addition to a complete amnesty, humanization of the prisons; protection of prisoners' rights; a purge of prison officers, police, and judges; and reform of the law and prison institutions. COPEL's first public move was the February 21, 1977, riot, but its activity dated back to when prison officers had raided the reformatory in Carabanchel where minors were being housed. On that day, some young inmates were ferociously beaten on the pretext that a pistol belonging to one of the warders had gone missing. Prison guards were banned from carrying their guns into areas meant for inmates, and the pistol later turned up in a wastepaper basket, but the viciousness unleashed on the youngest inmates in Carabanchel outraged the adult inmates, who declared a hunger strike on January 19. That strike lasted for seven days and was followed by a further crackdown. On the night of February 28, with all the prisoners locked in their cells, two members of the COPEL were beaten by a gang of prisoners who enjoyed favorable treatment. The warders opened the doors of their cells so that they might do their dirty work for them. Within days, the "abductions" started up. The overnight transfers known to the inmate population by this name continued until well into the 1980s and were effected without any court order (which is to say, unlawfully), without prior notification of the prisoners themselves and

---

4. *Bicicleta*, no. 1, November 1977.

without their lawyers or family members being informed. It was their lot always to be removed to the harshest prisons in Spain: Ocaña, Zamora, El Dueso, Huesca, Burgos, etc.

These "abductions" were behind the February 21 strike, which in turn catapulted the COPEL into the Spanish media headlines: "Tension could not be running any higher. The accumulation of punishments and unpunished assaults, the dereliction of the authorities vis-à-vis the 350 incidents reported to the office of the Director-General of Prisons by way of protest at these sanctions, the murky business of the pistol, which was hushed up, as well as the instigation of prisoner transfers to other prisons ensured that on February 21, having plumbed the depths of despair, rioting erupted in Carabanchel."[5] Just one month later, a royal decree was announced in the face of the protests triggered by the ineffectiveness of the 1976 amnesty, but this step, although widely cited by the politicians and the media, was construed very differently by those prisoners who were members of the organization: "As far as we social prisoners are concerned, the royal pardon was a blatant ploy to divide us and apply the brakes to the growing numbers and activities of the members flooding into the COPEL day by day."[6]

But neither the first moves designed to split the group nor the unrestrained and merciless repression, let alone the illegal transfers, could stop the rebelliousness. The riots, hunger strikes, and *plantes* (a collective refusal by prisoners to carry out their daily tasks, as well as refusing to receive visitors, attend the canteen, or make purchases from the prison commissary) were replicated across the prisons system, while the inmates of the various prisons embraced the COPEL demands as their own and used its initials when releasing their communiqués: "The reprisals, punishment cells and beatings failed to bring its gestation and birth to a halt. Let alone the transfers to other prisons. Quite the opposite. Not only did they fail to break the COPEL, but they had the opposite effect: it expanded. When its most pugnacious members were transferred, the spark spread to all the prisons—to Ocaña, Córdoba, Burgos, Barcelona, Cartagena, Puerto de Santa María, Zaragoza, Bilbao, Valencia, and others."[7]

On July 18, before the first anniversary of the initial revolt in Carabanchel Prison, a further riot occurred in the very prison where the COPEL was born. It was the third in a year. That afternoon a group of two dozen prisoners self-harmed: and while they were being removed to the infirmary, another large group of inmates showed solidarity with them by taking over the rooftops again: "Over four days, seizing their opportunity (according to the Justice Ministry, no less)

---

5. *Bicicleta*, no. 1, November 1977.

6. Communiqué from the COPEL in Carabanchel, April 1, 1977.

7. *Bicicleta*, no. 1, November 1977.

between three hundred and seven hundred prisoners rioted on the rooftops of the Madrid prison, and hundreds more inmates engaged in acts of rebellion across much of the prison map."[8] Finding the revolts more than they could cope with, the authorities decided to tighten the noose and riot personnel entered the prison, giving no quarter. One prisoner was killed, and many others sustained gunshot injuries. Forced down from the roof and marshalled in the yard, the prisoners carried on with their self-harming, slashing veins and swallowing blunt objects so as to secure transfer to the hospital and carry on publicizing their demands, while at the same time placing themselves beyond reach of the beatings and the torture. That month, both before and after many of the activists penned in Carabanchel were transferred, there were riots in the prisons in Valencia, Zaragoza, Basauri, Granada, Las Palmas, Tenerife, Barcelona, Cádiz, Zamora, Oviedo, Puerto de Santa María, Málaga, Valladolid, Almería, Burgos, Murcia, Seville, and in the women's prison in Yeserías. The powder keg that was the Spanish prison system had erupted once and for all: "No more human blood shed for rights that are rightfully ours as human beings. . . . We are desperate and ready for anything if this carries on."[9]

That autumn an amnesty was introduced but again it omitted the bulk of the prison population. The last Basque political prisoner to be freed, the autónomo Fran, stated once he was on the outside that December: "That I am the last of the political prisoners does not matter. That still leaves the social prisoners, the marginalized."[10] The rioting spread after that and in most cases turned violent, with the torching of prison buildings the general keynote. "The social prisoners are literally destroying the prisons by means of arson, riots, and escapes, insisting upon a general pardon, and have also organized themselves on the basis of assemblies."[11] Self-harm had also become everyday practice in every prison. This extended even into the courtrooms: prisoners quickly realized that it was a lot more effective to spill their blood in front of judges and journalists than to do so inside the prison walls where the censorship of news was an everyday fact.

Libertarian activists were direct participants in these struggles. First of all, from the streets, by showing solidarity with the prisoners, setting up or serving on the COPEL Support Committees, acting as spokesmen for the inmates, arranging support meetings, and using Molotov cocktails and explosives to attack the

---

8. C. Lorenzo Rubio, *La revuelta de los comunes*, 12.

9. *Bicicleta*, no. 2, December 1977.

10. Zirikatu, *Komando Autonomoak: Una historia anticapitalista* (Bilbao: Likiniano Elkartea, 1999), 69–70.

11. M. Amorós et al., *Por la memoria anticapitalista: Reflexiones sobre la autonomía* (Barcelona, Klinamen, 2009), 186.

judicial and prison authorities, which were offering no sort of solution to the conflict.

In the course of 1977 several devices exploded at premises associated with the judicial repression across Spain. On March 1, the Justice Ministry in Madrid came under attack. On June 13 an explosion rattled the courthouses in Barcelona. In November, the Territorial High Court in Valladolid had its turn. On December 28, devices hit the courts in Sant Feliu de Llobregat and, again, in Barcelona. Just a month after that, on January 23, 1978, in a coordinated simultaneous operation, the courts in Granollers, the Durán y Bas Home, plus the Modelo in Barcelona were all targeted. As the prisoner revolt spread, the GAAC appeared (Grupos Armados de Ayuda a la COPEL / Armed Groups in Support of the COPEL); in addition to carrying out a number of holdups at bank branches, they also claimed responsibility for bomb attacks in the Valladolid area.

During those same months there were many demonstrations in support of the prisoners and their demands, and some of these were quite violent; like the December 24, 1977, rally held opposite the Modelo in Barcelona, spreading through the whole of El Eixample, after a summons went out from the COPEL Support Committees: "Demonstrators threw stones, blunt objects, and Molotov cocktails at the Riot Squads deployed in large numbers in an effort to control the situation. . . . At the junctions of Calle Viladomat and Gran Vía, and Calle Valencia and Calle Vilamarí, through-traffic to other locations was completely halted as bus lanes were blocked."[12]

But the campaign was beginning to bear fruit. Some prison guards (a few) and doctors sided with the prisoners, refused to use force (for which reason they too were transferred to more problematic prisons), or even resigned from their jobs rather than be party to the policy of repression. The debate went public, and the inmates went so far as to ask if they themselves might take over the running of the prisons. Little by little, the COPEL was achieving some of its aims, and relations between the prisoners were becoming more decent and humane. The COPEL was denouncing rapists, publicly siding with less favored categories (demanding respect for gay people, foreigners, and prostitutes), and exposing cases of flagrant injustice, such as the case of Manuel Muela, a sixteen-year-old who by October 1978 had been in preventive detention for nine months for the theft of some cakes.

Inside prisons, away from the public spotlight turned on Carabanchel or the Modelo, the situation had not altered much, and conditions were still worthy of the nineteenth century. COPEL members transferred to El Dueso in February 1978 issued a statement according to which

---

12. *La Vanguardia*, December 25, 1977.

The living conditions in this prison are as precarious as can be. We have no water, no WCs, no washbasins in the cells, merely a bunk, a foul-smelling plastic potty that we can only empty twice a day, and a water-carafe of the same material; these are the only fittings in the cells. To grasp our situation better one would need to know that two people spend twenty-three hours per day in every cell. We have gone sixteen days without a change of clothing or a shower, which has given rise to several outbreaks of scabies. . . . We are refused access to all news media, as a result of which, plainly, we are enduring physical and sociological brutalization. We are denied family visits and visits by our lawyers, which not only places our home lives in jeopardy, but rides roughshod over basic legal guarantees.[13]

In the women's prisons, the repression was rather subtler, and force was not constantly employed. But the fact that the women who ran them were members of fundamentalist Catholic orders did nothing to diminish the suffering of the inmates: "The humiliation is relentless, and those who watch over us are doubly repressive: on the one hand, as jailers and, on the other, as members of a Francoist religious order such as 'The Evangelical Crusades of Christ the King.' To these women, we are not merely a menace to society but sinners to boot, and we represent the one and only release for their frustrations."[14]

On March 14, Agustín Rueda was murdered in Carabanchel Prison, which was evidence of the facts of life within the prisons. For all the talk of reforms, repression was the main response from the state, either to the prisoners' demands or to their attempts to escape. The warders were the same as they had been three years earlier and there had been no change in their methods.

March 22 brought the murder of the director-general of prisons, Jesús Haddad, and shortly after that Carlos García Valdés was appointed to replace him; initially, he suggested that he might accede to some of the prisoners' demands. What became known as "co-management" began—the running of the prisons jointly by the warders and the inmates.

In every ward, panels of delegates were set up. The sergeants in each ward were replaced by inmates. . . . Assemblies were held in the prison yards on a daily basis. . . . Cleaning teams were organized, and no inmate was exempted from service. Solidarity funds were raised to pay for tobacco, soap and milk for those without income, most of whom were African. Every time anyone

---

13. *Bicicleta*, no. 6, May 1978.

14. CNT Female prisoners and Grupos Autónomos, "Las Mujeres NO Queremos Prisiones Mejoradas," in *Comunicaciones de la prisión de Segovia*, 53.

received a little cash or goods from family on the outside, a given percentage of this was handed over to the common fund. Head counts were kept to a minimum, most of all because the prisoners themselves were the ones who signed off on them.[15]

But this reform was merely a mirage, or rather, a ploy to buy time for the planning of the definitive state response to the prisoners' demands. A mere five months later, García Valdés himself, in an exemplary display of audacity, replied to complaints from one inmate in the Modelo Prison: "The treatment received by the inmates . . . is correct, and I reject the charge that . . . beatings, provocations, insults and harassment take place. I would call upon you to abide by proper behavior from now on, radically different from the sort you have been displaying in recent months, and that will be the only route to ensuring a more permissive, more liberal regime within an ordered community."[16] Shortly after that, with the prospective opening of a brand-new top-security prison in Herrera de la Mancha, the discourse switched from mere audacity to direct threat. "Here you have a prison for people. A decent one. If you try to destroy Herrera, I can just as easily create prisons catering for wild animals and that's where you will go."[17] The prisoners realized that they had been deceived: "What is this reform about? We prisoners have the measure of this reform: Herrera de la Mancha as an example of repression."[18] All of the ground gained through the previous two years of struggle evaporated, and in the spring of 1979 one of the inmates active within the COPEL, Miguel Sánchez García, summed things up in an article in the magazine *Ozono*: "A lot of blood was spilled for so little return." At the same time the prisoners from the Fifth Ward in the Modelo issued an agonizing statement: "But above all there is the fear of beatings; the most recent ones we have heard of came last night and lasted for fifteen to twenty minutes apiece. . . . The nightly fear, terror and panic have now become unbearable."[19] That year, two warders in the Modelo stood out for their behavior, Agustín Morales García, aka "El Rompetechos," and Daniel, "El Cojones." On March 5, 1977, just a year on from his promotion to director of the state prison system, the magazine *Cuadernos para el Diálogo* published statements by García Valdés, who had these thoughts regarding the creation of the COPEL: "I can see a real case for unions or organizations

15. X. Cañadas Gascón, *Entremuros*, 42.

16. "Letter from Carlos García Valdés," September 27, 1978. See *Bicicleta*, February 1979.

17. Publication undetermined.

18. Statement from COPEL, Carabanchel, October 8, 1978.

19. Communiqué from the Prisoners on the Fifth Ward of the Modelo, May 1979, in *Bicicleta*, no. 16.

like those for enforcement of the rights of prisoners, be they in preventive detention or after conviction."

To ferocious repression, the new prison strategy added media misrepresentation in pursuit of its interests and the manipulation of inmates in order to sow discord in the ranks. During 1978, it became commonplace to see sensational and questionably accurate reports on the alleged murders of inmates after people's courts set up by COPEL members. News of the discovery of torture cells set up by prisoners themselves during the period of co-management was also commonplace. There was also the repeated release of specific prisoners, some of whom had been active members of the COPEL, but who made statements to the press after they were freed to the effect that the violence had to end and the campaign redirected down peaceful avenues. As part of this new wearing-down strategy, a group even surfaced that was against the COPEL's demands; this was the GIL (Grupo de Incontrolados en Lucha / Uncontrollables-in-Struggle Group). Far-right prison officers were behind this group, and it was made up of prisoners wedded to the previous prison set-up before the establishment of the COPEL. And the last weapon deployed was the final blow. With a strange simultaneity, heroin made its way into all the prisons. In December 1978 three prisoners were found dead in the Modelo. One of them had died by hanging: "He knew too much about (and apparently was dangerously inimical to) the traffic in hard drugs."[20] The other two died from overdoses: "The mother of one of the young men had written to him (García Valdés) on the subject just a few days before: drug dealing inside the Modelo bordered on scandalous."[21]

One year after his arrival as director of prisons, García Valdés's reforms had been reduced to paper and ink. He had achieved his real purpose, the breakup of the COPEL and the deterioration of living conditions for those who could not bring themselves to collaborate with the prison officers and to remain silent about injustices. Many of the leading members of the COPEL were transferred to the new top-security prison, where warders took revenge. The arrival of such prisoners in Herrera de la Mancha did not vary by one iota from the arrivals in prison five years before:

> Under a hail of blows, they ordered me to undress . . . insults, thumps, kicks. . . . It all came down on me, breaking my honor, my spirit and my morale while I stripped. Eight hand-picked jailers just for little old me. I found myself naked and up against the wall in the search position. I underwent that torture, and several times I fell to the floor, only to be trampled

---

20. *Bicicleta*, no. 12, January 1979.

21. *Bicicleta*, no. 12, January 1979.

and then forced up against the wall in the search position to suffer further blows. . . . The doctor . . . saw the torture and treated me for it, writing prescriptions, signing them off as "old injuries," "bronchitis" or "lost his footing on the stairs." The whole thing was a farce."[22]

The treatment in other prisons was the same.

The PSOE's accession to power in 1982 brought no positive change as far as the prison population was concerned. Any change had a negative impact on them: prisoners and their families were punished by means of surveillance and dispersion. "In 1984, things in Segovia Prison were greatly changed and bore no relationship to the living conditions back in 1979 and 1980. The PSOE had also made no changes in the prisons or rather, something had changed; now the regime on the inside was harsher than before and the food of poorer quality and lesser in quantity."[23] It was at this point that they introduced a "tightening-up of conditions for the so-called 'political prisoners,' the aim being to launch a psychological warfare that would end up destroying them."[24]

> "We cannot consider the prison system in isolation. It is, rather, the last word in a system of oppression that starts with the laws and in the very organization of society."
>
> —AGUSTÍN RUEDA

---

22. Anonymous complaint.

23. X. Cañadas Gascón, *El Caso Scala: Terrorismo de estado y algo más* (Barcelona: Virus, 2008), 68.

24. *Emboscada en Pasaia*, 206.

JUAN

Juan arrived in Barcelona in 1962, the year of the big snowfall that crippled the city. Juan had just turned nine. His parents had sent him up from Medina del Campo to find a new life and prepare for the arrival of the remainder of the family. After a time in the home of his aunts, he lived near La Ciudadella with a family that had a dozen adopted kids. The children sold carafes of olive oil door to door in return for a warm meal and somewhere to bed down for the night. He spent his childhood on the streets, and back in those days there was only one law: there is a price to be paid. Nobody mentioned education to him, nor cleanliness; the city and society were a jungle, and the only aim was to survive at any cost. By the age of fourteen or fifteen he saw the inside of the municipal cells, although his stay there was a short one. Two or three nights. When members of the Civil Guard arrested him for riding a motorcycle that did not belong to him, by way of punishment, they wanted to use pliers to clip his long hair which fell to his shoulders.

And then his parents arrived in Barcelona, but he refused to go and live with them and ran away to Madrid. One day in 1970, when still a minor, he was arrested en route to the city center boarding-house where he was living and placed in the reformatory in Carabanchel Prison. His father had reported him for running away from home. He remembers that winter, locked inside the freezing reformatory, as one of the toughest in his life. He served some months in the reform home, and shortly after his release he was rearrested, but this time finished up in the adult prison. That was in 1971. He had turned eighteen, and after a time in Carabanchel Prison he was moved to the prison in Ocaña up until 1977 when he was released. That last stay in prison changed his life. It must have been in 1976 when another inmate let him have a book. He cannot remember the title, but it was the first time had read anything about anarchism. The attraction was immediate. He was released in April 1977 and made his way back to Barcelona. One day when strolling through the city center, in the Calle Portaferrissa, he bumped into the comrade who had lent him that book in Ocaña prison. He was painting some premises and invited him to step inside. It was the CNT's Amalgamated Trade Union (Sindicato de Oficios Varios). At the time, Juan was working as a waiter.

He joined the union and quickly ended up on the Prisoners' Aid Committee. He was out to try to ensure that no one went through what he had been through. He collected clothing, food and cash that he took it upon himself to distribute among the libertarian prisoners so that they might go on to share it with the social prisoners needier than themselves. The situation on the streets was becoming unsustainable, and the aspirations for freedom and justice that seemed possible after Franco's death were vanishing spectacularly: the Moncloa Agreements, the COPEL, the Scala affair. Somebody put it to him that it was time to "glove up." He did not hesitate. The transition was forgetting about the poorest, the ones who suffered despicable living conditions in prison, which were the same under the new set-up as they had been forty years earlier. In slang "glove up" meant going into action: donning gloves so as to leave no fingerprints.

Months after that, in mid-1980, he joined forces with some other comrades to form a relatively stable group. Their first actions were in support of the comrades charged in the Scala case. Their trial was imminent. The money raised was used for the upkeep of their infrastructure and, once those costs had been covered, anything left over went to pay the lawyers of the jailed comrades, but Juan was never involved in the money side; every member of the group had his own organizational role. They remained active for around three years. They virtually always lived together in rented apartments procured by one of the comrades. They were not clandestines, but they did not hold down jobs eithers. These days Juan reckons that leaving their respective jobs behind and turning pro was one of their biggest mistakes.

When their actions started up, they made contact with comrades from another Barcelona group who offered to supply them with phony papers. At the same time, the members of a Valencia group, one of whose activists had worked with them on their initial actions, was supposed to provide them with several firearms, but the fall of that group in Valencia also led to the dismantling of the Barcelona group and Juan and his comrades were left with no documentation and weapons just as they were beginning to carry out their first expropriations.

They carried on with normal life and were often to be seen in places that made up part of the libertarian community of the time: La Rivolta, La Fragua, El Terra Alta. In fact, when arrested years later, they were shown some snapshots taken in La Fragua. Members of the group could be seen at leisure but there were no photographs of Juan. He was making an effort to be more discreet, and at the time, given his activity, his mind was made up to cut back on his social life. Two years later, one of his comrades fell during a holdup at a bingo hall on the Paralelo in Barcelona, but the remainder, having adopted their usual security measures, such as, say, instantly evacuating the flat they were all sharing, carried on for the next year gloving up. And then they stepped up their security measures: they stopped living together and got in touch by phone whenever they had to meet up to plan or carry out some action. They had no idea what the arrested comrade might have said, and they took it for granted that they had arrest warrants. At the time, Juan slept with two pistols stashed near his bed.

On just a few occasions they carried out vehicular operations, using cars, but as a rule they operated on foot. It was on one such occasion when, luckily enough, they had access to vehicles, that Juan lost a shoe during an expropriation. He did not realize this until he got back to the car, which had already started up. The tension at the time ruled out any follow-up to such petty personal matters. That day, his comrade had to take him as far as the door of their shared abode on the Avenida de la República Argentina, lest he arouse suspicion for walking the street with only one shoe. They carried out their actions unmasked, and when there was no need for every member of the group to participate in an action, those not involved were left out of the loop. For security reasons. At this point they were starting to receive—if the operation made it necessary—support from other libertarian comrades or even activists from the pro-independence left.

In the end, the group disbanded, and Juan spent nearly a full year out of contact with his comrades. One day, though, he received a phone call at home. One of the comrades, Willy, told him that he needed to speak with him as a matter of urgency and would ring back in fifteen minutes. Five minutes after that, BPS officers were knocking at his door. The comrade had been arrested the previous day in Valencia. One of the group's members managed to get away and went underground. In time, he left the country; the rest were arrested over a two-day period of police overtime. They were charged with a dozen holdups and with planting a couple of explosive devices at bank premises. No incriminating evidence or guns were found in Juan's place.

They spent nine days at the police station, with the usual violence from the police that that implied, and then a tour of the state prisons began. Those under arrest were moved to Carabanchel Prison and, after an initial night there, were placed on the Third Ward where Juan met with other comrades from the grupos autónomos and joined the libertarian prisoners' commune, a commune that managed some aspects of the routine life of the prison, such as the catering or cleaning. Protecting the rights of the inmates implied a relentless battle with the warders and the prison supervisory judges, but Juan was undaunted: in January 1984, a disciplinary report on him was written up after he referred to one prison officer as a "jailer." His punishment was six days in solitary. Juan presented a defense argument relying heavily on the dictionary of the Real Academia de la Lengua: *Jailer*—"*someone engaged in looking after and guarding prisoners in prison.*" That same month he was given three weekends in solitary as punishment for telling a prison officer "not to talk gibberish," which was regarded by the Prisons

Department as disrespectful. Having listened to his plea, the Prison Supervisory Court reduced that punishment to a single weekend.

Three members of his group served upward of a year and a half in preventive detention, but the law prescribed a maximum of eighteen months of preventive incarceration; for that reason, in order to insist that the law be observed, they mounted a hunger strike that lasted thirty-two days, at the end of which Juan was down to forty-one kilos. In the end, they stood trial, and Juan received a sentence of twenty-four years, nine months and seventeen days in prison for membership of an armed gang, possession of weapons, and five holdups. After conviction, he applied for a transfer to Segovia Prison, where there was a sizable community of libertarians. Twice he was refused a transfer until he informed the Prisons Department that, unless he was granted it, he would embark upon a further hunger strike. Within weeks he was transferred. There was only one language the prison authorities understood: pressure. During his time prison, the national prison network expanded. In Segovia, autónomos from Madrid, Valladolid, Barcelona, and the Basque Country found themselves neighbors, although at that point the Basques were starting to be targeted by extraordinary repressive measures. They were beginning to all receive the same treatment, meaning that all Basques were lumped together, as Basques, but were treated differently from the rest, no matter how autónomo or libertarian they were.

Juan strove to carry on with his activism from inside prison. These were the years when there was the squabble over ownership of the CNT initials and the trade union legacy. He had been a member of the union and went public with his support for the CNT against the *paralela* [eventually CGT] competitors. He also publicly denounced HB's stance on the Portugalete incident. A grupo autónomo had torched some PSOE premises, and HB vigorously condemned this, just as it had previously condemned the murder of Enrique Casas by the CAA. In addition, having served more than four years in prison, he mounted his last hunger strike, insisting that he be transferred to a prison in Catalonia. This time, after twenty-eight days without food, he failed in his effort. By then the state had won the battle inside the prisons. From 1988 on, representatives of the so-called Congress of Valencia CNT (today's CGT) opened negotiations with the government aiming to secure a pardon for libertarian prisoners, while more or less explicitly conceding that the libertarian movement's days of armed struggle were now over. On March 22, 1989, the Council of Ministers released eight of the prisoners. Juan had refused to sign the repentance papers; if all went well, he had about another year left to serve and refuse to bend the knee to the state.

He remained in Hueca prison for a little under a year; that was his last prison address before he was released back on to the streets on August 10, 1990. After more than seven and a half years inside, he was one of the last to walk away from the nightmare that was the Spanish state prison system in the post-Franco and neo-democratic era.

While he was in that last prison establishment, and in a good example of the Spanish state's courts being out of control, Juan was tried in his absence by the Barcelona Provincial High Court for some of the group's earliest actions. A verdict issued on October 13, 1989, acquitted him on the grounds that the statute of limitations had passed. In actual fact, he was tried for offenses for which he had already stood trial and been convicted by the National High Court, but the latter had failed to brief the Barcelona High Court on either that trial or its outcome.

On his release, he arrived back in Barcelona without a penny to his name. He had no one he could rely upon, but the comrades from the Ateneo Libertario in Gràcia welcomed him and helped him to start a new life.

Juan carried on supporting the prisoners for several more years through the KAP (Kol.lectiu Anti-Presons / Antiprisons Collective) in Barcelona.

THE RESULTS OF INFILTRATION

Eleven o'clock in the morning on January 15, 1978, marked the start in Barcelona of the first demonstration called lawfully by the CNT in forty years. Following the success of the demonstration called a couple of months earlier in Barcelona by the trade unions to protest against the Moncloa Agreements—a demonstration that had assembled several hundred thousand people—the CC.OO and UGT bureaucracies hurriedly called their Catalan delegations to order in order to dismantle the united trade-union front, which posed a threat to decisions made outside of the factories endorsed by those very same trade union bureaucrats. Once isolated in trade union terms and in the wake of the telling victory secured in the gas station employees' strike in 1977, the CNT decided to take to the streets alone in order to carry on standing up to new capitalist policies meant to stifle the working class's ability to respond. Several thousand people backed the union's proposal and marched the length of what is today the Paralelo (back then it was the Avenida Marqués del Duero) between the hours of 11:00 a.m. and 12:30 p.m. Over an hour later the fire broke out at the Scala nightclub in the Paseo de Sant Joan.

That fire utterly destroyed the nightclub and ended the lives of four workers, some of them CNT members (three quarters of the Scala workforce belonged to the anarcho-syndicalist confederation at the time). Sixteen hours after the fire broke out, members of the Policía Nacional's Anti-Anarchist Squad arrested a couple of young people—Xavier Cañadas and Pilar Álvarez in their home in the Nou Barris quarter and, minutes later, did the same to Arturo Palma, Xavier's workmate, a CNT member as Xavier was. Within hours José Cuevas, another Nou Barris resident, and Rosa López, his partner, were arrested. Xavier, Arturo, and José had all been involved in throwing Molotov cocktails at the nightclub's entrance but, of them all, José Cuevas was the only one with a police record. How had the people behind the attack been so effectively traced if the people initially arrested never even had police files? Years later, the man who prosecuted the case, Alejandro del Toro, wrote in the review *Cuadernos Jurídicos* in November 1994: "To an expert, the weirdest thing was the speed with which the police had rounded up the alleged perpetrators."

In order to get a handle on at least part of what really happened during those days in January 1978, we need to hark back to the year before. In January 1977 the same police squad rounded up dozens of activists during the FAI Peninsular Conference. These arrests, spread over time and space, led to the dismantling of the Murcian group and involved the fall of Joaquín Gambín, "El Grillo," a man already known in certain prison quarters as a police informer. Once in the Modelo Prison in Barcelona, Gambín met Cuevas, who had been picked up for his part in the FAI meeting. It was during that stay in the Barcelona prison that the sister of activist Josep Illamola, who had been in custody since August 1975 for his part in the grupos autónomos during the latter years of Francoism, tipped off the militant Luis Andrés Edo that her brother had told her that , according to another inmate, Gambín was an informer. It looks as if, in spite of Luis Andrés's efforts to alert the upper echelons of the libertarian organizations and expose the informer to the membership, no one lifted a finger to exclude him from the libertarian movement. The fact is that on January 11, 1978, four days ahead of the CNT demonstration, Gambín popped up in Barcelona again and, because of his age (he was in his fifties), his record (which included lengthy stays in prison) and the nickname by which he was beginning to be known in the city (the "Old Anarchist"), he attracted some interest from certain segments of the young libertarians eager to get to know anarchists with lots of experience behind them. The day before the demonstration, Cuevas invited Gambín to his home, and Cañadas, Palma, and their partners also showed up for the visit. They finished the evening in the home of Xavier and Pilar, where they readied six Molotov cocktails deciding to meet up at the demonstration the next day.

Once the demonstration had passed off without incident, Gambín egged the young people into throwing the devices at the night club, it being a symbol of the new Barcelona bourgeoisie. While he stayed with the girls, the three young men walked from the Avenida Mistral to the Paseo de Sant Joan. En route, they crossed paths with four young activists from the Rubí CNT, also acquaintances of Cuevas, and these tried to talk them into dumping the Molotov cocktails. In the end, though, they were persuaded into coming along with them to mount the attack. Within minutes, tragedy ensued.

Days later, as a result of the brutal interrogations to which Xavier, Arturo, and José were subjected, Luis Muñoz and Maite Fabrés, members of the Rubí CNT, were also arrested. Another two young people managed to slip across the border and put some distance between themselves and Spain. The squad's efficiency in the arrest of the young people from Nou Barris was in stark contrast with the arrest of the people from Rubí. The only difference between the two groups was that the latter did not know Gambín, nor did Gambín have any knowledge of their involvement in the action.

Once Xavier, José, and Arturo had been arrested and questioned, they
began to realize that they had been "played," and that the whole thing was part
of something bigger that was beyond their control. The police had information
that some of them did not even possess. When they met up eventually inside the
Modelo and were in a position to compare notes, they realized that the whole
thing had been painstakingly planned by Gambín, who had acted as an *agent
provocateur.*

Over time another misgiving arose: Could the utter destruction of the building and the complete burning down of the nightclub have been caused by a few
incendiaries at its entrance? It is hard to believe that, given the thousands of
Molotov cocktails thrown in Barcelona over the years, on this occasion these had
sparked an uncontrollable conflagration. Especially when one knows that, as *La
Vanguardia* reported on January 17, "by the time that the Fire Brigade emergency
services arrived minutes later, the interior of the premises was almost entirely
engulfed in flames."

Right from the outset, there had been contradictory reports and questionable actions: even though those arrested spelled out their ties to Gambín under
questioning, the police records never mentioned him. On the other hand the
youngsters from Rubí did get a mention, and arrest warrants were issued for them.
Joaquín Gambín's name hit the headlines a month and a half later, when the judge
drew up the indictment. But even though the press provided the full names of the
youngsters who were still on the run, they offered no details about Gambín, and
the police did their best to redirect attention away from him. It looked too, as if a
neighbor of the nightclub took numerous photographs of the fire from the outset,
but shortly afterward these were bought in the name of *El Noticiero Universal* and
vanished from circulation. Some accounts have it that those photographs show
that the fire had not started in the entrance to the club but toward its rear. That
version was given some merit by the counsel for the prosecution counsel himself,
who expressed surprise at the fact that Police Forensics "have not established the
precise place of origin of the flames."[1] According to the book *El Caso Scala*, some
residents reported having heard detonations, and another, a former Civil Guard,
gave a sworn affidavit to the effect that he had seen several well-dressed people
(ties and jackets, etc.) entering the premises with several suitcases, which they were
no longer carrying when they came out of the nightclub. Within days, that local
resident was found with three bullets in his head, and his notarized statement
was not accepted as evidence in the trial. Some accounts also pointed out that the
firefighters drew up a report according to which they had found traces of phos-
phorous in the rubble at the nightclub; that report too vanished. The National

---

1. *Cuadernos Jurídicos*, November 1994.

High Court requested an expert opinion nine months after the incident, by which time neither the Scala nor any rubble was left.

It is unlikely that we shall ever know the facts, but sixteen years on from the fire and thirteen after the trial, the article that the prosecutor wrote for *Cuadernos Jurídicos* does not leave much room for doubt. He himself queried whether the firebombs that these young people prepared could have been the cause of the fire. He states that the fire was the outcome of devices whose "huge incendiary capacity was indicative of a professionalism, which the accused obviously lacked."

It was two years before Gambín found himself jailed on October 27, 1979, in the town of Elche, Alicante, but, oddly enough, no one thought to advise the court that had issued his arrest warrant. It was lawyers for the Scala accused that passed on word that he had been arrested, but by the time, November 1979, the prosecution asked for him to be moved from Alicante up to Barcelona, he had mysteriously vanished from the prison. The counsel for the prosecution himself began to realize that there was something odd about this case because despite Gambín's having been tried "it was odd that in reports from the Policía Central on the person and antecedents of the accused persons, any reference to him had been left out, nor was there any acknowledgment that orders from the Central Court for him to be taken into custody had been received."[2] To put that another way, both the police and the higher courts were trying to avoid a statement being taken from him. On November 13, 1980, the prosecution forwarded a letter addressed to the National High Court requesting access to the case file and Gambín's record. The letter also asked for him to be tracked down and Luis Muñoz released, Muñoz having been held in preventive detention for two and a half years (he had been seventeen at the time of the fire). The response was wholly unexpected. Not only did the National High Court turn down all his requests but it immediately sought to have the prosecuting counsel replaced. Obviously, this case was one in which the delivery of justice was not a consideration.

The judicial farce eventually reached its climax after December 1, 1980, when a trial got under way in a climate of tension inside the courthouse and violence outside. Clashes between young libertarians and the security forces was commonplace. The Scala nightclub owners, the Riba brothers (who had received 800 million pesetas in compensation—some 130,000 euros) failed to show up to pursue a private action, nor did the families of the victims (who had also received compensation from the Interior Ministry). Everything boiled down to a straight fight between the accused and the state. Every one of the young people was convicted: José and Xavier got twenty-one years, Arturo twenty, Luis two and a half, and Pilar and Rosa six months apiece. Maite had been released months earlier and

---

2. *Cuadernos Jurídicos*, November 1994.

never even faced the court. She was not the only collateral damage: three days after the fire, a photograph of the faces of the detainees had made the covers of the newspapers and alongside them was a young girl by the name of María Valeiras Gómez who never had any connection with the case but who was thereby criminalized in the eyes of the general public.

In 1994, the prosecution counsel acknowledged that "fourteen years on, it was plainly a mistake to have denied the defense the right to call His Excellency Señor Don Rodolfo Martín Villa as a witness" and that "the fundamental issue [for me] is that my career not be reduced to a laughingstock."[3] Meaning that he explicitly conceded the importance of the interior minister's part in the matter while also admitting that his main concern had not been the delivery of justice and clarification of the facts but simply coming away from the trial with his career in good stead.

In December 1981, Joaquín Gambín Hernández was arrested in Valencia and, after much pressure was brought to bear, he was transferred to Barcelona to make a statement on the Scala case. In that statement he declared that that he had not been arrested but had handed himself over to the Policía Criminal because the Intelligence Squad had abandoned him to his fate after the failure of an anti-ETA operation in which he had played a part. Similarly, he acknowledged that he had been hired by the Intelligence Squad in 1977 for the purpose of infiltrating the libertarian movement. As for the Scala affair, after encouraging those young people to throw Molotov cocktails, on the very evening of the attack he had phoned his police contact in Madrid to furnish him with all the intelligence in his possessions, addresses, names. He stood trial on December 13, 1983, three years after the sentencing of the youngsters and nearly six after the events. Even though the prosecution had asked for a sixteen-year prison sentence, he was sentenced to seven years.

Less than three months after the nightclub fire, on April 1, 1978, four people raided the Catalsa supermarket opposite the Sants train station in Barcelona. Three people in hoods and a man over forty years of age, unmasked, made off with 2,600,000 pesetas (around fifteen thousand euros). Two weeks after that, on April 16, Gabriel Botifoll Gómez, employed at the SEAT plant in Barcelona, was arrested in his car while on his way to meet someone known to him by the nickname Juan "El Anarquista." At 8:30 a.m. the very next day, Manuel Cruz Carbaleiro, unemployed, sustained a gunshot wound but managed to get away. This happened in the Plaza Cataluña where Manuel was supposed to rendezvous with the very same Juan "El Anarquista." On the same date SEAT workers Manuel Nogales Toro, José Ramón Sánchez Ramos, José Hernández Tapias, and Diego Santos García were

---

3. *Cuadernos Jurídicos*, November 1994.

arrested, and, with them, the unemployed Agustín García Coronado and four or five more SEAT workers. A few days later, the police revealed that they had broken up an armed gang made up mostly of workers at the SEAT plant in Barcelona and going by the name of the ERAT. Manuel Cruz was arrested on August 28, four months later.

In addition to the April 1 holdup, they were charged with another four expropriations and two attacks that caused casualties, all of them carried out between December 31, 1977, and April 1, 1978. The group was a mixed bag, made up of militants from the revolutionary left who had almost all quit their organizations (the PSOE, PCE-ml, FRAP, FAC, CC.OO, etc.)—except for one who belonged to the CNT—essentially because of those organizations' reformist policies. The ERAT had been launched the previous year in order to support the workers' struggles and defend the autonomy of the assemblies against the onslaught from the trade union and political bureaucracies of the left-wing parties that they themselves had quit. Individually, its members referred to themselves as self-managerial socialists, independence supporters or revolutionary Marxists. After between three and four tough days at the police station, where they were subjected to the usual tortures (the *bolsa*, the *barra*, etc.), they were brought to the courthouse. There they were forced to make statements in the presence of their torturers, with no judge present, and were later transferred to the Modelo. Once inside the Modelo, where they met those jailed over the Scala case, they realized that they had been set up by the same *agent provocateur*, Juan "El Anarquista," none other than Joaquín Gambín.

In the early morning of April 1, six of the seven persons arrested had met up in Santa Coloma to take part in a demonstration called by the town's Unemployed Assembly. Once that was over, Manuel Cruz invited them to take part in a meeting with other comrades that afternoon. The meeting was held near the Plaza de España in Barcelona. Botifoll, Hernández, and Nogales met Juan "El Anarquista," who invited them to carry out the holdup at the Catalsa supermarket that evening, a holdup carried out by men wearing hoods, whereas Juan made no attempt to cover his face. The proceeds of the holdup, except for a significant sum with which Juan made off, was spread around unemployed assemblies and strike funds at firms in dispute. On June 30, 1980, the trial was held at the National High Court; the charges relating to attacks occasioning victims had vanished, but sentences were handed down ranging from four years for Agustín García to thirty-four years for Manuel Cruz, albeit that most of the accused were given twenty-seven years.

The charges were based on three shotguns, eight pistols, and three sets of handcuffs that the police claimed to have discovered in an apartment in the Calle Miró in Barcelona, an apartment rented by Juan "El Anarquista."

**ESCAMOTS
AUTONOMS
ANTICAPITALISTES**

Anticapitalist Autonomous Platoons logo

Sticker in support of imprisoned
autonomous group members

Publication edited by an autonomous group from Barcelona in
support of colleagues scheduled to be tried on November 15, 1979

Sticker made by an autonomous group from Barcelona

JUICIOS SUMARISIMOS EN EL TRIBUNAL MILITAR DE BARNA.

S.PUIG ANTICH.   O. SOLE SUGRAÑES. J.L. PONS LLOBET.

MILITANTES REVOLUCIONARIOS EN PELIGRO DE PENA DE MUERTE O DE LARGAS PENAS DE PRISION. ELLOS COMO TU DEFIENDEN LA LIBERTAD, LUCHAN CONTRA LA EXPLOTACION. TU PUEDES. COMO ELLOS, COMBATIR POR LA LIBERTAD, CONTRA LA EXPLOTACION. CONTRA LAS PENAS DE MUERTE, POR SU LIBERACION. TODOS A LA CALLE. EVITEMOS EL ETERNO CRIMEN FACISTA.

Prisoners Solidarity Committee poster
of the MIL of Barcelona

OTAGES

de la COUR de SURETE de l'ETAT
pendant 2 ans pour faire plaisir
au régime ESPAGNOL, en
COUR d'ASSISES maintenant
pour alourdir leurs peines
et denaturer le sens de
leurs LUTTES !..

tel est
le sort
réservé
en FRANCE
aux inculpés des GARI

GARI prisoner support sticker

Cover of the Mario Inés Torres album
in support of GARI prisoners

Maria Mombiola of the
refugee support network

Members of the refugee support network
that operated from Toulouse. On the
left is Hortènsia Torres and to her right
is Mario Inés (father) in Barcelona
before taking refuge in Toulouse

Spanish Bookstore in Perpignan, France. At the door, with a mustache, is Enric Melich

Leaflet in support of the members of the
Barcelona autonomous groups before
their trial on November 15, 1979

Agustín Rueda

Sticker in support of libertarian prisoners

Prisoners climbed on the roof of the prison during one of the
riots in 1977, on the banner see the COPEL logo

Demonstration for the amnesty of March 13, 1977 in Barcelona. One of the young
protagonists of this book is in the foreground, carrying a black flag with a circle A

5.

ARMED AGITATION

VALENCIA

"I want to make it clear that I am not claiming that this story will serve as a
lesson to anyone. On the other hand, within the account of what was going
through our minds, or what I now think was going through our minds
back then, one can see a certain silliness and ideological delusions with no
foundations beyond alienation which, when all is said and done, consists of a
distancing from reality."

—*POR LA MEMORIA ANTICAPITALISTA*

At the beginning of the 1970s, the Barricada and Bandera Negra groups surfaced
in Valencia, both in a student context. The former employed a language wholly
influenced by the Situationists and May '68 in France. They were mainly propaganda groups out to set up an autónomo or libertarian network, and over time,
they began to liaise with other groups around Spain such as Negro y Rojo in
Catalonia, Autogestión Obrera in Madrid, or Acción Directa in Zaragoza. These
connections facilitated the creation of a small escape line abetting the escape to
France of activists who found themselves "compromised" during the latter years of
the dictatorship. One example being a Valencian activist who served as a policeman. Once discovered, he managed to slip over the Pyrenees. The final years of the
dictatorship also saw the emergence of the Alcoy group (the group in which Felipe
took part) which eventually joined up with Bandera Negra, giving rise to a very
small coordinating body in Valencia.

These groups were still influenced by the historical record of the classical libertarian organizations, although, as a rule, they had no direct connection with the
latter's clandestine militants. Following the fall of the members of the MIL, and in
view of the January 1974 military tribunal, the first solidarity actions recorded by
the media were mounted. Take the one on January 19, when several Molotov cocktails were thrown at the Iberia offices in the city. In March, following the murder
of Puig Antich, the university campuses were paralyzed for several days running,

and there were tough, violent clashes between young demonstrators and the security forces. This led to the arrest of one young man who was sent to prison after being handed over to the military authorities. At the same time, the Alcoy group was smashed, but Seisdedos managed to slip away and tipped off El Alcoyano, who was performing his mandatory military service: in view of the risk of their being arrested, they both decided to run away to France. There they came into contact with the cousins Raimon and Felip Solé with whom El Alcoyano months later decided to return to Spain to continue the struggle. While the Catalans stayed in Barcelona, he settled in Valencia.

During these years, young Valencians used to meet up in parish clubs, groups whose evolution paralleled that of the society: "In many such clubs, the priests first lost control and then the bureaucrats, and in the end there was nobody left but the actual folk who ran them, which was akin to an assembly."[1] This was true of the parish clubs in Benimaclet, Benicalap, Orriol, and, slightly later, in the ones in Quart and Mislata. The young people who took over the management of the clubs were greatly influenced by the explosion in counterculture following the dark night of Francoism, and they decided to especially take pleasure in their day-to-day lives, beginning with changes in themselves: "As far as we were concerned, what mattered was the revolution that we were successfully making in our own daily lives and personal dealings."[2]

In many cases, The young people started off in neighborhood struggles, and little by little, especially from 1975 onward, they started coordinating with one another and sharing their experiences. It was natural for them to meet up at demonstrations and the parties afterward, and what prompted this connection was the fact that they employed similar approaches to those demonstrations, where "we were always the last to leave the streets and the first to clash with the police, whether the fascists or the stewards of the left-wing political and trade union bureaucracies.[3] "For one thing, some of these activists had not given up on their propaganda activities, and when, in late 1976, the campaign by the social prisoners came to light, they rallied in support of it. Through the COPEL Support Committees they organized lobbying and strike funds and produced publications offering a platform to what was the lowest stratum in society.

At the same time, these actions were being radicalized as a result of a number of factors. On the one hand, this was due to the realization that the network

1. *COPEL: Butrones y otras aportaciones de* grupos autónomos (Valencia: Desorden Distro, 2004), 7.

2. M. Amorós et al., *Por la memoria anticapitalista: Reflexiones sobre la autonomía* (Barcelona, Klinamen, 2009), 187.

3. M. Amorós, *Por la memoria anticapitalista*, 188.

involved a lot more people than they had thought when the various groups had been unconnected. On the other, because the pressure from inside the prisons was crying out for greater commitment by those on the outside. And, to finish off, they appreciated that they were living in historic times and needed to capitalize upon that: "Some of us agreed with the idea that our chance to 'apply the screws' was going to last only a couple of years, because of the instability resulting from the Transition, and we meant to exploit that instability as long as we could and then take off to Mexico . . . among others things, in order to dodge military service."[4]

In light of the reconstruction of the CNT, from early 1976 onward, the activists from these groups kept in touch and even supported some of that union's propaganda actions, while staying organizationally on the sidelines, without becoming members. It was then that some of these new activists came into contact with El Alcoyano, although the connection was intermittent: on February 17, 1976, he was arrested by Civil Guard personnel and taken to the Paterna barracks, where he was subjected to a brutal interrogation. This led to the discovery of a safehouse where weapons were being stored and, within days of that, the arrest of two youngsters from the Valencian network. That year, the last of the grupos autónomos that made up the network in later years sprang into action. Little by little, through their group network, they connected with Barcelona groups and, most notably, with people from Madrid and France. These connections boosted their capacity for action. Nineteen seventy-seven saw their struggle peak. Operations were mounted weekend after weekend. Between ten and fifteen two- to three-person groups mounted simultaneous attacks on bank premises to mark the anniversary of the murder of Puig Antich, show solidarity with German political prisoners, or back the struggle of the ordinary prisoners. By that point, they had a doctor they could call upon, who on one occasion removed a bullet from a comrade who had been wounded during an action.

That was the year when, faced with the escalating attacks from the grupos autónomos the GAR put in an appearance. The GAR used the same methods and claimed action in the same way as the grupos autónomos did, but it was supposedly the creation of some government source designed to track down the evasive unidentified youngsters whose ranks, being based upon affinity, had never been infiltrated. All their falls were the result of their own mistakes or inevitable accidents.

In January 1978, the first of the groups operating as part of the network fell. Four young people, including El Alcatraz and El Ventosa were intercepted, armed, in a stolen car. They were preparing to carry out a bank holdup. The ensuing days witnessed a general retreat. All the comrades who had built up connections with the people arrested vanished from the city for a while. That fall proved a turning

---

4. M. Amorós, *Por la memoria anticapitalista*, 187.

point, with some of the activists forced to go underground. From that arrest onward, they could count on the services of Alberto García Esteve, a PCE member who had a record of handling the defense of political prisoners in Valencia. They could also count on the services of the young lawyer Carmen Pertejo Pastor who involved herself with the activists in an extraordinary way. With links to the Anticapitalist Lawyers' Coordination, she had sampled the repression for herself, and was arrested in August 1975 after the Policía Armada located a safehouse where illegal propaganda was being printed.

A few months after the fall, those activists who had fled started to meet up again in the city, and it was discovered through the lawyers that the four imprisoned comrades were planning an escape from prison. Friends on the outside saw to it that they received small picks with which to dig a tunnel as well as walkie-talkies they could use to communicate and plan the escape down to the last detail. But on June 10 the tunnel was discovered, and those involved launched a violent riot, which inevitably involved the guards.

Paco fell a couple of months after that, following a double holdup in Lloret, and some comrades decided to move up to Girona in an attempt to break him out through the sewer system, with help from other French and Madrid activists. This escape bid too came to nothing. However, they were able to break out a couple of ordinary prisoners, neighborhood friends of some activists, from the hospital in Valencia. The two inmates had been removed to the hospital where a small saw was smuggled in, and they used it to saw through the bars on a window before making good their escape. They later went underground for a few days and, once the police pressure had eased somewhat, one of them was helped across the border.

During the final months of 1978 and throughout 1979, actions focused almost solely on helping comrades escape from Spanish prisons. These comrades were relentlessly swelling the numbers of inmates. On January 9, 1978, four activists were arrested while emerging from a manhole in the Valencian sewer network. They had just spent about two months working on an escape plan for a dozen people and had even had support from the odd member of the pro-independence organization Maulets. After an on-the-spot inspection, they chose to dig a fifty-meter tunnel into the prison facility. Every day they would climb down into a manhole in the middle of an orchard some two kilometers from where they had begun the tunnel and would trudge through the sewers to the worksite.

They had excavated ten meters until one day, as they were leaving through the manhole in the orchard, they found themselves surrounded by Civil Guards. There seemed to be every indication that some prison inmate, having found out about the excavation of the tunnel, had not been able to keep the secret. A couple of days before, prison officers had carried out a painstaking search of the prison and, finding no tunnel and nothing to suggest that one was being dug from inside the prison, they figured that the digging had to be coming from outside. On the day of the arrests this led to their mobilizing all available personnel to monitor all possible accesses to the sewer system, until they managed to catch the four young people. These activists, one of whom was Nano, spent only four or five days in custody. Except for Joan who, having been reported as a deserter from his military service, spent about three months behind bars, initially in Valencia and later in Huesca.

Even as these young activists were attempting an escape from Valencia prison, Felipe and some French and Catalan comrades were starting their planned tunnel in the Calle Vilamarí, in an attempt to break into the Modelo. Once the three youngsters arrested in Valencia regained their freedom, one of them moved to Barcelona to work on a fresh escape plan, but when that plan too was uncovered months later, most of them headed back to Valencia. It was then that Joan suggested that they organize the escape of an ordinary prisoner whom he had met during his stay in prison: on November 17, 1979, during the escape bid, Joan and Felipe were shot and arrested. That fall signaled the end of the Valencian autónomo network. A couple of weeks after that, when they made to leave the city, another four activists were arrested; among them were Nano and another of those arrested over the attempt to escape from Valencia prison eleven months earlier. The most dynamic members of the network had been captured

It was a further year before the last arrest of the Valencian autónomos took place. On October 12, 1980, the French activist Alain Drogou was arrested along with three Valencian activists, one of whom had belonged to the autónomo network that had been operating in the city since the arrest of the MIL prisoners. That group was in touch with one of the last Barcelona groups that were subsequently dismantled.

Joan Alfons Conesa i Sans (aka Joan) died on March 27, 1996, as the result of an accident inside the squatted Princesa cinema in Barcelona; he had been the main driving force behind the occupation of the premises. He never gave up on the struggle.

PACO (VALENCIA)

"We represent no one but ourselves as part of the radical proletariat."
—"RECUPERACION," MIAU-MIAU SECTION OF THE GATA,
GIRONA PRISON, OCTOBER 19, 1978

He arrived in Valencia in 1973 for the 1973–74 university year to study for his career, but, once established in the big city, that initial purpose quickly evaporated. He stuck it out in the department for a year and then dropped out. Of the various avenues open to a young nonconformist fresh in from a small Valencian village, some were more interesting than attending classes by those doctrinaire, or at the very least, boring lecturers. Paco, born in Oliva in 1957, found a whole new world opening up before him in Valencia.

During his first year at the university he ran across all the political alternatives (Trotskyism, Maoism, etc.), but many were beginning to suspect that these parties might represent the successors to Francoism. He struck up friendships with other youngsters as restless as himself with whom he started reading the few books on anarchism legally published in Spain, mainly by the Editorial ZYX in Madrid or the Catalan publisher Kairos. His life took a U-turn at the university. His main craving was for a radical alteration to the most mundane aspects of his day-to-day existence. What he was reading in these new countercultural publications that were being passed around among the student body was a lot more attractive to him than any of the lectures on offer from teachers who, in the main, wanted to churn out brand-new producers, tailor-made for serving the system. At the same time, music also helped transport him to different worlds. Furthermore, far from his family, he realized that the entire sex education he had received was wholly repressive and designed to emasculate him psychically in respect to any option other than the only socially acceptable one: sex for the purposes of procreation within the family. Society's hypocrisy fired up this inner craving for change.

January 1974 brought the passing of a death sentence on Salvador Puig Antich. Having nothing to do with political organizations, Paco was not worried about social evolution in political terms; like his pals, what drove him were human impulses. They knew nothing of the social links of the actions of Puig Antich and his comrades, but the death penalty turned their stomachs. So he started questioning the best way of reacting to atrocities of that sort. He did his best to find out about what the media were describing as "The Sten Gang" and got hold of a few of the texts they had been distributing, since these were gradually beginning to circulate among young folk opposed to the regime but not signed up to any of the Marxist-Leninist parties. It was at this point that he began to get organized with other young people whose analysis was similar to his own. When the school year ended, they decided among themselves that they would form an action group.

Together with four or five of those comrades they decided between them to start living as a community and enjoying life from a fresh angle. Paco gave up his studies. There was complete affinity among them. They started throwing Molotov cocktails and mounting propaganda actions, sometimes on their own, sometimes in collaboration with other young people acting similarly. They did not need to share the same thoughts about the future, the same social purpose; what actually was vital was that their approach to day-to-day work was the same. For that reason, on a number of occasions they worked with some youngsters from the Germania Socialista (Socialist Brotherhood), a maverick group that was a blend of nationalism, Trotskyism, and self-management, but which was run horizontally, along assembly-based lines. During that first year, with Franco still living, they came into contact with some of the young people who were part of the parish clubs in the Benicalp and Orriols barrios, youngsters with whom they quickly hit it off. During those years when the right of association was nonexistent, these parish clubs were one of the few openings young people had for getting together free of adult supervision and police harassment. In Valencia, in some of them, the young people drifted in the direction of workerism and autonomy.

In 1975, he and a comrade traveled legally to France. He passed through Perpignan, Toulouse and Paris and got his hands on some of the texts issued by the GARI in defense of its actions the previous year. Gradually, through such writings and the publications of the Situationists, he was being drawn into the world of autonomy, while drifting away from a more rigid, orthodox anarchism. Down in Valencia, small groups were making connections with one another and making contact with other like-minded groups in Madrid; together, they started marking the anniversary of Puig Antich. Such connections ensured that there was a proliferation of actions. The responses to the repressive actions of state repression (mostly the Spanish state but also its French and German counterparts), were turning more numerous and aggressive all the time. Independently of their clandestine activity, which was autonomous of other political factions, they carried on taking part in public protest demonstrations, while making no attempt to harness them for their own purposes. Of course, if the demonstration was crushed, they did not shy away from confrontation, but they were never the ones responsible for the violent clashes that occurred during some of the demonstrations. They strove to not stand out politically, and in public actions let themselves be carried along, reluctantly deferring to the organizers. At night, they carried on meeting up in bars such as El Racó, across from the Department of Fine Arts, where they listened to whatever music they liked, smoked joints, drank alcoholic beverages, and, essentially, hung loose, shaking off the decorous education they had received.

He also stepped briefly away from the hard facts of the dictatorship when, in July 1975, he and some comrades took off to the Barcelona town of Canet, although the arrival of the Canet Rock Festival—the reason for his trip—was unexpected. After spending the night on a nearby beach, on the morning of July 26, they made the decision to hitchhike the few kilometers between there and El Pla d'en Sala where the festival was held. Once on the road, a car belonging to the Canet municipal police pulled up alongside them, and a uniformed policeman invited them to climb aboard; they could hardly refuse even though they were not at all clear as to how this episode was going to end, especially given the illegal substances they had on their persons. The Canet police officers confined themselves to dropping them off at the entrance to the festival, and that night they were able to watch the performance of Pau Riba, their favorite singer at the time. In Valencia, the music side of the counterculture was reflected in May 1974 by the staging of the rock opera *L'home de cotó-en-pèl*, out of which grew the group Cotó-en-pèl. The local groups that Paco liked best were Buffalo, Paranoia Dead, and Cotó-en-pèl. When it came to singer-songwriters, Ovidi Montllor was his great favorite. As for comic books, his favorite was *Don Pixote de la Mancha*, the protagonist of which rode, not a horse, but a Vespa scooter. The hero's reckless behavior was not the result of his chivalry books but rather his relentless poring over the works of Lenin, and his trusty sidekick was a garbageman.

This one-day-at-a-time approach to life prompted the vast majority of young people organized in the many Marxist parties, which were out to bolster themselves by means of militant dogmatism, to look upon them as *pasotas*, empty-headed youngsters disconnected from the serious social issues. And if this was the view of some of the youngsters with whom they shared the streets during demonstrations, the security forces' opinion of them was no better. They realized that they had succeeded in erecting a screen around themselves and that their enemies could not even conceive of their actual social activities. After a few of their more sensational actions, the police stepped up the checks at the train station, on buses leaving the city, on the roads out of town. Meanwhile they held their own security meetings in the heart of Valencia, in the El Carmen barrio, where they would celebrate their successes over a few drinks in their usual bars.

In 1976, the CNT began reorganizing in Spain, including in Valencia, but Paco decided to keep it at arm's length. The internal bickering dating back to the years in exile (with which young people had absolutely nothing to do), the anarchist orthodoxy of some of the public faces (involving endless arguments), and the absence of any real plan (the reorganization was perceived as driven by its history) brought about a needless waste of time. As for trade unionism per se, Paco, being against wage labor, felt no need to join a union. His fight was to see life utterly transformed, and he was opposed to the whole capitalist system of production.

And then along came Paloti, the former partner of El Jebo, who had been killed months before when a device had blown him up in Toulouse. Along with her came Paco's first sporadic contact with some of the French *groupes*, but that year the situation around him started to change. The police had arrested El Alcoyano in Valencia, along with another two anarchist comrades they were linking with members of the MIL. And as if that was not enough, one of them was the fellow student with whom Paco had made his trip to France the previous year.

A point had arrived at which the Valencian grupos autónomos did actions as a network practically every Friday. About a dozen banks were raided simultaneously. But the invulnerability with which some of these groups had been operating had led to a relaxation of their security measure, and the reckless way in which they conducted their everyday lives was creating complications. Out of the blue, a "ghost" group of which they had no knowledge surfaced in the summer of 1977. It employed the same methods as they did and mimicked the manner in which they claimed their actions. The activists were starting to have their suspicions about it. The fact that not one of the people involved in the autónomo network had a police record made contact by outsiders impossible, and they discerned the hand of the Brigada Político Social in the creation of this group. They believed that its aim was to try to connect with them so that they could be broken up. Capitalizing upon the fact that the network had expanded after the summer of 1977 and the campaign to prevent the extradition of the ETA activist Apala, Paco decided to leave Valencia for a while.

This was the point at which he started leading a clandestine existence. In Valencia, his group could call upon a small network of safehouses rented using phony papers and used as dumps for gear that they could not keep in their own homes (propaganda, the *vietnamita* converted for use as a copy machine, weapons, etc.). The fact that none of them had a police record meant that they could blithely get on with their everyday lives. His trip marked a new phase in his struggle. A few months after he dropped out of sight, in January 1978, word came that four members of one of the Valencia grupos autónomos had been arrested, and he decided to get out of town immediately. This was the very first grupo autónomo ever dismantled in the city. A couple of weeks after that, he moved up to Barcelona, arriving there on the very day of the fall of one of the groups operating there; it was El Moro's group, which they were in touch with. A few more days went by, and then one of the Madrid groups had its turn to be hit by the police crackdown, another group with which they had had connections.

Paco traveled back to Valencia and sat down with his friends to look into the chances of organizing an escape of the arrested comrades who were being held in Mislata prison. At that point, due to his trip up to Barcelona, the network had expanded thanks to Paco's connections to some former members of the GARI who were beginning to operate in that city. Over that year, these French comrades became frequent visitors to Valencia. This was in 1978 when Paco slipped across the border with support from Petit Loup A comrade dropped them off by car to within reach of the border and, after they had crossed over on foot, another vehicle was waiting for them on the French side.

With the aid of groups on the outside that, through their lawyers, were supplying them with the necessary gear, the four comrades jailed in Mislata set about digging in the grounds of the prison. This was the first of the very many experiments in tunneling out prisons that members of the grupos autónomos were to have. Despite his criticisms of the security measures taken by some comrades, criticisms that had prompted him to quit the city the previous year, following a few disagreements with the lawyers, Paco decided to take a risk and go in and see the imprisoned comrades in person. His second surname was the same as the first surname of one of those under arrest, and he passed himself off as a cousin. The ploy worked and they were able to carry on planning the breakout face-to-face, from inside the prison itself. However, on the night of June 9, prison officers began to suspect that something was going on in the Fourth Ward. On Saturday June 10, in the early hours, they made to carry out a thorough search. Every Spanish prison was a powder keg back then, and the place erupted. The inmates tried to prevent the search from being carried out: "they piled up mattresses, beds, etc., against the iron gate on to the landing, along with five butane tanks, one of which was in the center of the barricade, to which they were going to set light."[1] According to *ABC* newspaper, after setting the barricade alight, the inmates in the Fourth Ward climbed up to the floor above and then set fire to the stairs. That way they had no way down, and the Policía Armada Riot squad and Civil Guard, who had already entered the prison to put down the riot, could not come up. The fire spread to the Third Ward before firefighters managed to extinguish it hours later. Whereupon the riot squad reimposed order in the prison, and they found the tunnel in cell 417,

---

1. *ABC*, June 11, 1978.

some fifteen meters from the streets. Shortly after that, when they got to the top part of the Fourth Ward, they realized that a group of inmates had taken to the rooftop and, when they refused to come down, smoke bombs and rubber bullets were fired. The following day, June 12, six prisoners, including the four activists who had been working on the escape, were located. They had been hiding between the ceiling and the Fourth Ward roof.

The escape attempt having failed, Paco decided to head back to Barcelona—his visit to Mislata prison, just days before the tunnel was uncovered, would scarcely have gone unnoticed by law enforcement. Several scattered members of the grupos autónomos that had been broken up were in Barcelona, and they had made up their minds to join forces; among them was a young man from Madrid who had a plan to break out his comrades, still being held in prison in Madrid. They needed a lot of money, but they knew where to get it. The question was how to get their hands on it. Paco and his partner La Bruja settled into an apartment in Sant Cugat while they decided what the best target was and made plans for their getaway. Then, in concert with comrades, they decided to mount a spectacular action. Raiding two banks at the same time. Two banks in a tourist-filled coastal town in the middle of August. It was a risky venture; that much they knew; but it was the only way of ensuring the desired outcome. They studied the matter in great detail; they planned the arrival, who would be first into each of the banks, how long it would take to carry out the holdup and their escape route.

On August 17, six comrades headed for Lloret de Mar. Three of them—Paco, Michel, and El Kilos—would enter a branch of the Banco de Madrid; another two would enter the Caja de Girona across the street, and a Mexican comrade who was coming along, La Chava, would be responsible for picking up the money-bags and vanishing into the crowd. She would then go to the port to catch a small tourist boat headed to the adjacent village, where, if she made it, she would be free of all danger. Things did not go at all according to plan. The five stepped inside the agreed bank branches but as they were leaving, they found that two police officers had been tipped off by a pedestrian who had seen them going inside. Shooting broke out, and while the Caja de Girona raiders managed to get away as planned, the other trio was thrown off balance by the unexpected shootout, got the street wrong and found themselves at a dead end. On top of that, Michel had been shot twice and was injured. No way out. All three were arrested.

They had a bad time of it at the police station in Lloret. The beatings were relentless, and their heads were continually dunked in water to nearly drown them:

> Over the first three days, they continually beat and kicked me on all parts of
> the body, genitals included. At one point, they beat me on the head with the
> butts of their pistols, leaving me bloodied. The blows were accompanied by

threats and insults. On another occasion, with my hands cuffed (I was held in handcuffs for three days, even when going to the toilet) behind my back and while three policemen were beating me on the body and pounded on my kidney, a fourth was punching me in the throat. They also had me swallow the contents of a bottle of Mexican hot sauce, which caused me great stomach pains.[2]

They had the questionable honor of being the first to suffer under the brand-new Antiterrorist Law, passed just a few days earlier, although they were initially unaware of the fact. After three days in the police station in Lloret with El Kilos (Michel having been taken to Girona Hospital), they were told to get ready for a trip; they believed that they were on their way to see the judge; instead, they were taken to Girona police station where they spent another week before appearing in front of the judge and being jailed. Ten days in custody was the maximum delay provided for under the new law before they had to be brought before a judge.

During the initial questioning sessions, in order to buy time so that his partner could clean up and empty the Sant Cugat apartment, Paco stated that he was living in a nonexistent French town. He had a surprise in store: he was not questioned again about his place of residence. The inefficiency of the security forces was such that they had not even authenticated that information; they were content at having captured some bank robbers and that was enough for them. Just to be on the safe side and unaware that the authorities did not know about the apartment, La Bruja and La Chava, who had managed to stick by the agreed plan and escaped with the proceeds from the Caja de Girona holdup, showed up at one of the CNT locals in Barcelona where José was. They filled him in on the situation and asked him to help them to clear out the Sant Cugat apartment. Although it ended up clean as a whistle, it was never raided by the members of the Anti-Anarchist Squad.

Paco and El Kilos were incarcerated in Girona Prison while Michel stayed on at the hospital. In prison, they made the acquaintance of Jacques André, a friend of Michel's and member of the French *groupes autonomes*. When Michel was moved to the prison a few weeks later, they issued two public announcements, one recounting their arrest and the treatment received in the police stations and at the hospital, and the other raising the alarm about what they saw as the CNT's (and, by extension, its publications') manipulation of the whole topic of the libertarian armed struggle. At the same time, on the outside, work began on attempts to get

---

2. Grupos Autónomos, "Sobre las detenciones e Interrogatorios a tres miembros de un grupo autónomo," in *Comunicados de la prisión de Segovia y otros llamamientos a la guerra social* (Bilbao: Muturreko Bututazoiak, 2005), 43.

them out through the sewers. Since the comrades were unable to establish which pipe led to the prison, they began, on an agreed date, to dump detergent into the toilets while the comrades kept watch at the main sewage vent which emptied directly into the river, so that they could track it. This gambit worked, but the difficulty involved in circumventing certain inclines and the narrowness of some of the pipework led to that escape plan's being abandoned.

A few months after that, in 1979, they were transferred to Segovia Prison, albeit that the transfer was quite odd. It took them a month to get to Segovia, since they were taken from Girona to the Modelo in Barcelona, to spend two or three days there. From Barcelona, it was on to Huesca for a few days. From there it was on to Carabanchel, the obligatory stopover for all prison transfers and, so on, until, from prison to prison, they arrived in Segovia Prison, where all the libertarian prisoners were being concentrated. There they were able to mingle with the comrades arrested in Valencia in January 1978, with some of those arrested in Barcelona that February and with those that fell after that in Madrid. About a dozen members of the grupos autónomos in all. And, along with these, some anarchist prisoners from Valladolid and those jailed over the Scala fire in Barcelona. Shortly after that, some of the activists from the ERAT were added, along with some FIGA members (arrested in Almería and Madrid) when they arrived in Segovia, plus other autónomo prisoners such as José, who had been caught in Figueras while they were en route from Girona to Segovia. By late 1979, there were about thirty libertarian comrades being held in Segovia.

Paco's time in prison was marked by the end of the era of prisoner revolts and by the uncontrollable influx (or rather controlled influx) of heroin into libertarian circles. On the inside as well as on the outside. Some comrades got hooked. Heroin was readily available within the prison through some inmates who were smiled upon by the prison officers, and beyond the prison walls there was a plague that caused devastation to the most combative ranks of that generation of young people. Little by little, but inexorably, the youngsters who had lost the battle found a deceptive, fleeting escape thanks to smack. Sometimes, the odd comrade on the outside managed to smuggle a sample inside at visiting time, not realizing at the beginning that, even as they were supplying brief glimpses of life (enabling the user to escape reality for a moment), they were pushing them nearer to death.

Paco was allowed out of Segovia Prison on several occasions. The first time, it was to go to Carabanchel for his trial, held on December 17, 1979; later he had another temporary change of scenery to allow him to visit the prison hospital in the Madrid Prison. These brief stays in the larger prison in Madrid were somewhat of a wake-up call. In Carabanchel, he came across all manner of things—whisky, hashish, movie shows. It was a break from the monotony of the smaller Segovia prison. Forced transfers after days of struggle or when the warders stumbled upon the tunnel that they had begun digging from one of the cells was a different kettle of fish. On such occasions, the warders would wake them up in middle of the night and, without telling them where they were taking them, would bundle them, handcuffed and in small three- or four-inmate batches, into an armored police wagon. Unable to see anything of the outside world. On the first occasion, when Paco arrived at the cellular prison in Ocaña, the prison officers were waiting for them. They formed two lines that they had to run through quickly, but not too quickly, because they had to dodge the trips intended to bring them down and thereby drag out their suffering. During the few seconds they were on the ground, the officers would unleash mindless violence.

On January 4, 1980, the verdict was brought in. Like his comrades, Paco was sentenced to what was commonly known as the "groovy" term: seven years, three months and one day. In Segovia, though, association with autónomo prisoners, many of whom were old acquaintances from before he was arrested, was crucial to his ability to hold up during the four and a half years he served behind bars. Their friendship helped him endure incarceration with some sort of dignity.

By the time he was finally released, the PSOE was ensconced in the Moncloa Palace. At the start, he felt drawn to the city and returned to Valencia. He enjoyed the crowded streets, being able to walk into a bar, order a glass of cognac, and look at the women, but all of a sudden such an explosion of life after nearly five years on the inside, left him in a daze. He very quickly decided to head back to his village, withdraw into familiar surroundings, and work in his father's orchards so that he could gradually ease himself back into society. He realized that it was very easy to get drawn into the deception of myth-making, the way freed political prisoners in some quarters were wont to do. That was wishful thinking. They had been defeated, changes in society had put an end to any meaning the struggle had had, and furthermore, they had turned into something they had never wanted to be: a sort of a revolutionary vanguard. He decided that there would be no going back.

MADRID

Don't try to catch me
I have learned to fly.
—BURNING, "QUE HACE UNA CHICA COMO TÚ"

In late 1960s Madrid, following the virtual disappearance of the CNT from labor disputes, the first libertarian groups out to raise the profile of anarcho-syndicalist principles among the working class emerged. Groups such as Autogestión Obrera, which popped up in the El Pilar barrio, had a presence in some metalworking firms and in the printing trades. They adopted the affinity-group format and mounted propaganda drives to present the libertarian ideal to the workforce in these forms. Autogestión Obrera was all but dismantled in July 1972, when fifteen of its members were jailed and a number of others were forced to flee the city. During the years 1971 and 1972, up popped the *Acción Directa* newsletter, which, espousing an anarchist approach, argued for autonomy of the student movement and proletarian revolution; that newsletter petered out a couple of years later following a conference at which the groups decided to support the reorganization of the CNT and launch a new newsletter, known initially as *Opción* and later as *Opción Libertaria*.

Simultaneously, also during 1971 and 1972, a range of grupos autónomos emerged: initially they were unconnected, nameless, and anti-authoritarian. Their aim was still mainly to distribute propaganda, and they were organized on the basis of either geographical affinity (like the Carabanchel and El Pilar barrio groups), workplace affinity (as in the construction or metalworking sectors), or student affinity (as with the groups from the various departments such as physics, medicine, or political sciences). These groups moved on from viewing the factory as the only theater of operations to queries regarding the various day-to-day issues of life under the fascist yoke. These groups revolved around a small core of young people, but were able to mobilize more people when it came to mounting concrete operations such a graffiti campaign, *saltos* protesting specific acts of repression, or holding rendezvous for the purpose of small-scale or mass distribution of leaflets—leafletting was carried out on a hit-and-run basis, given that it was an illegal activity. From 1973 onward, some members of these groups made contact at the universities and embarked upon something akin to coordination. The activists who kept the fight going came out of this environment, until the last of them were broken up at the end of that decade.

At that point, some of these groups started mounting offensive operations in an effort to respond to the regime's provocations and repressive actions. Out of this came what we might term Madrid's armed grupos autónomos. Two particularly significant groups came from the universities, one of them made up of young people who later crossed into Portugal; the other remained operational until it was broken up in February 1978.

One of the boldest actions mounted by these initial armed grupos autónomos was a car-bomb attack on the Army Ministry. After getting hold of a document that gained them entry to the area, right in the Plaza de Cibeles, they stole a SEAT 600 (one of the earliest SEAT production vehicles) and a comrade drove the vehicle into the parking lot of the ministerial building, having hidden an explosive device inside. He parked it in the courtyard outside the building. As he slipped away, since his intention was not to cause anyone injury, they alerted the authorities regarding what they had done, relishing the thought of how surprised the bigwigs would be, come the explosion striking at the very heart of the military dictatorship grinding Spain under its heel. We have not been able to find a single reference to this attack in the media. The regime did not want to encourage other youngsters to join the struggle as copycats.

As elsewhere in Spain, active solidarity with the MIL prisoners was a rallying point and in a way afforded their actions greater impact: on January 15, 1974, less than a week after the military tribunal before which Puig Antich and his comrades were tried, two banks in the city came under attack. On March 4, the day after Puig Antich was executed, the police had to clear several departments at the Universidad Complutense, whose campus was brought to a standstill for an entire week, and overnight there were several *saltos* and clashes in the Argüelles barrio.

During one such action in solidarity with the MIL prisoners, following the murder of Puig Antich, some of the activists had to slip over into Portugal. There had been a revolution that brought the dictatorship there to an end, and they enjoyed the support of the Portuguese libertarian groups. On 16 July, in the middle of GARI's summer campaign, as these youngsters were setting up shop in Portugal—among them El Jebo and Paloti (two of the main players setting up the important network that would subsequently permit contact with activists from elsewhere in Spain and other countries)—another group calling itself GAR-5 (a direct nod to the GARI) kidnapped Juan Antonio Astarloa, the twenty-six-year-old son of the owner of a major dairy company. That night, three young people, one of them in a black Policía Municipal uniform, entered the family's luxurious home and, after leaving a few papers behind claiming responsibility for the action, made off with the young man. They forced him into one of the family vehicles and fled the scene. The young man was released the following night.

At the same time, the *Federación* newsletter appeared; it was published by people who were coordinating some of the student groups, and its propaganda contents were intended for internal as well as external consumption. As a result of its publication, some of the groups operating in a disconnected way discovered that there were other young people sharing their same concerns. The newsletter started publication in late 1974, and its final edition, dedicated to the MIL, appeared in 1977. Another publication issued by one of the university student groups was *Socialismo*. Its publishers, like those coordinating *Federación*, decided to steer clear of the issue of reconstruction of the CNT. Toward the end of 1974, the feasibility of such reconstruction began to be debated among some sectors of Madrid's libertarian youth. Most of the remaining Madrid grupos autónomos had opted to support the rebuilding of the libertarian trade union. In issue no. 4 of the underground publication *Acción Anarcosindicalista*, published in France for distribution within Spain, one of these student groups called for the creation of a CNT-linked student federation, although at the same time it declared that it would carry on "collaborating actively with the newspaper *Federación*." In January 1975, the newsletter *Libertad* appeared; it was published by the grupos autónomos of the construction workers agitating for the establishment of an autonomous workers' federation.

Meanwhile, about ten refugees had arrived in Lisbon. When the activists discovered that the Madrid police were on to them, they crossed the border and set up shop in the Graça quarter, where Titina showed up in January 1975. Titina had found out from a comrade that the police were looking for her. In the wake of one arrest, that comrade had been shown a snapshot of Titina and been asked who she was and what her connection was with underground activities. Shortly after that, Titina was briefed and crossed over into Portugal. Once in Lisbon, she met with the comrades who had been fleeing Madrid throughout 1974 and found out that they had begun work on a publishing project. Vigo also turned up in Lisbon. Born in Bilbao, "Vigo," had fled as a way of getting out of his military service. He was arrested in Germany with Portuguese papers on him, and was therefore deported to that country. On arrival in Lisbon, he contacted the libertarian structures and slotted right into the Madrid group.

Portugal was in ferment, with three tendencies in ongoing competition with one another. The reactionary factions out for a return to the dictatorship, the capitalist factions out to create a bourgeois democracy, and those groups that were out for revolution, even if that revolution was as yet none too well defined. Each group had members serving in the armed forces and had its own intelligence agency. One day in the spring of 1975, Vigo and a comrade were picked up by a squad of soldiers after a chase during which they had been obliged to jump from an apartment, resulting in Vigo breaking his collarbone. A comrade's father, a high-ranking serviceman, was able to get them released after four or five days, but the activists felt that they were in danger. They realized that there were forces at work that were beyond their control, and the entire group vanished from Lisbon.

It was then that one of the groups that had remained on active service in Madrid mounted a couple of spectacular operations. The first came on March 3. On the first anniversary of the killing of Puig Antich, the Monument to the Fallen in Madrid sustained damage after a device exploded. The second operation was even bolder: while the Caudillo was officiating as master of ceremonies at the VIII Trade Union Festival, held to mark the First of May in the Santiago Bernabeu Stadium, an explosive device planted inside a vehicle parked outside the ground went off.

At the same time, back in Portugal, some of the young people had settled in the Algarve, where lands and houses were being squatted, and in one village they started running a cinema. It was then that they came into contact with the LUAR, an openly armed organization that sought to defend the revolution by force of arms. They stayed there until, in November 1975, their house was raided by the police and all the occupants arrested. A painstaking search was made of the premises, but no weapons were found, and so the young people were freed after a few days. Once they were out, they decided it was time to wind up their Portuguese adventure. Franco had died, and it was time to go back and spread the revolution to Spain.

In mid-March 1976, these groups got some tough news. On March 8, El Jebo had died in Toulouse. Following the debacle in Lisbon, El Jebo had gone back to Madrid, and in the summer of 1975 had crossed over into France where, in the capital of Languedoc (Toulouse) as well as in Perpignan, he came into contact with members of the GARI and Catalan and French libertarian activists. Along with one of these French comrades, Robert Touati, he was preparing an action when the device they were handling went off. The explosives had been furnished by Catalan comrades from Perpignan. A number of documents from Lisbon, dated June 1975, proposed an association or coordination body for anarchist grupos autónomos. Papers which, while never linked to El Jebo nor to other Madrid autónomo activists, reached the Catalan grupos autónomos operating on French soil. The fact is that in the interval between his arrival in France in the latter half of 1975 and his death, El Jebo had put some of those Madrid grupos autónomos in touch with the Catalan and French activists.

As for Madrid, the activists there were carrying on with their actions. On July 25, six bank buildings were struck by incendiary devices and, on August 5, another savings bank was held up, a holdup that resulted in the death of a security guard, who tried to thwart the robbery of the payroll of a leading construction form. A month and a half after that, on September 28, the day following the first anniversary of Francoism's last firing squad victims, Molotov cocktails went off in the El Corte Inglés department store, and the day after that, September 29, four Civil Guard barracks in Madrid and their environs were attacked with firebombs. However, it is very hard to follow the trail of these groups. This is because of two facets of their activities, to which must be added news censorship in the Spanish capital: their members played no part in traditional libertarian structures, and they enforced tight security measures, which prevented their being tracked by the police agencies. Another thing, in 1977, by which time they were in contact with other groups around Spain, and in light of the explosion of demands coming from inside the prisons after the COPEL was formed in Carabanchel, we can confirm that their actions became more widely known, although we cannot be sure that they had actually been stepped up.

On March 1, the Justice Ministry came under attack, and a week after that, on March 9, four bank premises were attacked with Molotov cocktails. The same thing happened to another place the very next day.

May 2 saw the so-called Malasaña incidents in which about thirty young people were rounded up after three nights of clashes, including an attempt to storm the police station in the barrio. On July 15, election day, there was a bomb attack on an electricity pylon and on July 24, in an operation intended to expose several firms using prison labor in a modern form of slavery, five devices went off in locations belonging to those firms, El Corte Inglés being one of them. Before the month was out, on July 28, a group traveled out to the province of Seville to rob the National Social Security Institute in Alcalá de Guadaira; and, two days after that, it attacked a transport firm in Madrid.

On October 31, in another risky operation that was indicative of the capabilities of these groups, a large printing firm was robbed. According to the newspapers of the day, five armed individuals drove a vehicle into the industrial estate in Leganés and, while one of them restrained the doorman, the rest drove the vehicle as far as the building containing the payroll offices. On reaching the entrance to the building, one of the young men remained at the wheel while the other three, brandishing a submachinegun and two handguns, carried out the robbery. It was the day when the workers were due their monthly wages, and the proceeds came to around four million pesetas (about twenty-four thousand euros). Within days a campaign had been launched to expose the German crackdown on the members of the RAF. It included Molotov cocktail attacks on the Porsche showrooms, the Mantequerías Alemanas firm on November 11, and a device exploding at the Colegio Alemán on November 19.

Shortly after that, some of these activists relocated to Barcelona, resulting in the short-term dismantling of their group. When, in late January 1978, El Moro and his group fell, some of the Madrid activists with whom they had met up a few weeks before went down with them. This led to panic among the Madrid youths who saw their numbers reduced. These were the very months when three activists relocated to Madrid to mount an attempt on the life of Arias Navarro, the dictatorship's last prime minister. One Madrid activist had happened upon his home address, and this information reached some ex-members of the MIL through Pepe, a Madrid activist who was living in Paris at the time. The ex-members of the MIL held a meeting near Toulouse to weigh up the timeliness of the action and its potential fall-out, and after two days of intense debate, they decided to give the green light to the attack and put together a team made up of the three activists who were to have carried out the operation. These then traveled down to Madrid on a couple of occasions in order to lay the preparations. For the retreat, they were relying on backup from the activists from the Madrid group who had evaded arrest. The weapons were already in the city and the logistics were set to go, but in the end the omens of the fall of El Moro and his group in Barcelona, the dismantling of the Madrid group and the suspicion that in Barcelona information had been leaked to certain CNT officials forced them to desist.

There were still traces of these groups around in August 1978 when El Kilos fell in Lloret, and in February 1979 three of its members—Paco, Juanjo and Titina—fell in Barcelona, but by then the network had been taken apart, and any activity was beginning to become nominal.

On May 17, 1981, the media reported the arrest of five libertarian youths in relation to some alleged attempt to escape from Carabanchel, which they had tried to reach via a tunnel from the outside.

PACO (MADRID)

At five they opened the door
And in came the cops.
Since no one had invited them,
The party stopped right there.
—BURNING, "UN POQUITO NADA MÁS"

His university career started off in the Department of Philosophy at the Universidad Complutense in Madrid in 1972. Along with a bunch of his friends from the barrio, he had decided that this was the subject for him, but his time at the department was short-lived. A year on, they had grown bored by the narrow-minded lecturers who never spoke to them about the philosophers they were drawn to but only about stale theologians from whom they had nothing to learn. But during that time they made contact with other young people from the departments of Physics and Sociology, departments where the ethos was much more subversive and, among these, El Jebo and his partner, Paloti, became his acquaintances. They started carrying out propaganda actions together and also dabbled for the first time in mass launching of incendiary devices, the so-called *cocteladas*, in which a group of activists would assemble at a certain hour to throw a barrage of Molotov cocktails at a single or at several targets, helping to sow confusion in the ranks of the security forces. Paco was born in 1955. He was seventeen and had just started reading the anarchist classics (Bakunin, Kropotkin, etc.). At the same time, he and his comrades were trying to look into how things had been for the last generation of anti-authoritarian fighters against Francoism (people such as Sabaté, Facerías, and other libertarian guerrillas).

For a year or so, he divided his time between his activism and his interest in progressive music. One day he would attend a concert by some group such as Máquina or Om, his favorites, and the day after that he would be cooperating on an armed action meant to denounce the oppressive environment for young people. On Sunday mornings, he used to enjoy the rock matinees held in Aravaca and involving groups like Smash, after having taken part, the previous night, in the planting of an explosive device. He was young and life was for living. In those early stages, he had no firearms, and in his actions he used homemade explosives assembled using legal materials bought in drugstores. A year or so after those initial actions, following an operation in which his role was merely informational, he was forced to go into hiding. In the spring of 1974 El Jebo moved away to Portugal, and Paco followed suit a short time later.

The two met up in Lisbon where they were subsequently joined by Paloti and other comrades. They lived in the homes of Portuguese libertarian comrades whose hopes were running high in the wake of the April 1974 Revolution of the Carnations. The Portuguese libertarian trade union, the CGT, emerged from the underground and took over a large building in northern Lisbon where they set some room aside for the young refugees from Madrid who lived as a commune and even tended their orchard. While the older Portuguese anarcho-syndicalists resumed publication of their historic newspaper *A Batalha* from that building, they also set up a little publishing outfit and started making Portuguese translations of books such as Max Stirner's *The Ego and Its Own*, readings from Wilhelm Reich, and even George Orwell's *Homage to Catalonia*. But this integration into their host country did not mean that they had forgotten where they stood in their own struggle, and their chief concern was planning their return to Madrid.

After a few months, the group broke up, and Paco set off for Costa da Caparica. There he was welcomed at a sort of a refugee camp where young Chileans on the run from the Pinochet dictatorship rubbed shoulders with Portuguese ultrarightists who had had to clear out of Angola following the advent of independence in that African nation, a Portuguese colony up until that same year. It was a time of unforgettable social ferment. Farmers were taking over farms that had been in the possession of the oligarchy for centuries. Workers were occupying firms after the owners had fled, and the revolution was on the march. In Costa da Caparica, he met a Trotskyist comrade from Madrid and, some months later, the pair of them, along with a Chilean and a Portuguese, planned to steal explosives from a nearby quarry. Under cover of darkness they drove a van out to the quarry, but were arrested after the police intercepted them at a routine checkpoint. They were caught in possession of two pistols, and the van was stolen.

The Chilean and Paco wound up in Montijo prison while the other comrades were taken away to Monsanto prison. They were held in medieval conditions, but at no time did anyone lay a finger on them. In Montijo, he found out that the Spanish embassy in Lisbon had been attacked in retaliation for the five shootings carried out in Spain on September 27. Shortly after that, they were transferred to Setúbal, where conditions were no better: they had only a half an hour's exercise in the morning and another half an hour in the afternoon, and their cell was absolutely filthy; it held eight prisoners with just a bucket for use to answer the call of nature. It was in Setúbal that he found out about Franco's death. After they had been in custody for almost six months, they went on hunger strike in order to force a trial, and after six days the authorities caved in to their demands. They knew that during the trial things might go in their favor due to their being revolutionaries. Portugal had just been through her own revolution. After the trial, by which time they had served over six months in prison, they were released.

Paco and his Trotskyist comrade chose to head back to Madrid. They slipped over the border, but the information supplied to them proved inaccurate, and they got lost in the darkness. They woke up absolutely soaked in dew and clueless as to where they were. They got up and trudged on, carrying an unfortunate-looking trunk. All of a sudden, they realized that they had been sleeping in a field full of bulls, and a number of the bulls were staring at them. They scuttled out of there and, as best they could, vaulted over a ditch they had no memory of having crossed the night before. They snatched a few minutes' rest to catch their breath and then tried to work out the right direction. Shortly after that they passed a worksite, and all the workers put down their tools to look at them; with that slovenly luggage they could scarcely pass unnoticed. In the end, they managed to get hold of a car in which they arrived in Madrid, but things did not go smoothly; during the last leg of the journey, they were passed by masses of police vehicles with sirens screaming in the direction opposite to theirs. On arrival in Madrid, they caught on; it was April 6, 1976, and that morning, MIL member Oriol Solé had been murdered. He had broken out of Segovia Prison with another twenty-eight political prisoners the previous afternoon.

In Madrid, he spent a few days looking up old friends. By that time, he knew that his name was not known to the police, who were searching for him under his nickname. He made up for lost time and enjoyed a few crazy nights that he had not been able to enjoy during recent months in Portugal. Days after that, he got some bad news: a month before his arrival back in Madrid, El Jebo had been blown up by the device he was handling in Toulouse. Once he got over that shock, he picked up the threads of his life again. On Sundays, he would venture out to the Rastro, the heartland of the Madrid counterculture, and at nights he was a regular at the music bars that played the records of prog-rock bands, including Weather Report, which was still his favorite. Little by little he was rebuilding his old contacts, and by the end of the year had joined a group that was carrying out actions for a while; its members had been in touch with El Jebo, and they knew Paco by reputation. Nineteen seventy-seven saw him back in action. They lived beneath the radar and supported themselves by means of expropriations while carrying out political actions using explosives they had secured in France.

In 1977, social circumstances led to an expansion of the group, which is how Paco came to meet Juanjo; he was also trying to bolster the autónomo network, and he met Michel and El Moro on one of the pair's trips to Madrid. Although they were living in fairly strict clandestinity, from time to time they visited a few sympathetic bars in the Malasaña barrio. Paco did not remain aloof when, during the May 2 celebrations, a mini-revolt erupted , triggered by police stepping in when some young people stripped naked and climbed a statue in front of the crowd. On June 24, they attacked several firms involved in the exploitation of prison labor; these included El Corte Inglés and Adidas. These actions were attributed to FRAP by the media. Months after that, on October 31, they attacked a major company in Leganés in a holdup that netted them upward of four million pesetas (about 24,000 euros) which was used for the purchase of a powerful offset printer so that they could step up their propaganda activity. Not that they got the chance to enjoy the benefits. Three months later, El Moro was arrested in Barcelona, and within days, personnel from the Civil Guard's 111th Command raided the Galapagar chalet where four of the members of the group were living. Thanks to their security measures, half of the activists managed to get away. The ones not living in the chalet had made it their business to live in safe locations. The apartment that Paco was living in was known to just one of the activists The day after the raid, Paco had a rendezvous to keep with one of the group's members. When they were together, he phoned the chalet to speak to the comrades there, but an unfamiliar voice answered. The stranger stated that he was a friend of the residents, and Paco then hung up.

They tried to get out to Portugal right away. A friend drove them to the banks of the Guadiana river, and as the pair waded into the water, the driver crossed over the border to wait for them on the far side. This was in February. The water was icy, but they made it across. As they were doing their best to dry themselves off, now on Portuguese soil, they were arrested by personnel from the GNR, the Portuguese police. They were held, dripping wet, for some hours in a cell at the customs post before being handed over to the Spanish police. Luckily, they quickly grasped that their names had not come up during the interrogations of their arrested comrades and were not on the wanted lists. So they concocted a far-fetched story: Paco had been trying to flee from his father's control. Even though he was twenty-two years of age, this gambit worked. The police phoned his father who confirmed that, yes, his son had run away from home. Therefore, the police escorted them to the nearest railway station and put them on a train bound for Madrid. Once in Madrid, knowing that he was not on any wanted list but fearful of what might befall them, Paco decided to catch a plane and fly to Lisbon just to be on the safe side. In Lisbon he was reunited with other comrades on the run from Madrid, and they were joined shortly by his partner who was pregnant.

Weeks later, they decided to visit London. Then she returned to Madrid to give birth, while he stayed on in the British capital for a few more weeks.

By the time he got back to Madrid he was paranoid. He had no idea what his comrades might have said, and getting in touch with them was complicated. He passed a few utterly chaotic days before he got hold of some detailed information. He was on his own, penniless and cut off. This was when he met Sebas, who was on a fleeting visit to Madrid with an eye to assassinating Arias Navarro. Out of the blue, word came of the Carabanchel escape plan. Paco sought out some friends with whom he might organize support. Since the escape came at a price, and as they did not have the money needed, his role was purely logistical. The got hold of some papers for the escapees and harbored them for a few days until the heat had died down. Once the escapees were gone, he turned his attention back to revamping the network with the support of some old contacts established in France through the good offices of El Jebo, Paloti, and Michel.

One of his comrades moved to Barcelona for a few weeks, but Paco declined to go with him because he did not have good vibes about the city. When he came back, it emerged that Michel and El Kilos had been arrested during a holdup, and a Valencia comrade by the name of Paco had also fallen. Another two Madrid comrades had made good their escape. Months after that, by which time it was 1979, he arranged a meet with Juanjo in Barcelona. They scarcely had time to do anything as they were both arrested three days after his arrival. He just about had time to meet up again with Titina. Titina and her partner, "Vigo," put them up in their home in the Gràcia barrio. Two days after arriving in the city, while heading home with Juanjo, they crossed paths with two young people who brazenly stared at them; Paco had a funny feeling and mentioned it to his comrade. They both went to bed uneasy. At 7:00 a.m., they were wakened by a voice speaking through a megaphone. The voice insisted that the house was surrounded. They swallowed the most compromising papers and, being unarmed, since their firearms were being stored in a safehouse, they made up their minds to give themselves up. Paco was the first to step outside in his underwear. He was taken aback by the police deployment. Even from the stairs there were armed police with submachineguns trained on him. As he emerged from the building, he could see that they had sealed off the streets and the entire block was surrounded. Titina had been arrested minutes earlier while getting ready to go to work. While the comrade slept in, at 7:30 a.m., the bell rang, she opened the door and was arrested in a flash, and not allowed to step back inside the house, albeit that the police did not dare to step inside either.

This arrest was not like the arrest he had undergone in Portugal. The police brutality was unleashed the moment they reached the Via Laietana station. Paco was subjected to several different forms of torture: drownings, punches, kicks, the *barra*, etc. Once they were convinced that that they had extracted all possible intelligence from him, they took him to the cells where he was reunited with Juanjo and "Vigo." It was there that he met the other comrades rounded up as part of the same swoop, people like the Basque Alberto, who had been caught in possession of a list of the particulars of fascist prison officers in the Modelo, such as El Cojones. Ten days later, they were brought before the judge. Paco and other comrades, the ones that had receive rough treatment at the station, asked to see the police physician. The judge later ordered them committed to prison.

Their arrival in the Modelo was also a complicated affair. They were held in isolation for a few days, during which time they had a visit from El Cojones and the other warders mentioned in the list found on Alberto. Having found out about the list, these warders threatened them. When they were moved onto a ward, Juanjo and Paco ended up in the same cell as an ordinary prisoner who had escaped from Carabanchel with Juanjo and been arrested again in Catalonia months later. On the inside, they met up again with El Moro, the ERAT comrades, those arrested in connection with the Bultó affair, and, after some months, they welcomed the comrades from the Barcelona grupo autónomo arrested that August. By that time, they were cellmates with El Moro, whose family put up Paco's partner whenever she traveled to Barcelona to visit him. His time in the Modelo was tough. Prison conditions had been tightened up after the mass breakout of June 1, 1978, but the fact that he was able to associate with his comrades, plus the support received from the outside from El Moro's humble family—often in the shape of food—made his stay more bearable. His spirits were raised when word came from the outside that the comrades were planning his escape and had started digging a tunnel. They were kept fully informed of the plan and celebrated every time fresh news reached them from the outside. But Paco was soon released. His lawyer managed to get him out on conditional release as a result of a technicality. He was greeted on the outside by his brother and his partner. That was in October. He had spent eight months behind bars.

The very next day, he went to look up the comrades working on the escape plan, determined to do his bit of the work, but he never did get into the tunnel. A day after that, the landlord called Felipe—who had originally rented the premises to dig the tunnel—and arranged a visit to look into some complaints from the neighbors. The place was swiftly abandoned, and those involved got out of Barcelona. Paco headed for Madrid.

He ceased all activity and settled down with his partner and their son in his parent's home, initially, and later in his partner's parents' place, until he was able to rent an apartment of his own and live independently again. He took his son to the daycare at the Mantuano Cultural Center. The Escuela Popular de Prosperidad operated there, a popular educational alternative that to this day still offers its services, although the cultural center, which back then was self-managing, has been taken over by the City Council and these days operates as the Nicolás Salmerón Cultural Center. During his first three months back in the city, plainclothes policemen tailed him everywhere he went. One day, when he was feeling a bit friskier, he tried to shake them off, but no matter how hard he tried, he could not. A year after that, in the late summer of 1980, he was arrested again and this time his partner fell as well. They were processed under the Antiterrorist Law and spent ten days in the cells at the Puerta del Sol, after which time Paco was sent to Carabanchel and his partner to Yeserías. This was a preemptive step. The comrades arrested in the Galapagar chalet back in February 1978 were going to be tried on October 29, and the police were leaving nothing to chance. Meeting up with those comrades again was an emotional experience and a source of happiness, in spite of its being behind bars. While in prison he became acquainted with El Kabra, Txomin, and other Basque comrades from the CAA. He was also able to spend a few days with El Moro, who had been moved to the Madrid prison on account of his trial before the National High Court. Three months after that, Paco was set free. The Galapagar comrades, acquitted on all counts, also walked free before the year was out.

The return to the hard realities of democracy was complicated. He rented a small apartment in the Chueca barrio and found work as a pollster. Later, over a six-month period, he carried out a study on behalf of the SGAE. After that, he stumbled across the Trotskyist comrade he had known in Portugal with whom he had shared so many adventures. This pal, who was running a bar in the Malasaña barrio, provided him with work for a couple of years, work that made it possible for him to revert to a more or less normal existence.

In September 1989, over ten years after his arrest, he had to move to Barcelona because of the trial over the matters that had led to his imprisonment. He was greeted by some comrades who shared an apartment opposite Toti Soler's place. Which is how he came to make the acquaintance of that musician who had thrilled him so much back in the days when Toti was playing with the band Om. After a major campaign in a few media outlets, which wondered about the point of a trial focusing on matters from such ancient history, the trial never even took place.

THE BASQUE COUNTRY

Estatuari gerra, gerra beti, pakean utzi arte.
(War on the state, always war until they leave us alone.)
—HERTZAINAK, "PAKEAN UTZI ARTE"

In the Basque Country, too, there were groups back in 1974 that showed solidarity with the MIL prisoners by means of taking direct action; they did the same in protest at the murder of Puig Antich and later took part in the backlash against the murders of members of the RAF or in support of the demands of ordinary prisoners. Although they might seem similar to those elsewhere in Spain, their dynamic was marked by the recourse to armed struggle by ETA (ETApm and ETAm alike) and the violent repressive response to nationalist demands and nationalist actions, such as the ventures into worker self-organization in industrial areas of Vitoria, Iruña, or the Urola Valley, where villages such as Azpeitia or Azkoitia are located. The murders of militants and workers (many more than elsewhere in the Spanish state) and the deployment of police as if they were colonial troops, in forms as explicit as the takeover of Errenteria on July 14, 1978, caused a large part of the population to embrace the need for an armed backlash.

After Franco's death, the political parties strove to highlight their differences, the aim being to capture future power structures, but several sectors realized that neither the reformist options on offer from the all-Spanish parties nor the Basque statist options offered by the nationalist parties, could meet their aspirations. At the same time, just as was happening in the rest of Spain, a start had been made on the rebuilding of the CNT, which was supported by several grupos autónomos, such as Askatasuna. Askatasuna was an unorthodox libertarian group that had autónomo, councilist, and anarcho-communist tendencies in its ranks. It also published its own review from 1971 onward. It stuck with the CNT for about eighteen months, during which time it called for a global organization far removed from classic trade unionism. It joined in mid-1976, but was expelled from the libertarian trade union in January 1978, in part, because of its stance on the Basque national question. Its approach was that the Basque Country CNT should be in voluntary federation with the all-Spain CNT, but not subordinate to it.

During the first few post-Franco years, there came a series of splits inside the various popular organizations and sectors. Over time, this led to the creation of a coordinating body that came to be known, in the context of armed struggle, by the initials CAA: "A substantial group of militants from ETApm and satellite organizations . . . set about developing political structures open to armed activity, mingling with those factions that repudiated the Leninist LAIA (bai) and the conciliatory approach of the KAS [Koordinadora Abertzale Sozialista / Socialist Patriot Coordinator]. Also involved in this convergence were movements linked to significant areas of autónomo struggle . . . plus groups drawn from areas with a great working-class tradition that had moved on from classical anarchism."[1]

It was in late 1977 that several such groups decided to coordinate with one another and to take the confrontation to a new level. This coordination allowed groups drawn from both the autonomous working-class sector and the libertarian sector to step up their capacity for reactive violence, moving on from sabotage and Molotov cocktails to an armed confrontation, something that was already familiar to groups drawn from anti-authoritarian nationalism due to their earlier experiences in the ETApm. Driven by circumstances, these groups found themselves drawn into a spiral that marked both a beginning and an end: "In the discussions between autónomos, we very often stated that we did not need to reproduce the same structure as the enemy, that nothing new could be created by aping enemy structures, organization and practices. That an army-type structure as an avenue to a change in society was not to be countenanced. And then, all of a sudden, what did we see? The emergence of the Komandos Autónomos with their similar or at any rate somewhat similar structure."[2]

On April 13, 1978, a powerful explosion ripped through the offices of the Guipúzcoa Entrepreneurs' Association (Adegui). One of the commando members was injured by the shockwave and fled, hijacking a taxi at gunpoint and forcing the driver to take him to the border at Irun. A few meters from the borderline, the attacker forced the driver out of the car and then crossed the border at top speed, smashing through the customs barrier. Once on French soil he checked into the hospital and just a week later was handed over to the Spanish police. Thus formalizing the first political extradition of a Basque activist. The attack on Adegui was

---

1. *Comandos Autónomos: Un anticapitalismo iconoclasta* (Bilbao: Likiniano Elkartea, 1996), 9.

2. Espai en Blanc, *Luchas autónomas en los años 70* (Madrid: Traficantes de Sueños, 2008), 194.

part of the struggle workers were waging to negotiate a contract with employers that would embrace decent working conditions. That same day, in an action that was unrelated but which unmistakably reaffirmed the line of action of this armed group, workers attacked the premises belonging to the CC.OO and UGT, causing considerable damage.

Back in those days, the struggle in response to government repression in the Basque Country was still an all-Spanish affair. The government had not yet begun its differential treatment in all matters relating to the dirty war (prisoners, para-military gangs, occupation of the area, etc.) nor had the Basque population broken away by beginning to live as a parallel society (in the sense that its social model was characterized by issues exclusively affecting the Basque people: issues like taxes, language, armed struggle, etc.). For that reason, due to the Basque people's part in the wider conflict arising out of forty years of fascist rule, the earliest grupo autónomo prisoners there (Bixente Aldalur, who had been injured in the Adegui attack, and Enrique Zurutuza) were still being acknowledged as libertarian pris-oners by the Spain-wide libertarian support network, as were autónomo prisoners from Valencia, Madrid, and Barcelona, the CNT prisoners and the Scala prisoners.

From the very outset, the media decided to play the disinformation and mis-representation card in order to ensure that other youngsters would not identify with the armed anti-authoritarian, assembly-ist, and pro-independence faction, and for that reason it frequently represented the autónomo activists as belonging to ETA. Later, that approach was constantly replicated in an attempt to identify the members of the autónomo commandos as merely the most extremist faction in ETA or as a breakaway group of die-hards; at all times, the media avoided report-ing their true nature. Even though, as we have stated, some of them actually had at one point been members of that nationalist organization, the CAA cannot be regarded as a breakaway from ETA, much less as that organization's most extremist wing. Moreover, as happened elsewhere in Spain, the fact that operations carried out by the autónomo activists were not being claimed prompted other organi-zations to try to claim them for themselves. ETAm did this following the attack mounted on May 16, 1980, against the deputy personnel chief of the Michelin company in Vitoria, Jesús Casanova, who was shot five times near his home and severely injured. For years, the firm had been embroiled in serious labor disputes, and that sort of operation was well regarded by certain segments of the workforce, which is what prompted ETAm's attempt to cash in on it.

Not that that was the only link between ETAm and the CAA. The response from the "*milis*" (as members of ETAm were called) and the parties backing the Alternativa KAS in response to the emergence of another popular armed faction on their home turf—and this armed faction was opposed to the KAS political program—was not confined to an attempt to claim public credit for its actions, but also included verbal attacks, slander, and open condemnation of some actions, to the point where they too eventually started to entertain the idea of using force to put an end to the autónomo movement.

This escalating aggressiveness started with the murder of the informer Germán González by one *comando autónomo* on October 27, 1979. As it turned out, González was a member both of the PSOE and of the UGT but the communiqué claiming responsibility for his killing left no doubt as to the reasoning behind it. It was then that "the most catastrophic disavowals [started to come] from the KAS bloc as it attempted . . . to assert a monopoly on armed struggle."[3] One of its component parties, the ESB (Euskal Sozialista Biltzarrea/Basque Socialist Assembly), even insisted that "the assassination of Germán González represents yet another link in the dirty war of the Spanish paramilitary special services."[4]

The fact of the matter is that over the previous year, following a meeting between CAA activists and ETAm activists, the differences between the two groups had grown. Whereas in August 1978 CAA activists who had taken part in the meeting reckoned that "[ETA] regards us as a military organization on the ground and one to be reckoned with,"[5] an internal ETAm document dated a months later was sounding the alert that "armed activity in the Basque Country has taken a fresh and dangerous turn over the past month . . . We refer to the armed activity of the so-called 'Comandos Autónomos.'"[6]

In June 1980, tensions peaked when, following a meeting with ETAm members, the autónomo activist Naparra, also known as 'Bakunin,' went missing. During the spring of 1980, Naparra, who had taken refuge in Iparralde in 1978 following the dismantling of a *comando autónomo*, had come into contact with an arms dealer who was also supplying other armed organizations. His aim was to improve the quality of the Basque autónomo network. ETAm members, having found out about the contacts between Naparra and the dealer, tried to talk Naparra into severing his links with the arms supplier. When the autónomo activist refused, ETAm members invited him to a meeting. On June 11, another autónomo activist accompanied Naparra to the town of Saint Jean de Luz, where the meeting had been arranged, and left him in the company of the ETAm members. Naparra was never seen again.

The reports thereafter were completely contradictory, and every faction did its best to make political capital out of the matter. Two weeks later, the fascist

---

3. *Comandos Autónomos*, 24.

4. *Comandos Autónomos*, 25.

5. Zirikatu, *Komando Autonomoak: Una historia anticapitalista* (Bilbao: Likiniano Elkartea, 1999), 39.

6. *Comandos Autónomos*, 45.

Batallón Vasco Español (Spanish Basque Battalion) claimed responsibility for his abduction. Within days, the EFE news agency was reporting that the activist had been murdered by his own comrades for embezzlement of funds. His comrades responded immediately with this communiqué: "The EFE report comes when no one believes the Batallón Vasco Español claim, and it is designed to discredit Naparra and the autónomo movement of which he was an active member."[7] A month after Naparra's disappearance, the CAA issued a further communiqué in which they made veiled reference denouncing the possible involvement of ETAm members in the operation "especially when we have been continually threatened by some organizations that they will sink us, by fair means or foul."[8] To this day, who was behind the disappearance of Naparra remains a mystery, and his body has never been found.

The CAA's activities lasted for around seven years and declined for essentially three reasons. For one thing, there were two quite different groups within the ranks, and the differences between them were exacerbated as time went on. There was an autónomo faction which championed autonomy as a political idea, and into that camp fell the libertarian activists from the network. Then there was a faction that championed autonomy vis-à-vis ETA's monopoly, but which was also at the same time the faction closest to ETA and its tenets. Second, this was due to the loss of a popular base because of the social changes within the new post-Francoist society. This also happened to grupos autónomos elsewhere around Spain, albeit a few years later. The grupos autónomos were becoming an elite, a proletarian vanguard—something they had never wanted to become. Finally, it was down to repression, the repression that had always been a feature of their existence.

The material targets of their attacks were very similar to those of the grupos autónomos elsewhere in Spain: pillars of the education system, centers collaborating with the prison system, firms in disputes with their workforce, and the economic assets of big capital, but the big difference in their actions was the blood-letting; albeit that this distinguishing feature was the explicit result of there being two warring camps, that of the autónomo activists and that of the forces of repression. The main targets of the CAA's attacks on individuals were those behind the repression: those who planned it from behind desks, members of the intelligence agencies, informers, and those responsible at company level for the surveillance and monitoring of activists. At the same time, those activists were the chief target of the security forces and the paramilitary groups. Roberto, Zapa, Fran, and Peru were murdered at the hands of the state. But they were not the only victims; on August 13, 1983, Nazkas and Piti perished when a device they

---

7. Zirikatu, *Komando Autonomoak*, 81.

8. Zirikatu, *Komando Autonomoak*, 83.

were handling inside a car went off in the village of Usurbil. The most extreme case came following the murder of the socialist senator Enrique Casas by a grupo autónomo on February 23, 1983.

The murder of Casas was the CAA's response to the launch of the GAL which, in December 1983, had begun operating openly in the south of France. Casas, a leader of the PSE (Partido Socialista de Euskadi / Euskadi Socialist Party), took part in the meetings at which Plan ZEN was devised. This plan gave the green light to para-police activity designed to terrorize Basque refugees living in Iparralde. In the wake of the action, the entire ETAm and KAS community bent over backward to condemn the assassination and align themselves with the parliamentary parties, who called a general strike to repudiate it. The response of the autónomos was not long delayed: "We denounce the campaigns by a certain *abertzale* (KAS) coalition which, setting itself up as the spokesman for the entire national liberation movement in Basque Country, did not hesitate to disown and defame revolutionaries in favor of Basque independence, in order to save face for their political opportunism that led them to issue condemnations and call a general strike."[9] A month after that, on March 22, four autónomo activists (Txapas, Pelu, Pelitxo, and Kurro) were murdered in the Pasajes district in a planned ambush by Policía Nacional personnel. On March 19, members of the latter corps had abducted an activist from Guipúzcoa; she was tortured over two days until she eventually agreed to set up a rendezvous in a location near the port of Pasajes with activists hiding out in Iparralde. As five activists neared the rendezvous location on the night of March 22 in a rubber dinghy, they were riddled with bullets. Initially, three of them survived, but once on dry land, and after the only one of them who had had a hand in Casas's murder—Joseba Merino, known to his comrades as "Durruti"—had been picked out, the other two were gunned down. Days earlier Ricardo García Damorenea, the general secretary of the PSE in Vizcaya, had declared: "Attacks will be repaid five-fold!"[10] Some months later, that summer, Antxon, credited by the police with having fired the shots that killed Enrique Casas, was himself murdered. García Damorenea's threat had been carried out. The CAA's activity from then on was merely vestigial and it effectively petered out months later.

But not all Basque autónomo armed action was linked to the CAA. There were also other groups that steered clear of the network or at any rate were involved in other structures or groups that were not confined exclusively to the Basque Country, geographically speaking. This was the case with Manuel Muner, an activist arrested on February 23, 1979, during the dismantling of a Barcelona grupo autónomo involving activists from Madrid, plus Catalans and Basques.

---

9. *Comandos Autónomos*, 42.

10. Zirikatu, *Komando Autonomoak*, 155.

Manuel fell again two years after that in late May 1981, when a network operating in the Basque Country, Catalonia, and the Valladolid area was dismantled. In the same crackdown, ten activists were arrested in Valladolid, Vitoria, Bilbao, Barcelona, and Errenteria. Among other operations, they were linked to the blowing up of FN headquarters in Valladolid, a year and a half before. Muner was arrested yet again in 1985 and on that occasion was connected to the CAA. Another important crackdown was mounted March 13 to 20, 1984, only a few days prior to the slaughter in Pasajes. The arrests began in the Basque Country following a thwarted holdup in Caleruega, Burgos. Three days later, the scene shifted to Barcelona where two Catalan autónomo activists were arrested; they were linked to a holdup carried out months before in Granollers. And on March 19, another three activists were arrested, among them Mario Inés Torres and some former members of the CAA who had been trying to set up "a brand-new network coordinating the grupos autónomos."[11] Under the ferocious torture used on them, one of them said, "I told them I would sign a note claiming that I was committing suicide, just so that they would put a bullet in me."[12]

> Behind the uniform, anonymity
> In the barracks a cup is raised, four this time around
> Mr. Governor, wash your hands
> Everything was done right, success guaranteed.
> —BARRICADA, "BAHÍA DE PASAIA"

---

11. Zirikatu, *Komando Autonomoak*, 163.

12. Zirikatu, *Komando Autonomoak*, 163.

MIGUEL

Anonymous fighter, guns will never be the solution
But when learning to weep for something
One also learns to defend it.
—BARRICADA, "NO HAY TREGUA"

On that late evening in February 1974, that stretch of the Gran Vía in Bilbao seemed particularly busy. All of a sudden, two youths loomed on the pavement while one of them blew on a whistle. Instantly, a young girl who looked pregnant produced from her belly a placard that she unfolded with help from her companion. It was a call for Puig Antich to be set free. Immediately, several dozen young people started handing out leaflets and chanting slogans in support of the imprisoned autónomo and against the death penalty. The whole thing lasted about five minutes, after which the large crowd of youngsters dispersed, but not before they had arranged to reconvene thirty minutes later in the Plaza de Rekalde. By the time Miguel reached the square in his barrio half an hour later with two of his comrades, he was startled to see the political squad from the Policía Armada had got there ahead of them, but neither he nor his comrades were able to make themselves scarce without alerting the rest of the youngsters, invited there by word of mouth, to the police presence. At which point, an undercover group of "*secretas*" came over, having recognized one of the youths with Miguel, who was in their line of sight. One of them said, "This guy is a goner. No matter how many demonstrations you mount you won't be able to save him." That said, the action ended without any arrests.

Four or five days later while at work in the mid-morning, one of his comrades told him that Puig Antich had been executed. Miguel locked himself in the firm's restroom and wept inconsolably. At twenty years of age, he was eaten up by his powerlessness.

Six years earlier, he had arrived in the Basque Country with his family, from a farming village in Salamanca. Born in 1954, on arrival in Bilbao he experienced his very first strike, a strike that, in 1968, brought manufacturing to a halt for a couple of weeks. The workers' struggle was highly politicized, and months after that he started work in the Basque shipyards where he got his feet wet as an activist. A couple of years after that, he was active within the MC (Movimiento Comunista / Communist Movement), a breakaway from ETA with its roots in the most radical sector of the Jesuit circles. He set off in the early morning to hand out clandestine propaganda to the workers starting work, but it was very high risk and over time he came to realize that the party leadership was using young folk like him as cannon fodder. Gradually, he drifted away from that political struggle and was drawn to social struggles being waged around the residents' associations. Under that umbrella, youngsters got together and tried to create structures of their own, while staying within the law; it might be a dance group where, rather than dancing, they debated the various modes of struggle, or a hikers' group, the pretext for their taking to the hills to hold meetings.

Toward the end of 1974, Miguel suffered his very first arrest. It came during a neighborhood demonstration: on November 18 in the port of Santurce a corn depot had exploded due to poor safety standards, leading to the deaths of several residents. The demonstration called to protest the lack of safety provisions was brutally broken up by the police, who murdered one pregnant woman and arrested dozens of youngsters, including Miguel, who was then placed in Basauri prison after being tortured in the barracks. He served about a year within the prison walls, where around half of the inmates were inside for political reasons, mainly membership in ETAm. After that he was brought before a military tribunal, but was set free just after Franco's death. When he got out, he joined up with other comrades with whom he mounted his first actions, mainly expropriations of propaganda equipment, photocopiers, offset printers and copying machines that allowed them to convey their views to the public.

In Rekalde during the latter years of Francoism, there was no organized libertarian presence, but whereas some young people were divided up in the PT (Partido del Trabajo / Labor Party), the ORT, or the MC, others organized themselves along assembly-ist lines while rejecting the oversight of those same parties and trade unions. The same dynamic was at play in many barrios and villages. Unconsciously, these youngsters were starting to lay the foundations for what would turn out to be, over time, the grupos autónomos. When the young people in Rekalde, having drifted away from the residents' associations because of the moderate nature of their demands, set up the People's University, the first practical clashes occurred. Party activists would approach them, attempting to negotiate with university leaders in their midst, and the young people were very clear that, outside of themselves, there were no leaders to consult. They were the People's University. They collected books and later sold them off to be able to buy the books they really wanted to have on the library. They engaged with professors who might give talks on matters of interest to them; and so they were gaining a social and political grounding free of outside meddling and structural manipulation unconnected with matters of concern to them. This learning process lasted for three or four years until, in light of the crisis caused by industrial restructuring, the shipyards and the other major firms reliant upon them started to close down. Such closures led to masses of job losses on a hitherto unprecedented scale. Workers, especially the younger ones who were less experienced, found themselves tossed onto the streets overnight with no financial means, and they started organizing themselves into unemployed assemblies. Which is where the first economic actions came from—mostly the recovery of company payrolls and expropriations of small banks, carried out by groups organized around their members' affinities. And so, separately but parallel in time, the groups that would eventually form the CAA were emerging.

These groups brought together anti-authoritarian youths, many of whom had their cover "blown" after their passage through a range of authoritarian Marxist tendencies; Trotskyism, Maoism, etc. Groups drifting away from protesting in order to switch to direct action. Without infrastructure, they sometimes found themselves having to fake it. Like the time, during a strike in late 1975, when they planted a parcel at the Universidad de Deusto, supposedly containing a device with a clockwork timer. They managed to bring the right bank of the river to a standstill as the police decided to play it safe and tried to deactivate the device by shooting at its wiring. They fired from the Deusto bridge which was closed to traffic for several hours. Such groups were impromptu and came together and broke up again depending on whatever each action required. After 1976, when the first falls came, they started to specialize and focus more specifically on armed actions. It was at around this time, in June 1977, that Miguel was obliged to go on the run to France. After carrying out an expropriation, just as he was removing his ski mask, he had some inkling that a passerby in the street outside had recognized him; something in the passerby's eyes suggested as much. Miguel realized that his cover was now blown and that he was readily identifiable in certain circles on account of his social campaigning, so he decided to play it safe. Within hours, in fact, he discovered that the police had visited his home looking for him.

He arrived in Bayonne and realized that the place was not for him. The Basque refugees were living together, in blocks of apartments inhabited exclusively by refugees. Buildings that could readily be monitored, where collective identity acted as a an assurance of safety as well as a risk, by making them easily traceable. Miguel decided not to apply for asylum as this implied surveillance by the French state from the moment any such application was submitted, and within four or five months, by late 1977, he quit Iparralde for Toulouse.

There he spent several months during which he got to know and spend a lot of time with María Mombiola and Hortensia Torres as well as coming into contact with one of the groups that had been part of the GARI. He also came into contact with other autónomo activists from Spain who were living in exile or using French soil as a supply base and a place to rest. These French comrades who had access to a little string of houses that they used as bases on both sides of the Pyrenees, helped him to cross the border via the Catalan zone for the first time.

They accompanied him as far as Can Puig, the Maçanet de Cabrenys farm-house that was discovered by the police in February 1978. Once he had successfully completed the most exacting part of the trip, he spent a couple of days resting in the farmhouse before pressing on to Barcelona, where he made contact with the Catalan grupos autónomos. There he set up a little structure to assist the entry of the active groups who were in France. It was this that enabled him to carry out actions in the years thereafter, when, after spending three or four months in Barcelona, he headed back to France for fresh supplies of materials he needed and carried on bolstering coordination efforts. Along with those activists, he helped set up a coordinating body for several groups operating in France, the Basque Country, Aragón, and Catalonia, and for almost two years, he devoted himself to crossing the Pyrenees (again via Catalonia), trekking across the mountains until he came to medium-sized towns where he caught the train on to Barcelona. During these years, he popped back to Bilbao occasionally, simply to visit the family and always appropriately disguised; once, after a stay in Barcelona, he got to Bilbao and knocked at her door, his own mother failed to recognize him. Miguel knew that as far as the Basque Country was concerned his cover was "blown," and his presence a danger to anyone in his circle who might run into him.

In 1979, he was arrested for the second time. This was in France on the bor-der with Belgium, after he had picked up some weapons from Brussels. He was held for about six months in prison in Valenciennes, where he met comrades from the Italian autonomo movement. On his release, he was deported to Switzerland. On the train there he bumped into some Italian activists who had been attending the extradition hearing of *Potere Operaio* founders Franco Piperno and Lanfranco Pace, who had taken refuge in France, where they had been arrested. On arrival in Switzerland, Miguel decided to travel on to Italy, by which time he had been inducted into Prima Linea, an armed organization that had popped up in the cir-cles around Lotta Continua. In Italy, there were constant direct confrontations between armed leftist organizations, armed right-wing organizations, and the state. Miguel stayed around three months until he got hold of fresh documentation, whereupon he made the decision to return to Barcelona, now an Italian subject.

In Barcelona, he took part in the restructuring of the groups on both sides of the border; out of this reshuffle came the EAA, a Catalan organization that carried out important propaganda work. Over 1980 and 1981, the EAA claimed several bomb attacks in retaliation for the repression of armed groups all over Europe. Subscribing to no homeland and acknowledging no flag, this organization was an attempt to respond to attacks no matter where mounted, and if a direct representative of the aggressor state was within reach, it struck. On February 18, 1981, faced with the deportations of Basque militants, a TNT charge exploded at a branch of the Crédit Lyonnais in the Avenida Diagonal in Barcelona; on March 26 a jeep belonging to the Civil Guard in L'Hospitalet was blown sky high as a response to the attempted coup d'état spearheaded by that corps; on April 22, another device caused serious damage to the German firm Hoechst in the Travessera de Gràcia as a protest at the death of the activist Sigurd Debus during a hunger strike against the isolation of German political prisoners; and a couple of weeks later, another explosion struck at a British banking firm following the death of the Irish militant Bobby Sands. Unexpectedly, before the month of May was out, a crackdown was unleashed, and it resulted in the capture of a portion of the network of grupos autónomos.

On May 20, two activists were arrested in Bilbao, one of them Portuguese: between May 21 and 22 three comrades fell in Valladolid, and the following week there were ongoing arrests in Bilbao, Vitoria, and Errenteria, resulting in the arrests of four comrades, one of them Alberto, who had been caught in Barcelona a couple of years earlier; he was in touch with Miguel and a comrade from Rekalde. Finally, before May was over, Miguel himself was caught in a safehouse he was occupying in Barcelona. The arrests continued in Catalonia with other comrades from the Escamots Autònoms who were operating out of a commune in Arbolí in Tarragona Province.

In the Modelo, Miguel's incarceration was very different from his prison experience in France two years before. In France he had been held incommunicado for six months in a single-occupant cell that was four square meters, enjoying an hour's yard exercise just two or three times a week. The surroundings there had been designed to drive him crazy; there was no conversation, so he could not even hear the sound of his own voice; he could not walk without bumping into the walls, and he had turned the mirror around so that he could not see his own reflection. In the Modelo, comradeship was an important factor. The inmates were still living in communes where they could organize some of the day-to-day tasks for themselves, and at the same time, on occasion, this allowed the seed of the battle for dignity to germinate. Which is how it was after that summer, by which time he had been in prison just four months.

That summer there were several deaths among the inmates. The reasons for a few of these deaths were rather dubious, whereas others were the direct outcome of prison officers' passivity in the wake of suicide attempts. The already strained situation erupted when a group of prison officers brutally thrashed an ordinary prisoner before the very eyes of several political ones, including a number of libertarian autónomos. The situation inside the prisons had not improved much since the battles four years earlier, and hunger strikes and "*plantes*" were being called in an organized way across many prisons in Spain. This was one of the last signs of the prisoners' collective fight. In Barcelona, they exploited media attention in order to openly denounce some prison officers and the failure to purge the officer corps during the six years since the death of the dictator. While some warders were out to ensure that the inmates' time behind bars was as decent as possible, others had precisely the opposite ambition, especially where the left-wing political prisoners were concerned. One group of these warders, gathered around their ultrarightist ideology, ventured to arm a tiny gang of fascist prisoners held in the Sixth Ward so that they could count on their support in putting down struggles. Miguel was one of the spokesmen for the Modelo prisoners who spoke out, calling for humanitarian changes to the everyday routine and denouncing the fascist prison officers: when the struggles died down, some of these officers tried to exact revenge. Then, when they tried to send him to the Fifth Ward as punishment for matters in which he had had no hand, Miguel slashed his wrists.

On March 16, 1983, Miguel faced his first trial. He was thrown out of the Barcelona Provincial High Court "for expressing his lack of confidence in the courts."[1] He was accused of having planted the device that struck the Crédit Lyonnais premises in Barcelona. Months after that, on August 11, he secured a transfer to Carabanchel to undergo a routine medical check-up in the prison hospital there, a check-up that was just a pretext to ensure his transfer out of the prison and a chance to implement a plan on which Miguel and his partner had been working for months.

After fifteen days in the prison hospital, Miguel was moved into Carabanchel Prison. When he got there, his partner applied for a private visit (which was known in the prison world as a "vis à vis"). That initial visit actually proved to be a trial run. The point was for them to time things once the visit was over. She had to time how long it took to reach the streets, and he would check how long it would take for them to take his fingerprints and verify his identity. Eighteen days after that they had a further "vis à vis." This time, though, in addition to his partner, one of Miguel's brothers would come to see Miguel, a twin brother of whose very existence no one in Miguel's activist circles was aware. Once inside the prison facilities, the two young people were painstakingly searched and had to wait for a few minutes before being escorted into Miguel's presence. The moment the prison officers shut the door, Miguel's brother peeled off his clothes and the

---

1. *Punt Diari*, March 17, 1983.

phony wig, beard and moustache, while Miguel was being helped by his partner to dress up the way his brother had a few hours before. Once they had done this satisfactorily, they summoned the warder, who escorted Miguel and the partner to the exit, while the brother was walked to the hall where he was to have his fingerprints sampled. He delayed things as much as he could and expressed surprise and at the same time outrage when the prison officers stated that his fingerprints and Miguel's did not match. In the end, the officers realized that this young man, facially identical to Miguel and who even had the same way of talking, was not Miguel. They swiftly, in a panic, raised the alarm but by then Miguel and partner were far from the prison facilities, hiding out in a Madid apartment where they went underground for a couple of months.

His brother spent a couple of hours in the prison until the Policía arrived to place him under arrest. They then removed him to the station, where he spent two days, after which they hauled him up in front of a judge who released him provisionally. The brother was a direct relative and in the event of an escape Spanish law acknowledged that this was an extenuating circumstance. Miguel and his partner crossed over into Portugal and spent some time there. But seeing how things were progressing in southern Europe, with various groups falling, they decided to cross the Atlantic and headed for Latin America, where they supported different social struggles. Year later, by which time the statute of limitations had passed for all of the charges against him, Miguel, his partner and their daughter decided to return to Spain. By then Spain had finally entered the twenty-first century, and Mateo Seguí, the Barcelona lawyer who had been handling his affairs since his last arrest, verified that Miguel was indeed at liberty to return with no fear of forfeiting his freedom.

They came back in 2002, and their first stop was Bilbao, where Miguel was arrested within days of his arrival. He was accused of involvement in a brawl in a Madrid bar at a time when he had already left Europe, in 1985. Somebody had simply decided to use this outstanding case as a pretext on which to harass him further. Quick action by the lawyers from the outlawed Gestoras Pro Amnistía organization managed to persuade the judge that the whole thing was a set-up. The judge herself urged Miguel not to leave the house so as to avoid further attention and that he might find himself being rearrested, until such time as the matter had been sorted out and this fresh charge (of which even his lawyer Mateo Seguí had no knowledge) could be stricken from his record. Three months after that, the charge vanished from his file, and Miguel was able to venture outside again, although he had realized that the police agencies would not do anything to make his stay in the Basque Country any easier. Furthermore, Gestoras Pro Amnistía had never refused him help when he needed it, but, in light of the situation which the *abertzale* movement and its community was in, he decided to move back to Barcelona.

In Barcelona, his world collapsed. The city had changed and so had its inhabitants. Virtually nothing of the libertarian network remained. The ateneos could be counted on the fingers of one hand, with fingers left over. To all intents and purposes, the unions were no more, and the working class had been supplanted by a consumer class. He realized that living in this brand-new designer city was meaningless and made up his mind to launch a new self-management project.

CONCERTED AGITATION

The Valencian, Madrid, Basque, and Catalan grupos autónomos were not the only libertarian groups in Spain to opt for armed agitation during those years. Along with them, the newspapers were filled with alleged armed groups from the FAI, the FIGA, and even from the CNT, which had been broken up following a range of activities scattered across a range of locations across the peninsula.

One of those significant falls in terms of the numbers arrested, sentences handed down, and bearing on the grupos autónomos was the one in Valladolid. Throughout 1977 and in early 1978, in and around the city, various actions had been mounted in support of the prisoners and COPEL's demands, expropriations and attacks meant to raise the profile of the struggles of those oppressed by the Spanish court and prison system. In November 1977, a device went off at the District High Court; a month after that, on December 24, Valladolid witnessed ferocious clashes during the day of support called by the COPEL Support Committees; and on March 11, 1978, the railway tracks were blown where they crossed the city in an operation claimed by the GAAC. Furthermore, there were constant clashes with far-right militants in the city and, on March 9, 1978, a meeting called by the CNT at the University was interrupted by a fascist group, the members of which clubbed several of those attending. The events of May 1 triggered the crackdown.

Days ahead of the demonstration called by the CNT to mark Workers' Day, it was hit with a ban; when, on the day itself, dozens of people tried to mount the demonstration, riot personnel were given a free hand to stop it. During the ensuing clashes, one of the demonstrators used a pistol to make the riot police back off. The media were scandalized by this, as were the political parties. It was one thing for demonstrators to perish year after year under the gunfire of the security forces, but for those same demonstrators to use the same approach in self-defense was quite another matter. That same evening, eighteen people were arrested; three of them were released the following day, even as a further arrest was carried out; the arrests continued over the ensuing days until, on May 5, nineteen people were processed. Twelve of them were jailed, including Fidel Manrique. They were charged with four bank expropriations and three explosive attacks, including the one at the District High Court in November of the previous year. A month and a half later, on June 22, a further clampdown was implemented leading to fresh arrests and jailings, and several comrades went on the run. These young people's campaigning carried on inside prison, and, on July 2, eleven prisoners in Valladolid prison declared a hunger strike, insisting that the Antiterrorist Law be repealed. Seven of the eleven were libertarians jailed in connection with the First of May incidents and the ensuing falls. A year and a half later, on November 1, 1979, three young people who had dodged the clampdowns in Valladolid were arrested in the Canaries: they included Álvaro del Río, whose sister had been arrested in June the previous year.

On January 30, 1980, four activists mounted a high-risk operation. As night fell, they made their way inside an apartment in the city center and seized the two occupants. From that apartment they moved on into the adjoining premises, which was the FN's headquarters in the city, where they planted several incendiary devices that caused considerable property damage. That May 1981, when the autónomo network coordinating activists in the Basque Country and in Catalonia was broken up (this was the breakup in which the members of the EAA in Catalonia and Manuel Muner in the Basque Country, among others, fell), three more people were arrested in Valladolid as well. On May 31, the media reported that Juan Antonio Senovilla (one of the Valladolid arrestees) and José Antonio Téllez (arrested in Vitoria) were two of the people responsible for the raid on the FN headquarters, although during the trial they were not convicted on that count. José Antonio Téllez had previously been arrested and jailed in Valladolid back in 1978.

Fidel Manrique was discharged from prison on July 7, 1986, under a pardon, following five trials and upward of eight years locked up.

Álvaro faced three separate trials, two in the Canaries in July 1982 and February 1983, plus another in Valladolid in February 1988. He was sentenced for five robberies to upward of eleven years' imprisonment. On March 22, 1989, he was pardoned and freed five days later, having served nearly ten years in prison.

José Antonio Téllez was brought to court in November 1981 for possession of weapons, robbery, and car theft and sentenced to a ten-year prison term. He was pardoned along with Álvaro after serving nearly eight years.

The other armed group whose presence was recorded in the media and whose members shared a ward in the state prisons with autónomo activists, was the FIGA. On June 18, 1979, following a holdup of a bank in Almería, the search began for the perpetrators, who were subsequently tracked down to an apartment right there in the city. When surrounded by the police, one of the young suspects, in an attempt to climb into another apartment via the balcony, slipped and fell, which fall cause his death: this was Agustín Valiente Martín, twenty-three. Within moments Alejandro Mata Camacho was placed under arrest. Over the days that followed, the clampdown spread across Spain and twelve people in all were arrested in Almería, Madrid, and Barcelona. The media then reported that an unknown armed anarchist gang called the FIGA had been broken up; it was credited with twenty-one expropriations of banking firms. For months after that, on October 25, the media were reporting further arrests made in connection with the FIGA, every one of them carried out in Madrid. Nearly three years later, the National High Court scheduled a trial for sixteen of those arrested on May 14, 1982, by which time only two of the activists—Alejandro Mata and Francisco Sevilla—were still in prison. But the trial was postponed and months later, in 1983, they were both freed on provisional release. In the end, some of these young people were tried before the National High Court, which in March 1983 sentenced Fernando Román to eight years and six months in prison and Alejandro Mata to thirty years and three months. By that point, however, Alejandro had gone underground again, and he did not show up for his trial.

On June 19, 1985, the FIGA leapt back into the newspaper headlines. Following the arrest of two activists in Almería that April, the police were back on the trail of Alejandro Mata, who was arrested in Barcelona on June 15, along with the Frenchman Alain Drogou and four other activists, among them Carmen Valiente, sister of the comrade who had fallen to his death six years before. Another two comrades were arrested in Almería. On July 2, 1987, the National High Court postponed the trial for the incidents that led to these arrests. Ultimately, that trial affected six of the activists and was held on September 24 the same year, although only five of the young accused attended, since Alain Drogou, who had been granted provisional release in January that year, failed to show up. Five days after that, the National High Court announced its rulings, sentencing José Enrique Pérez Navarro and Matías Ripoll Ramón to eighteen years in prison and Alejandro to twenty-four years.

The four jailed members of the FIGA, Fernando Román, Alejandro Mata, José Enrique Pérez, and Matías Ripoll, were pardoned on March 22, 1989, along with the Valladolid comrades and ordinary prisoners Alfredo Casal and Pedro García who, while serving their sentences, had always associated with the libertarian prisoners and whose statements had ensured the conviction of Agustín Rueda's killers.

The FIGA disbanded itself in 1986. During its years in action, it was regarded by libertarian activists as the FAI of the Congress of Valencia-CNT, meaning what is today the CGT. It was members of the CGT who negotiated the pardon.

As for the FAI itself, discounting the January–February 1977 clampdown, the most significant fall connected with the organization came in December 1981, when eight individuals were arrested in Andalusia, Extremadura, Galicia, and Catalonia, but every year the press carried various reports of arrests linked to the organization.

6.

THE END OF A DREAM

JUANJO

He fell in February 1978, when, following the arrest of some comrades in Barcelona, a small part of the network had its cover blown. The address and phone number of the Galapagar chalet, which Juanjo and his comrades used as their center of operations and living quarters, were found in the Calle Zaragoza apartment occupied by the Barcelona comrades.

That day, he was feeling pretty queasy and had therefore spent the night in his parents' home rather than in the house in the residential area on the outskirts of Madrid. In the evening he had a date with a girlfriend to go to the cinema, and some sort of a sixth sense prompted him to bring the rendezvous forward. That change almost allowed him to escape arrest, but not quite. As he left the house in Carabanchel where he had spent his teenage years, they were waiting for him. He was quickly overpowered and bundled into a police car.

Born in 1956, Juanjo's activism began at university where several groups of students decided to stand up to, first of all, the dictatorship and, later on, the transfer of powers overseen by international capitalism. After those initial assemblies, the student groups realized that they needed some basic security during their clandestine get-togethers, and they decided to set up security arrangements mapped out by a self-defense group, a group of which Juanjo was a member. Roughly a year before the death of Franco, this self-defense group had begun carrying out actions independently of the rest of the students. Like the majority of the groups that started their actions during the dictator's lifetime, its number-one purpose was propaganda activity, and for that reason they started contributing to the bulletin *Federación*, a publication by the comrades trying to coordinate some of the activist groups.

Once Franco was dead, a lot of those groups, which had been operating under the radar and autonomously up until that point, decided to support the creation of a more broad-based movement that revolved around the CNT, for which reason they took part in its rebuilding. Juanjo's group did not. Its members decided to stand aloof, prosecuting its own policy line, withholding its identity from the affiliated groups, and clinging to autonomy and anonymity, so vital for its survival.

It was a dynamic group and one of the most effective in the whole of Spain. With a very high capacity for action and an almost provocative boldness. Actions followed fast and thick: its main targets being Francoist monuments, financial entities, barracks, police stations, and firms that were refusing to accede to workers' demands. On many occasions, the police's preference was to blame their operations on the orthodox Marxist groups rather than set off a chain reaction, as on July 24, 1977, when a number of devices were planted at five Madrid businesses, including El Corte Inglés. Two days later, the press was crediting FRAP with an action for which some of the activists from the group were sentenced in 1979. On the other hand, its chief purpose was still propaganda related. In addition to texts they produced themselves, they amassed dozens and dozens of texts by French, Italian, and Portuguese comrades that they intended to publish. Then, instead of stealing the required machinery to boost their output of written propaganda, they bought a state-of-the-art copier with which they meant to print exceptionally high-quality examples of all these materials. The plan was to set up a legal printworks that would provide them with the requisite front. Obviously, the money used for the purchase came from the proceeds from expropriations.

The group was also remarkable for its mobility. Sometimes they would pop over to Portugal for supplies because, in order to do so in France, they needed the backup of Barcelona comrades, and this did not sit well with them. They reckoned that the libertarian movement in Catalonia and the south of France was riddled with "plants," whereas, being an affinity group, the only threat to them would be a mistake of their own making. Which was how they came to fall. The month before the group was broken up, Juanjo and some comrades had gone to Barcelona, where they carried out some fund-raising operations and linked up with one of the city's groups, the members of which they had met during an earlier stay in the south of France. When that Barcelona group was dismantled a few days later due to treachery, it took the Madrid group down with it. Along with the group, the four-color offset printer they had bought weeks earlier also "fell" before they had had the chance to use it.

Considerable chaos greeted them at the police station. The operation team in charge of their arrest had been formed only recently and was made up of young men devoid of any sort of experience. While they made a start on interrogating them, some confused reports came in, to the effect that another chalet had been located and that shooting had erupted between its occupants and police personnel. The young men in uniform questioning them were all aquiver, and when the team leader issued the order for them to fetch their rifles, chaos took over the room. Compartmentalization, however, proved a real help to the activists. Their arms dump was not in the Galapagar chalet, and the chalet where the shooting had erupted was occupied by common criminals who had nothing to do with them.

Some days later, they landed in Carabanchel where they met Agustín Rueda and Felipe, who had arrived a few days before them. Together, they began work on a tunnel in order to try to escape; that tunnel was uncovered, and for that reason Agustín was murdered by prison officers. Given the upheaval that that brutal killing sparked, members of the group spread out through the various workshops in the prison, keeping an eye open for the best way of breaking out. Juanjo was working in a shop where the inmates were building miniature boats and where, as the weeks slipped by, he and other inmates working in the same workshop, noted that there was a chance of their escaping: every few days a van would arrive to pick up the manufactured goods for distribution outside the prison walls. They worked out a plan and how to go about implementing it: it was a matter of fitting the van with a false compartment. There, they would have to get as many people as they could into that tiny space, packed tightly together and motionless. Finally, in mid-May, the day came. Six ordinary prisoners who had made the preparations for the plan were the first to squeeze in, and the seventh person was Juanjo; there was no room for anyone else. Worriedly, he watched Felipe closing the lid of the false compartment. There was no turning back, and his fate now was in the hands of destiny. What he had not been expecting was that before leaving the prison grounds, a member of the prison officers' corps would climb into the van. This only added to Juanjo's growing worries. In a whisper, he asked the comrades what they could do, unarmed as they were, faced with the prison officer guarding the van, but his fellow escapers kept cool. When they reached their destination, the officer climbed out of the van and wandered a few meters away from it. He turned his back and saw nothing untoward. Whereupon Juanjo caught on that the officer had been bribed and was in on the escape plan.

It took the prison a few days to realize that some of the inmates were missing. Following the eruption of prisoners' demands the previous year, the position was that this had led to a sizable part of the prison being controlled by the inmates themselves, and head counts were far from reliable. A lot of cells had holes punched in the walls to connect them, holes covered over with posters. For one week that year, the inmates had successfully hidden two Corsican prisoners wanted by Interpol. Added to this situation where the prison officers were not in control was the fact that the remainder of the prisoners, egged on by Juanjo's comrades, made the head counts all the more chaotic. The prison officers, although aware now that there were prisoners missing, could not quite establish how many of them, nor indeed which. A few days later the media put out the story that there seemed to be every indication that an escape had occurred. The following day, the number of escapees was reckoned at three. Finally, on May 28, it was publicly acknowledged that seven prisoners had broken out.

And then Juanjo dropped out of circulation.

He popped up again nine months later. On February 23, there was a series of dismantlings leading to the arrest of eleven comrades, among them two from Madrid, Paco and Titina; two Basques, Alberto and Vigo; and a veteran anarcho-syndicalist militant who had been involved in the CNS, namely José Cases from the Barcelona Entertainment Workers' Union, who was released around three months later along with a female French comrade arrested during the same operation; she was the niece of El Moro.

His interrogation was much tougher than at the time of his previous arrest. The personnel from the Barcelona Anti-Anarchist Squad were not greenhorn youngsters, and tightening the noose did not give them a second thought. After a few days in the police station, he realized that his situation did not look likely to get any better, and, weary of the police violence to which he was subjected, without any guarantees, Juanjo decided to go for it. Capitalizing upon a moment's negligence, he threw himself at one of the policemen, breaking a couple of his fingers. As a result of the mayhem, he was able to get to an officer to come, and this officer brought an end to the violent treatment meted out to him since the moment of arrest.

After serving some months in the Modelo, where his time overlapped with that of some Catalan and French comrades arrested between February 1978 and August 1979, he was transferred via Carabanchel to Segovia, where he ran into some of the comrades caught with him in Madrid a year earlier. In Segovia, the libertarian prisoners' commune was very sizable and, except with regard to relations with most of the prison officers (out-and-out fascists led by a fellow known to them as "El Nazi"), the situation was relatively stable, and they enjoyed a measure of calm. On December 17 that year, he appeared at his first trial. The National High Court tried him and the three comrades arrested following the double robbery in Lloret de Mar in August 1978. Juanjo was acquitted for lack of evidence as there was nothing to place him in that town in Girona Province on the day of the robbery. Ten months later, on October 29, 1980, he had his second appearance before the National High Court. This time he was on trial for armed actions carried out by the Madrid comrades prior to his fall in February 1978. Again, he was acquitted. On November 26, the media reported that "the Court has some very well-founded suspicions that some of those tried may have played a part in the incidents imputed to them," although it was pointed out that "it seems crucial and unforgivable that, in the trial, not enough evidence was adduced by the prosecution to impress upon its mind a complete and utter certainty that the accused had played a genuine and real part in the incidents".[1]

Then, nearly two years after his last arrest, having been tried and acquitted twice over, he was released, but still had a third trial hanging over him, stemming

---

1. *ABC*, November 26, 1980.

from the arrest in Barcelona. That trial arrived nine years later, on September 21, 1989, more than a decade after his fall. By then everything had changed. One of the accused had died, the rest had their youth far behind them. Capitalist democracy was a fact of life. The Frenchwoman comrade failed to show up, and some of those accused featured prominently in various media articles during the days leading up to the trial. In the end, the prosecution counsel decided to drop the charges, and all of the suspects were freed without charge. Having spent upward of two years in the prisons of the democracy, Juanjo was never convicted.

CLANDESTINITY

Clandestinity was one of the great ordeals faced by that generation of young people in their self-education. The decision to cross the line and abandon all public existence was one of the most transcendent decisions they had to make. It was a first step, and in taking it they were leaving behind the barrio where they had grown up and their childhood friends, they were walking away from family and many of their loved ones, leaving the bars and childhood recreational spaces where they had matured as human beings; in short, they were bidding farewell to life as they had previously known it.

The transition into clandestinity was a leap in the dark, a step in the direction of a breathtaking, near deadly anxiety. It was a step in the direction of nonexistence. That decision left its mark on many of the activists: paranoia ensconced itself in their brains. Security measures were an unspoken code that these days, thirty-five years on, lingers still in many of them. They knew that under such extreme circumstances they would not be able to stay of sound mind for long, but there was no going back, and the other path that was opening up in front of them—namely going on the run or into exile—was something that, at the time, they were only ready to embrace as a temporary stratagem.

There were a number of stages to a clandestine life. The first stage involved engagement with activism, implying involvement in clandestine actions that did not require any clandestine structures to prepare and prosecute their actions. During this stage, everything was within the law, except the action itself. During the second stage, and the first properly clandestine stage, there was recourse to a clandestine support network from where the groundwork was laid for actions—safehouses, weapons, stores of stolen license plates, etc. During this stage, individuals had not yet gone under the radar, but activists were breaking laws, not just in the moment of the action. This added to the risks and, in the event of arrest, to the sentences. During the first two stages, activists could carry on working or studying or could live with persons unconnected with their activities. Meaning that they could carry on with their everyday lives. Aside from their oppressive living conditions and their own characters, the only thing that was directly

responsible for pushing them into activism was themselves and their determination not to be trampled underfoot by the system of repression. By the time the
third stage came along, it was already marked by police identification, or the activist's suspicions of it, and this meant the transition to absolute clandestinity. From
which point on they could not show their real papers in any situation and thus
had to create a phony identity to secure all the necessary wherewithal for living—
accommodation, transportation, etc.

Initially, clandestinity mainly meant taking precautions, and it required the
involvement of friends who could not be directly implicated in armed agitation,
in securing certain structural backup such as, say, renting an apartment. Such
safety precautions included rendezvous with comrades: several rendezvous in a
row would be arranged and when the comrade failed to show up at the first, the
activist was supposed to wait no more than two or three minutes before moving
on to keep the second rendezvous. That way, if somebody was arrested and forced
to "cough up" the time and location of the rendezvous, he could ensure that the
police would turn up a few minutes late, thereby allowing his comrade time to
make himself scarce. Such rendezvous were set in busy public locations where two
young people could pass barely noticed and where, in the event of trouble, they
could run away and blend in with the crowds.

At the start, such activists, still flying below the police radar, could carry on
using their own papers should they be questioned at some routine checkpoint,
but as more comrades were arrested, it meant there was a chance that their names
might crop up during interrogation sessions, so they had to get hold of phony
papers. From that point onward they crossed over into a stricter clandestinity.

A lot of these groups started living together in communes. Such a collective
lifestyle entailed lots of risks, although, at the same time, it offered significant
human support in hairier times and could help dispel possible misgivings about
certain comrades. In any event, the best option was to lead an independent existence and prevent the network of safe accommodations from becoming known
to the bulk of the membership. That way, a lot of groups were able to compart-
mentalize their operations. Their members lived separate lives, each in a different
location, with only one of the members knowing the address of another comrade's
home. This ensured that the only way the entire structure would fall would be
if the majority of its members were arrested and the whole network dismantled.
During the period of strict clandestinity, apartments were being rented using
phony papers, and whenever someone who knew the address of a safehouse was
picked up, they had to try to hold out as long as they could without "singing" so as
to buy time for his comrades to clear the place out and remove all prints.

As for vehicles, during the first stage, with the activists as yet unidentified, cars
could be stolen as necessary in order to mount an action. The license plates were

then swapped for others stolen from another vehicle of the same model and then jettisoned after an attempt had been made to wipe away all prints. Later on, when the activists had access to phony papers, there was also the possibility of renting vehicles, which allowed them to make use of them at no risk, in the early stages.

A clandestine lifestyle also entailed taking measures against possible detection by the police, and the most important of these was countersurveillance. Activists had to check whether there was anyone tailing them. In the event that they should spot such tails, they had first to verify and then shake them off. That way, they could tip off their comrades and organize a little countersurveillance exercise that would enable them all, as a group, to verify whether the comrade had indeed been identified. That exercise consisted of picking out a few public areas (such as a bar or a bookstore) into which the comrade would drop at a set time, at which time the other comrades could discreetly check if indeed that comrade was being monitored by the police.

As far as these young people were concerned, clandestinity meant losing touch with the social lives they had grown up with. At the same time, it entailed a radicalization of their actions—as clandestinity entailed extreme financial need, and as it required activists to live without incomes, they had to support themselves solely on the proceeds of expropriations. All of which helped generate the first personal, internal frictions as these young people came around to the realization that because of their clandestine existence, they were turning into a sort of a revolutionary vanguard. The sort of vanguard that they had rejected when formulating their initial principles. However, they realized that, in times to come, there were only two ways out of this temporary, clandestine phase: arrest, and a more than likely a prison term, or else, exile.

And this was the reality, although the latter option was only chosen in extreme circumstances, when arrested activists successfully broke out of prison and, finding themselves on their own, with all their comrades in custody, saw that their only way out was, first, to effectively evaporate from the area in which they had been active, to wit, Spain, and then to quit the area under its influence, to wit, capitalist Europe. How long that exile was going to last depended on the actions in which the activist in question had been involved, but in some instances, it meant an irreversible departure from the country for which these young people had been fighting. Some of them have never returned to a Spain governed by the monarchy and capitalist system that they fought against.

MICHEL

If you live like a human animal
And if ever you spare a thought for the rest
If there is freedom behind those eyebrows
Then I confess, you're an intriguing fellow.
—LEÑO, "ENTRE LAS CEJAS"

In the dying days of the autumn of 1973, when he hitchhiked down from Paris to spend a couple of nights in Toulouse, a city he was visiting for the very first time, he was taken aback to find that the members of that group of youngsters were all living on the same street, on the Rue des Blanchers. Petit Loup had his own apartment; Ratapignade was living in another one, sharing with some comrades, just across the way at No. 11; Cri Cri lived a bit further down, Sebas was living with Aurora and, as if that was not enough, further away but still in the same street, in No. 34, was the premises use by the comrades from La Imprenta 34. A few days after that he was back in the capital of Languedoc, this time with Sabata in tow, and their purpose was to work out the details of their first actions with the GAI, one of the groups that gave rise to the establishment of the GARI a few months later. Within days, Sabata and he were stepping into a bank branch in Alès, a town in France's southeast, and robbing it. That was Michel's first ever armed action, and it netted them the cash that would allow them to launch their campaign in support of the comrades who had been arrested down in Barcelona.

Born in the Santa Margarita barrio of A Coruña in March 1946, Michel spent his youth in the family home in the same quarter. It was a big house. His father and mother occupied the ground floor, his grandmother had the first floor and, insofar as he was able, Michel staked his claim to the attic. His father, a traveling salesman for a firm making crockery and cutlery, would leave home on the Monday morning and not return until late on the Friday night. Michel particularly remembers when he was five or six years old, and his mother let him play hooky from school to keep her company all day as she did her daily work. That world caved in when his mother died when he was seven. Father and son muddled through with the aid of his grandmother. Two years later, his father remarried, but relations between the second wife and Michel were never as good as they might have been. A year after that, after he returned from a vacation with some relatives living in Lugo, the atmosphere deteriorated considerably, and Michel began to lose all interest in his schoolwork. However, he started secondary school and even manage to complete the first two years, but by the age of fifteen, before finishing his third year, having been suspended on several occasions, he quit school. At the age of sixteen, he started work as an apprentice in a textile workshop. It was then, on realizing that his future prospects in Galicia were not looking too bright, he began dreaming about the possibly of traveling up to Lyon, where an aunt of his father's was living. Shortly after that, he finally managed to talk his father into signing the parental permission form and letting him go to France unaccompanied. That was in the early spring of 1963.

On arrival in Lyon, he witnessed his very first demonstrations. One was meant to prevent the murder of PCE member Julián Grimau and the other, months later, was in support of the anarchists Granados and Delgado. He was surprised that, whereas the former had the support of hundreds of people, the latter managed to mobilize only a few dozen. In Lyon, he qualified as a lathe operator and within months had found work. He had been employed for only a few months when, out of the blue, his father and grandmother showed up in the city; their home had been repossessed, and they reckoned life might be a bit easier for them in France. This family reunion struck him as a bit of an intrusion. They lived together for a while, but when the time came for him to perform his military service, he had to decide between doing it in France or in Galicia, and he chose to return to Galicia to enlist as a volunteer with the A Coruña Motor Pool where his father was acquainted with one of the officers in charge. There, in the army barracks, his incorrigibly anti-authoritarian personality was forged. He was repeatedly confined to the cells or going AWOL at night throughout his time at the barracks.

His military service over, it was suggested to him by his father, who had moved back to Galicia, that he stay on there and work alongside him, but Michel would have none of it, and in August 1969 he arrived in Paris, settling in a corporation-run hostel in the Montreuil district. He had a few casual jobs until he was taken on by a firm making aircraft components and, shortly after that, when the University of Vincennes was opened (an experimental university and product of the student demands from the 1968 unrest), he signed up for the Cinema and Sociology course. He worked until 5:00 p.m., and attended lectures between 6:00 and 10:00 p.m. It was then—prompted into it by his character—that he began to feel a degree of affinity with the young anarchists who were plentiful on the

campuses. He began stealing books to further his social education, books ranging
from those of Leon Trotsky to Nestor Makhno, not forgetting Rosa Luxemburg
and other more or less classical European left-wing writers. It was also at that point
that he began taking part in student demonstrations and realized that certain factions were only out to make political capital out of them. During a demonstration
in protest at the killing of a striker at the Renault plant at the hands of a company
security guard, and after attacking a bank with some other comrades, he had his
first run-in with Trotskyists from the Ligue Communiste acting as stewards in
the demonstration. During the years after the upheavals of 1968, there was a proliferation of impromptu demonstrations during the weekends in Paris and, over
the course of these demonstrations, he began coming into contact with anti-authoritarian factions. These factions were beginning to set up self-defense squads
equipped with walkie-talkies and monitoring the movements of the CRS (French
riot police), keeping demonstrators up to date on escape routes when the usual
clashes kicked off. Among them there were many youngsters from Spain, and with
a few of these he set up an informal group that met in the premises of the FL at no.
79, Rue Saint Denis. Sabata joined that same group when he arrived in Paris in the
summer of 1973.

As the summer drew to a close, Sabata, Michel, and the other comrades heard
about the arrests made in Barcelona and within weeks had launched the Paris
branch of the MIL Prisoners' Support Committee. At the time, they were meeting
on the ORA's premises in the Rue Vignoles. At one committee meeting, Michel
met Cri Cri and Sebas, who had managed to evade the clampdown in Barcelona,
and he decided to start working with them toward the release of the imprisoned
comrades. Which was how he, Sabata, and other comrades from the affinity group
decide to resort to armed agitation to press for the release of the jailed MIL comrades. Which was what brought him down to Toulouse that autumn.

Besides the holdup at the bank branch in Alès in 1974, Michel was unable
to take part in any of the other actions mounted by the GAI from February
onward or those claimed on behalf of the GARI between May and August. On
January 16 in Paris, he was arrested along with Cri Cri, who was driving a stolen
car. Tonton and Ratapignade, traveling behind them in a second car, were also
arrested. In Michel's pocket, a piece of paper was found with instructions on the
manufacture of a suitcase bomb and that, together with the fact that they were in
a stolen vehicle, ensured that he and Cri Cri ended up in prison, whereas Tonton
and Ratapignade were released. They were held in custody until October 15, when
they were tried and sentenced to ten months in prison. Even though the judge
had ordered them freed, Cri Cri was not able to walk free. As a draft dodger, he
was handed over to the Military Police, who took him into custody. During the
trial, Michel was startled to see some of his comrades, especially Sabata—he knew

by then that Sabata had taken part in some of the GARI actions, which was why Michel was not surprised when he found out that he had been picked up in a café near the courthouse. When Cri Cri was freed a few days after that, Michel was waiting for him at the entrance to the barracks. They both moved into the home of Claude, the illustrator of some underground comics published by the magazine *Anathème*. Later, Cri Cri headed back down to Toulouse, and Michel got in touch with one of the Paris comrades, Dimitri, who set him up with a rendezvous with Sebas in the Place de la Nation.

Virtually all of the comrades who had belonged to the GARI had been arrested by then, and Sebas, Aurora, and their child had moved up to Paris. The only surviving group from the coordination, a group made up of five or six comrades, revolved around them. That group had an arms dump in an establishment in the Place de Pigalle, near the police station. One day, they decided to clear it out, and Michel, who had been living in Paris for years and was familiar with the police's nighttime routines, refused to have anything to do with the removal of the arms to a new location, due to his not agreeing with the logistics. The issue was the time chosen for the relocation. That night, Sebas and the two comrades accompanying him were arrested. That left just two or three comrades without any police records. Plus Michel. One of these comrades told him that down in Montpellier there was a couple of activists eager to meet him, and he chose to leave Paris. Which is how he came to make contact with El Moro and Jacques André. That was in the spring of 1975, and he stayed with them for about three weeks.

He spent a year moving around southeast France. Between Montpellier, Toulouse (where he stayed with María Mombiola), and Perpignan. Although, from time to time he would make the trip up to Paris, where he shared an apartment with El Pechinas, a comrade from the Maresme area who had decided to head back down to Barcelona that summer since he had not been pinpointed as one of the members of the network of libertarian activists. One day when he was visiting Paris, El Alcoyano showed up at his apartment; he said he knew "Montes," one of the ex-members of the MIL. El Alcoyano was just passing through. He was on his way to Belgium, where a UGT miner was supposed to hand over a Sten submachinegun that he intended to ferry back to Valencia. In the end, given that El Alcoyano did not speak French, it was Michel and El Pechinas who made the trip to Belgium, while El Alcoyano stayed in their apartment in Paris. Once the contact had been made, the Sten gun retrieved and they were back in Paris, El Alcoyano set off for Perpignan. A few months later, in March 1976, Michel and El Pechinas got word that El Alcoyano had fallen in Valencia, along with that Sten gun that they had collected.

Whenever he traveled down to Perpignan, Michel used to take advantage of the weekend visits that so many from Catalonia were making just to see *Last*

Tango in Paris, which was banned in Spain, and he would break into cars with Spanish license plates to steal passports that helped him add to his resources of documentation. He made a lot of connections in 1975. In María Mombiola's house in Toulouse, he met Joan Conesa, a young man from Barcelona who had crossed the border to get out his military service, and in Perpignan he met Gerard and other activists who had fled from the crackdown unleashed in Barcelona the year before. Among these young people, one individual stood out because of his age, being fifteen or twenty years older than the rest; this was Eduardo Soler who immediately fell under suspicion because he was working in a casino, a position of responsibility rarely open to newly arrived Spanish refuges. Despite such suspicions, he agreed to a holdup at his casino, which was in an old ship that had run aground on the beach in Barcarès years earlier and the plans of which Soler had provided to him.

He was supposed to carry out the holdup in January 1976 with El Jebo, who he had known since the latter arrived in France the previous year; another two comrades would be waiting for them in a getaway car. All four headed to Barcarès, and on arrival, El Jebo and he got as close as they could to the ship before donning the ski masks. They started to sneak across the beach, intending to get to a side door by which they meant to get into the casino. All of a sudden, they had a feeling that somebody was watching them. A couple on the balcony of a nearby apartment had sighted them. They hid the guns they were carrying, Michel a Sten, and El Jebo a pistol, and they abandoned the mission. Then, making their way via small country lanes, they made for Toulouse. The following day they were surprised to read a report in *La Dépêche* according to which action by the Perpignan city police had "blown" an antiterrorist operation by the gendarmerie. On another page it was reported that Eduardo Soler had been arrested in Perpignan, an arrest carried out by the city police. Michel put two and two together and began to think that the holdup had been "the bait" and he and El Jebo the fish for which the gendarmerie, with Eduardo Soler's assistance, had been angling. A couple of months later, after a crazy night in Paris during which Michel had dropped some acid, he found out that El Jebo had been killed in Toulouse when a device he had been handling exploded. Suddenly he came down off his trip.

During those early months of 1976, he was contacted by some members of the German RAF, who suggested that they coordinate a few joint operations. He declined. Attacks against people were a far cry from the sort of actions he found palatable and, above all, effective. So, in the belief that there was a lot more scope for operations within Spain, and after he had set up a more or less stable network through the many contacts he had made over the previous year, in the summer of 1976 he settled in Barcelona, using the identity of a French fashion designer. The passport had been supplied to him by Sebas prior to his arrest in December

1974. He stashed his two pistols in his knapsack and then took the train as far as Perpignan; there be boarded the bus bound for Le Perthus and then another bound for Figueras, which was rarely ever checked. From there he caught another train that took him all the way to Barcelona. In Barcelona, he met up again with El Pechinas with whom he carried out his first expropriation in the city. One weekend they broke into a travel agency in the Travessera de Gràcia while it was closed and made off with two printers. They were wearing blue overalls as if they were cleaning staff, and nobody paid them any heed. Two days after that the printers were in the hands of members of the GOA. It was at this point that Michel met Llengües. Later, when the dispute at the Roca plant in Gavà erupted and paramilitary gangs attacked the workers' homes, Michel made contact with them through the GOA activists and let them have the two pistols. Over those months he was putting the finishing touches to the coordination: on occasion he would travel up to Toulouse; he traveled to Madrid to deliver weapons to the Madrid comrades; he went all the way to Valencia to offer that city's autónomos three hundred thousand pesetas (about 1,800 euros). The autónomo network spread throughout Spain, and Michel was in the eye of the hurricane. And then he was contacted by El Largo.

El Largo came from Madrid, and Michel had met him in Paris; he was into buying stolen checks and then forging the payees' papers so that he could cash them without thinking twice about it. During the two months that Michel had been living in the south of France and in Barcelona, El Largo had come up with a way of perfecting his strategy for a wider scale operation. He had counterfeited a significant number of French postal money orders and had dozens of phony documents ready and waiting. The plan was to share these money orders out around dozens of young people, who would split up, go to several European countries and cash them all at the same time, so that by the time the French post office bank caught on to the counterfeits, the operation would already be over. The young people would be broken up into teams of three. Each group would visit one or two countries. One of the three in each group would hold on to the money orders, the ID documents and the cash proceeds, while the other two would, separately, enter the post offices of various cities to cash the money orders. Furthermore, every time a youngster changed money orders in an office, he would do it using a different identity. Such measures made it hard to uncover the con but, if it was revealed at some point, the huge network behind it would be safe.

In February 1977, the group that Michel was part of was made up of El Largo's partner, who would hold on to the money orders, papers, and cash, and a fellow from Barcelona just out of prison and known to them as "El Barquero." It fell to them to start their work in Italy and if all went well, repeat it in the Scandinavian countries. In Italy, things went off without a hitch, and after visiting Turin and

Milan they left by plane, flying—just to be on the safe side—on a new identity and in separate seats as if they did not know one another, as far as Copenhagen. When they landed on Danish soil, they ran into their first glitch: El Barquero was held back at customs and refused entry to the country. Michel and his companion then moved on to Malmö and from there on to Stockholm. They arrived in Stockholm late into the night, and at that point they called Paris, as all the teams were supposed to do every day, to report that everything was going well and that the operation should continue. They spent the following day calling in at all the post offices in Stockholm. The excessive workload prevented them from making that security phone call, although they made it the next day in the early morning from the train station where they had already bought their tickets to move on to Gothenburg, where they intended to press ahead with their activities. They discovered during that phone call that Gerard, who was part of a different team, had been arrested in Amsterdam, which meant all the remaining groups were to abandon the operation. Michel's comrade still had fifty checks left, and they could change up to ten checks per office. She and Michel both reckoned that they were a long way away from Amsterdam and that there could not be any risk involved in visits to five Goteborg post offices. Once in the city, Michel changed the checks, but in the third office that he visited, he caught on that something was up. He felt like making a run for it, but in a strange city with an impressive snowfall on the ground, he reckoned that he had little chance of getting very far.

He was arrested with forged papers and spent three months in police custody. During the first few weeks, he received police visitors from all over Europe trying to identify him. In order to postpone that identification for as long as possible he made no effort to contact anyone abroad. In the end, after six weeks, his identity was established. After three months, he stood trial and was sentenced to eighteen months in prison, served in Tidaholm prison. While in Tidaholm, he started to receive visits from two young people from Barcelona who were living in Sweden as refugees; one was a member of the GOA and the other a draft dodger. When Michel's lawyer appealed his verdict and the date was set for a second trial, these young men set up a support group that helped him highlight the political motives of the operation for which he had been arrested. His sentence was reduced by three or four months. The prison conditions were a far cry from the conditions he had known in France: the inmates had radios and TVs in their cells, had access to a sauna, and once a month they even enjoyed a dance with the prison's nurses. Despite these conditions, he served some time in solitary after going on a hunger and thirst strike in solidarity with some RAF comrades who had raided the German embassy in Stockholm two years before and who had just been sentenced to life imprisonment. Eight months after he was arrested, he was released and expelled from Sweden.

He was taken under escort to Stockholm, and on a temporary passport issued
by the Spanish embassy, he bought a plane ticket to Barcelona, where Lluís María
Xirinacs and the lawyer and PSC (Partit dels Socialistes de Catalunya / Socialists'
Party of Catalonia) deputy Rodolf Guerra would be waiting for him. The purpose
of the reception committee was to forestall anything untoward with the Spanish
police. His plans first went awry when he was informed that a mechanics' strike
had grounded the Swedish airlines planes. In light of this, he had three options: go
back to prison until the strike ended, change his ticket for an Iberia airlines flight
to Seville or take the Iberia flight to Madrid. He went for the last of these. That was
at the beginning of December 1977, and he arrived at the airport in Madrid to find
three members of the Regional Intelligence Squad waiting for him; even though
he was not facing any charges in Spain, they arrested him and took him to the
underground cells at the Puerta del Sol. His detention in the Madrid catacombs
was like a medieval punishment. The police tried to implicate him in the cashing
of counterfeit money orders by other comrades in Madrid, even though they knew
that Michel had been in Sweden at the time in question, and when they failed to
come up with any information in that regard, he was imprisoned in Carabanchel.
There he received support from Alfredo Casal and Pedro García Peña, COPEL
members who were to witness Agustín Rueda's murder some months later. He
lived alongside them for the almost four weeks that he remained locked up without charge.

When freed from Carabanchel, he went to the Malasaña barrio, where he
knew some of the places where the Madrid comrades used to hang out. With their
assistance, he moved away to Barcelona, where El Moro had embarked on armed
actions after setting up a little structure and contacting the transport workers,
Boni being one of these. El Moro had an apartment in the Calle Lepanto; Michel
moved in and, during the first few days in January 1978, a meeting was held there
with a group of Madrid comrades, including Juanjo. By then a coordinated network was up and running, and material and information were being traded on a
daily basis between activists from Barcelona, Madrid, and Valencia.

Some weeks after that, the El Alcatraz and El Ventosa group fell, and when
El Moro failed to come home one day in late January after a rendezvous with
Boni, Michel began to have suspicions. That same night some Valencian activists
turned up—Paco, La Bruja, and El Morito; they had fled from Valencia following the fall of their comrades, and when the four of them found out that Boni,
El Moro, and their partners had been arrested, Michel settled them into a safehouse in the Via Júlia, while he went into hiding in the Poblada Roca with the
comrades whom he had let have those two pistols a year or so previously. The
falls of Boni, El Moro, Nanda, and Conchi were followed by the arrest of the
Madrid group with whom they had had that meeting a few weeks before. Such

was the beginning of 1978, a year that would prove decisive for that network of autónomo activists.

Michel then got in touch with Joan, the Barcelona comrade whom he had met two years earlier in Maria Mombiola's home. Joan had worked alongside El Moro since the latter's arrival in Barcelona. Joan and Michel then both traveled to France along with Titina, and there Sebas, who had been freed from prison a few months earlier after spending about three years inside, let them have the low-down on a bank which they expropriated. The proceeds from that robbery enabled the French comrades to buy the guns they needed in order to resume their actions, after almost three and a half years of inactivity following the breakup of the GARI. Shortly after that, in May, Michel went back to France for the purpose of procuring arms for the Catalan groups. He got in touch with Jacques André, the comrade from Montpellier whom he had met back in 1975, and they planned the action together. They got hold of the arms, loaded them into a vehicle and set off for Perpignan, where they split up. Jacques André would drive the car and the weapons over the border, while Michel would follow his usual practice of catching the Le Perthus-Figueras bus. They arranged to meet up in Figueras at the train station a few hours later, but Jacques André failed to show up. Michel had to alert the French comrades, letting them know by phone that his friend had had an accident. Actually, Jacques André had been arrested at the border and was jailed in Girona a few days later.

In Barcelona, Michel carried on talking part in the actions mounted by those comrades from El Moro's group who had not been arrested. At the same time, he kept in touch with the French, Valencian, and Madrid comrades. That same May, a Madrid comrade turned up in Barcelona with the suggestion that they raise six million pesetas (around 36,000 euros) to bribe a prison officer to turn a blind eye to an escape by the comrades held in Carabanchel. Having no weapons, Michel, along with Alberto, a Basque comrade living in Barcelona, crossed over into France again in an attempt to get his hands on the money. This time, though, things did not go well. With weapons slung over their shoulders, they both crossed the border via the mountains. They then came to a town in the Ripoll area, where they were able to catch a little bus that brought them as far as Ripoll. From there they caught the train to Barcelona. With these weapons they decided to mount a double holdup in Lloret de Mar.

The holdup went awry, and Michel was arrested after taking two bullets that wrecked his leg. He was taken to the clinic in the town, and the doctors there decided to remove him to Girona Hospital where he spent about two months, during which time he was visited by the Anti-Anarchist Squad of the Policía Nacional in Barcelona, who had a particular interest in how the autónomo network had been formed and how the groups were coordinating. He was also visited by Mateo Seguí, the lawyer who defended most of the autónomo activists arrested in Catalonia, and a left-wing Catalan senator. He regained his physical health after two operations and was admitted to the prison in Girona. There he was reunited with his comrades Paco and El Kilos, who had been arrested during the holdup, and Jacques André, whom he had not seen since they had parted ways in Perpignan station half a year earlier. After three months in Girona Prison, he was moved to the Modelo, where he was able to spend a few hours with El Moro, before moving on the next day to Carabanchel, arriving there after a night spent in Huesca Prison. He was in Madrid for about a month, after which he was transferred to Segovia, where the majority of his comrades were being held.

He found imprisonment in Segovia very different from his previous experiences of being locked up. Pressure from the inmates meant that supervision by the prison officers was quite loose; prisoners could let the first roll call go without moving from their beds. Cell doors were left open during the day, and they were free to move around. Come the summer, they could sunbathe stark naked in the prison yard. Months later, on December 17, 1979, the National High Court sentenced him and his comrades to seven years, three months, and a day's imprisonment.

He served out the last part of his sentence in Carabanchel, where the Coordinadora, the prisoner network that strove to pressure the PSOE into improving the quality of life of prisoners, was formed in 1983. That pressure extracted a few changes to the prison legislation, such as having the sentence counted from the time of arrest (whereas previously the count was only from the moment a firm conviction was secured) and a reduction in older sentences, a step that made it possible for several thousand inmates to be released. In Carabanchel he took part in a brand-new educational initiative, the CEPA (Colectivos de Educación Permanente de Adultos / Adult Lifetime Learning Collectives), taking part as coordinator of the classes in the prison. Classes were delivered in the wards themselves since the prison school had been taken over by riot control units since the recent unrest in 1981 and 1982, which had given rise to this brand-new prisoner coordinating body. With the advent of the PSOE in government, prison gates opened up for the first time to cultural and artistic activities, and Michel was able to do a bit of woodworking in the prison yard.

When he left Carabanchel, El Kilos, who had been released three months ahead of him, covered the cost of his plane ticket to Barcelona, and when he arrived there Michel was awaited at the airport by Irma and Conchi, El Moro's partner (El Moro was behind bars in France after he had been arrested during another forged-check-passing operation). Michel quickly picked up on Irma's addiction and realized that during the almost five years that he had been inside, things on the street had changed and the collective battle had been lost. Shortly after that, when he traveled up to A Coruña to obtain fresh documentation, he discovered that he was a wanted man. After arresting Alberto, the Basque comrade with whom he had made his most recent clandestine crossing of the Pyrenees, the police got wind of this crossing. However, it was not a criminal offense, and his lawyer was able to get the paperwork straightened out.

Six or so years later, in April 1990, Michel was under arrest again, this time in Madrid, along with El Largo and another two individuals, after mounting his latest check-counterfeiting operation, complete with the usual ID documents.

INSIDE

"I was nothing, not even a number, because I had no number, and it was not like in the movies with the striped uniform and the number on your back and cap. No, here I wore my own clothes and I was nothing, worse than nothing, I was a dead man walking."

—XAVIER CAÑADAS, *ENTREMUROS:
LAS PRISIONES EN LA TRANSICIÓN DEMOCRÁTICA*

From the first moment of incarceration, members of the armed grupos autónomos embraced the demands of the other prisoners, but this was most especially the case after January 1978, when the second generation grupos autónomos (the ones who launched the actions during 1974 and 1975) were beginning to be dismantled. Their members, the young people who had shown immediate solidarity with the prisoners when the latter decided to confront the state in pursuit of their demands, swelled the numbers of state prison inmates. Once they were put behind bars, there was no wavering in their discourse nor in how they acted. They played an active role in internal organizing, clamoring for improvements to prison conditions while striving to coordinate the solidarity networks. They also took part in the rioting and hunger strikes aimed at securing these improvements: "He said that we had foisted the assembly upon them. Now we have foisted everything upon them, from strike committees to labor commissions. The real gains may not be glittering, but they are beginning to look upon us as individuals with a capacity for organizing."[1]

Two autónomo activists plus two of the people implicated in the Scala fire took part in the group self-harm exercise mounted in the Modelo in February 1978: "Some three hundred of us inmates cut our veins open. . . . We used the blood to fill buckets and daub graffiti on the prison walls. We did not agree with

---

1. January 1978 letter from Agustín Rueda in Girona Prison to his sister.

the self-harming, but there were only two things we could do: lock ourselves in our cells so that we didn't have to see anything, or show solidarity and cut ourselves too."[2] Three weeks after that, Agustín Rueda was dead. After his brutal murder and the police takeover of the prisons, the prisoners lost heart: "Since the recent riots last January, things have petered out greatly, and the prisons have been under emergency conditions for two months. So far, this has usually meant a crackdown by our tormentors . . . beatings and torture."[3] Despite the collapsing morale, some inmates (especially the libertarians and the founders of COPEL) were still in the thick of the process of self-organization and showing solidarity with those in the greatest need. In April 1978, after selling a detailed report on Agustín Rueda's murder for thirty thousand pesetas (about 180 euros) to the magazine *Cambio 16*, they forwarded ten thousand pesetas to the COPEL comrades who had been transferred to El Dueso prison in retaliation for their activism, five thousand to those held in punishment cells in Cartagena and the remaining fifteen thousand were shared out among the neediest prisoners in their own prison, Carabanchel.

Months later, on June 10, a riot erupted in Mislata prison down in Valencia. The four young members of the grupo autónomo arrested in January that year played an active part in the disturbances, which were launched in an attempt to thwart the discovery of a tunnel that they had begun digging with help from other inmates. Once the riot had been crushed, those four activists and another two of the prisoners involved in the escape plan managed to hide out in the roof space of the landing, where thy remained for a couple of days before they were found. But for the support and active engagement of comrades on the outside, escape attempts would not have been feasible: "To dig a tunnel you needed something to use as a pick. Back in those days, things could be smuggled in through the lawyers, and picks were among them. A walkie-talkie was even smuggled in so that we could communicate directly with the people working in the tunnel."[4]

Activists who finished up in prison during the social prisoners' restlessness never staked a claim to political prisoner status: "Only a few cranks among us claimed to be politicals. . . . We identified more with the ordinary inmates than the political ones."[5] But they set up their own communes inside the prisons: initially as a matter of affinity and later for security reasons, when the prisons reverted to living under the law of might is right, once the rebelliousness of the years from

---

2. X. Cañadas Gascón, *El Caso Scala: Terrorismo de estado y algo más* (Barcelona: Virus, 2008), 37–38.

3. Letter from Felipe from Carabanchel Prison to his brother, March 21, 1978.

4. *COPEL: Butrones y otras aportaciones de grupos autónomos* (Valencia: Desorden Distro, 2004), 7.

5. *COPEL: Butrones y otras aportaciones de grupos autónomos*, 10–11.

1976 to 1978 had been defeated. It was some years after that, starting in 1983, when the PSOE came to power, that embers of the last dismantled grupos autónomos and libertarians found themselves obliged, however reluctantly, to apply for recognition of their political prisoner status in order to ensure that they could run things for themselves inside the prisons and try to avert the various risks involved in living alongside heroin-addicted prisoners ready to sell them out for a dose. At the same time, it was the only way to avoid feeling completely isolated, because they were getting no support of any sort from the outside other than family support. The libertarian movement had been crushed and was completely at odds with itself. These were the early years of social democratic government when the communes experienced a second golden age, albeit not as intense as in the years after Franco's death. All these activists were held longest in Barcelona's Modelo Prison and Segovia Prison. In Barcelona's case, this was only natural as it was the city where most young libertarians had been arrested, and always the first prison in which they were processed; in the case of Segovia, the government had decided to concentrate the greatest number of anarchist prisoners there from 1979 on. All of those charged in relation to the Scala affair, all CNT prisoners and FIGA prisoners, plus virtually all the autónomo inmates passed through Segovia. The other main stop was Carabanchel because, during transfers, it was an obligatory transit point where prisoners were held for the duration of trials heard before the National High Court. Besides that, it was where the main prison hospital was located.

Their main weapon in the fight inside the prison walls was the hunger strike, a weapon that had already been used successfully by members of the GARI imprisoned between 1974 and 1977 in French prisons. The four autónomo prisoners in Mislata who were held in two separate wards declared a hunger strike on March 15, 1978, asking to be held together in the same ward. The following day, a hunger strike in protest at the killing of Agustín Rueda broke out in the women's prison La Trinidad, in Barcelona. On April 8 libertarian prisoners in Carabanchel launched a fresh hunger strike in support of the comrades down in Valencia; in addition, they were demanding an end to the torture inflicted upon an autónomo comrade from Madrid (after being roughed up during her arrest, she had been placed in the Psychiatric Hospital) and they were also protesting at the killing of Agustín Rueda. This time, the news spread around the libertarian inmates. On April 12, the comrades in the same women's prison joined in and at the same time a number of comrades held in the Modelo and others held in Alcalá joined the strike. Together with the ones who had begun a strike in Valencia, that came to around thirty activists across several prisons. Their two demands were granted. The Valencian comrades were moved to the same ward, and the comrade from Madrid had her mistreatment ended. In late June that year, eleven inmates in Valladolid prison, seven anarchists among them, began a fresh hunger strike to protest the Antiterrorist Law and, once it came into force, Modelo prisoners (from the grupos autónomos, the ERAT, and the Scala affair) started another on October 1 to press for it to be repealed. Toward the end of 1979, with a large number of libertarian prisoners already being concentrated in Segovia Prison, twenty of them went on hunger strike in order to have three comrades released from the isolation cells; at the same time, they pressed for one activist still being held in solitary in Herrera de la Mancha to be moved to Segovia and for a range of improvements to be made to their living conditions, including the transfer of a prison officer known as "El Nazi," whom they hoped to get rid of for a while. After twenty-three days, they won all their demands except for the transfer of that prison officer. Those were not the only nor the last strikes, and well into the 1980s libertarians persisted in demanding improved conditions or, bluntly, for the law to be adhered to. That was what lay behind the thirty-two-day hunger strike mounted by three activists (two of them members of the same Barcelona grupo autónomo, plus a militant arrested with them who was charged with membership of Terra Lliure). This hunger strike started on August 6, 1984, at which point they had served the maximum period in preventive detention and still had not been brought for trial.

Isolation was the worst of the tortures they faced. Those conversant with conditions in the democratic and forward-looking French, Swedish, or Dutch prisons realized that physical violence was not necessary in order to break one's fighting spirit. Solitary was enough to accomplish that. The crude violence of Spanish prison officers was relatively bearable as long as one had companionship, but isolation drove one inexorably into madness. There were comrades in Spain who served nearly six months in isolation cells; also, since, as a rule, such long stints were enforced in Ocaña or Burgos prison, the punishment was triply effective: there was the isolation, plus the ongoing violence from the prison staff and the absence of the most elementary standards of cleanliness in such ancient and obsolete prison establishments. In the Modelo, unfortunately, the cells in the Fifth Ward, where the punishment cells were, and where beatings were doled out methodically, were notorious: "The Policía Nacional softened us up with daily beatings; even-numbered cells on even-numbered dates, odd-numbered cells on odd-numbered dates. They delivered us two sessions of beating per day, one in the morning and another in the afternoon."[6]

But possibly the ones targeted for the greatest physical violence were the younger inmates when they were transferred to Ocaña prison, a prison set aside for minors. One night in September 1979, five underage prisoners, two autónomos and three of the Scala affair prisoners, were "abducted" in Segovia Prison. They

---

6. X. Cañadas Gascón, *Entremuros*, 46.

had been involved in a number of struggles and a couple of escape attempts. On their arrival in Ocaña, the police were in the corridors waiting for them: "The entire corridor was lined by around sixty members of the Policía Nacional in riot gear with green bandanas around their necks; positioned on both sides of the corridor they waited, grinning and thirsting for blood, for me to arrive. The first thing I felt was an electric discharge over my head, coming from the right-hand side, and it threw me into an iron gate; immediately dozens of electrified prods rained down on my back, countless kicks switching between my testicles and my legs; after that I felt nothing, meaning that I could feel no more pain. They all assaulted me as many times as they wanted."[7] When the modern top-security prisons were later introduced, the heartlessness of the Spanish prison system started to resemble that of the rest of the advanced European countries.

Back in those days in Segovia, Herminio Rodríguez Maheso, aka "El Nazi," stood out for his viciousness. There, in July 1980, Jorge Benayas Manzanares, an anarchist activist who had fled to Perpignan in the mid-1970s was found dead: he had been jailed six months before charged with defrauding the post office bank where he worked. Two days prior to his death, he had signed a sworn affidavit detailing how he had been scapegoated by a far-reaching scheme of corruption just for being an anarchist and for having dodged his military service. His death was presented to the public as a suicide. Not that he was the last libertarian to perish in a Spanish prison. On October 30, 1983, in Carabanchel Prison, the lifeless body of Terrassa-born Jacinto Avalos Cardona was found. He had been arrested in January 1981 and charged with responsibility for an attack on the Muebles Casarramona store belonging to a well-known fascist in the city, following a gun attack mounted by ultrarightists on the premises of Els Amics de les Arts. Sentence to five years in prison by the National High Court, he had already served more than half of that sentence, and furthermore his case was being appealed at the Supreme Court. He had only months to wait before being released from prison, where he shared a cell with El Ventosa. As in the case of Jorge Benayas, it was reported that death was due to suicide.

The activists never accepted that their circumstances were final. They always gave some thought to the chances of securing their release by means of an escape, and once inside prison, their chief preoccupation was with trying to dig their way out again. They tried it in the prisons in Figueres, Girona, Barcelona, Valencia, Carabanchel, and Segovia. They were never successful using this method, but some of them did regain their freedom illegally rather than serve out their sentences. People such as Pep Caro, who arrived in the Modelo from Carabanchel on October 27, 1981. On that date, the police van decided not to enter the prison

---

7. X. Cañadas Gascón, *Entremuros*, 81.

grounds as it normally did and parked opposite the prison gates. This circumstance was exploited by the activist, who hit the pavement and sped off down the Calle Entença, until he slipped on some oil and two bullets fired by his Civil Guard escorts slammed into his body. This led days later to a number of demonstrations mounted by local residents since the indiscriminate firing by the Civil Guards had also resulted in a number of parked cars being struck, triggering panic among pedestrians. Despite his injuries, Pep Caro pulled it off on February 6 the following year. He escaped from the Clinical Hospital after an operation to remove the two bullets. Other escapes widely reported in the media were Juanjo's 1978 escape from Carabanchel with another six inmates; or Miguel's, a few years later, when he traded places during a "vis à vis" with his twin brother. And there were others such as José or Petit Loup who, after being let out on provisional release, decided to cross the border and not risk going back to Spanish prisons, of which they had had their fill.

The remainder of the imprisoned activists derived varying benefits from the prison facilities: "Those benefits had to be wrested from the prison authorities as the members of that institution were unevolved, politically speaking."[8] The first ticket of leave granted to these young people went to Felipe in the summer of 1978. Felipe, in light of the earlier murder of his comrade, decided that he would not be going back to serve out the reminder of his sentence; later, given the new judicial and state prison approach to dismissing the inmates' demands, many years went by before another period of leave was granted to any libertarian prisoner. In an ongoing and systematic way, the state circumvented all the laws and regulations regarding prison facilities in the case of these young people, who had lost all outside support from libertarian organizations that were themselves finding it hard to survive.

Finally, starting from the PSOE's second success in the parliamentary elections, talks were opened between high-ranking members of the socialist administration and lawyers for some of the prisoners with an eye to securing their release. On March 22, 1989, the cabinet pardoned eight of the fifteen libertarian prisoners still behind bars, which, as we have seen, applied to the FIGA prisoners, the libertarians from Valladolid, and Alfredo Casal and Pedro García Peña, the COPEL members who, having been beaten along with Agustín Rueda in Carabanchel, endured all the pressure, beatings, and torture until they made sure that their comrade's killers were convicted. However, they did not all agree to sign the paper renouncing the struggle or expressing repentance for their actions just to regain their freedom. It took Juan a further year and a half to win back his

---

8. L. Andrés Edo, *La CNT en la encrucijada: Aventuras de un heterodoxo* (Barcelona: Flor del Viento, 2006), 368.

freedom legally, on August 10, 1990, after he had served upward of seven and a half years in prison.

"Today, the grupos autónomos are no more, but the grupos autónomos stand out as a proletarian experience, a revolutionary experience. Capital has isolated them, and they failed to dissolve into the workers' movement. Their isolation was their undoing."[9]

---

9. "Carta Abiebrta a Quienes Sepan Leer," *Opción Libertaria*, no. 3, October 1974.

VÍCTOR

A year after Víctor was born, his father passed away. He came from a military family. His two uncles had careers at the Via Laietana police station in Barcelona during the early part of the 1960s. The cool reception that his mother received from her husband's family, together with her problematic financial circumstances, led to Víctor's being placed in the Ciudad de los Muchachos (Boys' Town) home out in Collserola. He stayed there until he turned ten, at which point his mother, having remarried, was in a position to take charge of the boy again.

Víctor went home and started hanging out with the OJE group in his barrio of Sant Antoni, drawn to it by his love of nature and his attraction to all things related to climbing. It was while in the OJE that, as time wore on, he was recruited into the Círculos de Formación Política (Political Education Circles) and began reading books of political theory. He went to the Milà i Fontanals high school, and due to the frictions between the various OJE factions, he and his comrades started asking the same questions as his entire generation. Questions unanswered either by the official history delivered in the schools or by the official propaganda of General Franco's fascist regime.

The yearning for freedom and answers prompted that bunch of young lads to join the JGR (Joven Guardia Roja / Red Young Guard—the youth section of the PT), but still their questions went unanswered. On the occasions when they dared pose them openly during meetings of the organization—they always seemed to be the youngest ones there—they sensed that they were a bother to those in charge of the group. Their learning needs meant that these five *bachillers*, as high school-ers were called back then, often found themselves together reading literary works that were still on the banned list. Mainly all the classic works of Marxism. At the same time, on the orders of the leaders of their cell, they joined the Barrio Chino Residents' Association. Gradually, as they deepened their theoretical knowledge, they began asking if they might switch to more practical matters. The JGR was still small. These teenagers were calling for action against totalitarian rule, and the best the organization could come up with was for them to learn the slogans that were later chanted at demonstrations: "Party of Labor, party of combat!"

Given that their suggestions were forever being rejected by their superiors, these youngsters started acting on their own, and sessions of daubing propaganda graffiti with slogans not approved by the organization, which they were beginning to drift apart from, grew more frequent. At which point Víctor got to know the shoemaker.

The shoemaker was an older man, and he had a workshop near his stepfather's bar. One afternoon, Víctor ventured inside and asked him if he could repair his bag, the small schoolbag that he carried to high school. He had scrawled on it in very tiny lettering a phrase with which he identified: "Freedom is not begged for, it is won." The shoemaker read this but said nothing; he simply repaired the bag and started talking to the young lad, the stepson of the bar owner on the corner, as an equal. Days after that, Víctor went back to the workshop of the man who had made him feel so special by the way he treated him. From then on, whenever Víctor had no political education session with his comrades, or before he set out to pepper the barrio with slogans raging against the system, they suffered under, he would drop by the workshop and spend entire afternoons chatting with that decent fellow. And then one day the shoemaker produced some papers hidden among his shoe-repair materials and offered Víctor a copy of *Solidaridad Obrera*, the mouthpiece of the clandestine CNT.

Apart from the magazines *Star*, *Ajoblanco*, and *El Viejo Topo*, Víctor and his comrades started reading Errico Malatesta, Bakunin, Proudhon, and other historical libertarian theorists. He was strangely drawn to the young people who were standing up to the *grises* ("grays," or the armed Francoist police) during demonstrations and who often carried black flags. Through the shoemaker, they were able to start hanging out in such outlaw, clandestine circles. They wanted to sign up but were greatly taken aback when the answer came: "No." The CNT was a trade union and only workers were eligible for membership. Víctor and one of his comrades did not hesitate. They dropped out of high school, and set about looking for work. Two weeks later, Víctor became a member of the CNT's Amalgamated Trades Union which had only recently been reestablished at a clandestine meeting in the Sant Medir Church in the Sants barrio.

Finally, the three *bachiller* comrades joined the union. Eager to learn, they sat quiet at all the meetings. The brains of those three adolescents were quickly registering and absorbing what they were listening to. All those discussions. The most diverse arguments. When they had built up a little confidence and understood how the organization operated, their youthful energy and youthful appetite for action drew them to the Confederal Self-Defense Groups. These groups made it their business to frustrate the actions of the riot squad during demonstrations, facing them head-on, which meant that their members were the first to feel the repression. It was at this point, in early 1977, that one comrade invited them to take part in an FAI conference to be held toward the end of January in Barcelona. Víctor's comrades wanted to take part, but he roundly refused. Their activity as an affinity group was below the radar, and the conference was premature. The conditions just were not ripe for such a gathering. Self-discipline, which they had embraced as members of the JGR, and which was also a product of their reading of the classics, was eventually accepted by his comrades. When word reached them a few days later that all those taking part in the conference had been arrested, they we able to see how correct he had been in his decision. But over time, the members of the affinity group, who had already gone over to acting along autonomous lines, carrying out small-scale expropriations to raise funds for their clandestine propaganda activities, were drifting apart due to each of them taking up a different trade. The meetings held in a room (their preferred meeting place) in one of the most secure buildings in the city—the Civil Guard barracks in the Calle de Sant Pau—came to an end. Two of Víctor's comrades had fathers who were members of the Civil Guard Corps.

They each launched a new action group inside their union, but often ran into one another at meetings of the Self-Defense Groups. Víctor's first group had multiplied.

At that point he met Irma in the CNT Construction Workers' Union, although he had often seen her before at demonstrations. Irma was hard to miss. She was one of the few women who stood in the front line, and her figure did not help her escape notice. That year he also took part for the first time in several labor disputes, like the Roca dispute and the gas station workers' dispute. It was actually during the gas station workers' dispute that he first cooperated with El Moro on a range of actions.

Because the CNT had a confederated structure back in those years, the fight against repression was decentralized, and all the unions had their own prisoners' aid committees. In dealings with these committees, he got to learn of the actual situation within the prisons and the treatment of prisoners straight from the horse's mouth, reading letters written by them to the committee. The facts came like a slap in the face. Also, as time passed, he branched out into the network of libertarian ateneos and all the collectives making up the Antirepression Coordination, on which he served through the Barrio Chino's Ateneo Libertario. The mission of that coordinating body was mainly to do with propaganda and organizing public actions against the excessive repression and unspoken torture that followed in the wake of the arrests of activists. At its meetings, even as they were planning their public response to repression, Víctor was encountering those who were to become his comrades in action over the ensuing years. Ideological affinity, in terms of how to respond to the state's relentless onslaughts, carried the day. Out of his involvement with the Coordination a grupo autónomo emerged made up of five individuals of different backgrounds but sharing the same purpose: fighting capitalism, which they already sensed bore the main responsibility for the repression of self-organization by working people.

These five comrades started meeting up and debating the aim of their struggle and which steps they had to take to keep things moving along. The need for total trust in comrades and collective responsibility led to their sharing an apartment in Poblenou along with a couple of other friends who had nothing at all to do with their actions. They made up one of those typical youth communes that were around in the late 1970s. Only one of the members of the group held aloof, preferring to retain his independence. The time had come to step their struggle up a notch. Víctor dropped out of active membership of the CNT. His reading matter had evolved, and *Star* or *Bicicleta* had been joined by *¡Palante!* and *El Topo Avizor*.

El Químico was an enthusiast. Chemical substances held an inordinate attraction for him. His passion for them outweighed any other interest, and naturally he started to experiment a little. In fact, El Químico and Víctor had already conducted some initial experiments up the mountains, and prior to the formation of this new affinity group they had been associating with one another for a time. One of the comrades showed up one afternoon with a pistol. For some of them, it was the first time they had ever held a firearm in their hands. The time to ask for a deeper commitment was drawing closer. They decided to use that pistol to procure one of their own. One day they took up positions around a building in L'Hospitalet. One of the comrades stationed himself in the stairwell of the apartment bloc with the gun, another two remaining on the street outside. When the municipal police officer approached and opened the door, the two comrades jumped him. The one in the stairwell trained the pistol on him as the other two wrestled with him. On hearing the sounds of the struggle, the residents started to emerge on to the landing. The comrade ordered them to go back inside and shut their doors. In the end, Víctor hacked through the officer's cartridge belt with a knife and the trio took off running. They had obtained the group's first pistol. The comrade who had snatched the pistol, one way or another, started making new contacts, and even though this put the rest of the comrades' noses out of joint, since it posed a threat to their safety, they knew that it was the only way of securing arms or new contacts through whom to get some. Through these connections, they got hold of a Cetme rifle one day; another grupo autónomo had let them have it.

For around two years, they were involved in nonstop struggle. Not that they ever claimed any of their actions citing any name or set of initials. They were not out to grab the limelight; they merely wanted to help sink the power structures. The group's security measures were very tight. The self-imposed countersurveillance tactics meant their taking a different route each day, and they usually moved around on a couple of high-powered motorbikes. Víctor carried on working in a large factory, the factory where, prior to the setting up of the group and during his days as a union activist, he had helped grow the CNT and where he was the union rep. On days when an action was in the offing, Victor would arrive at the factory, punch in, and when the time came, he would vanish without anyone noticing his absence. He would carry out the action and go back to work, thereby guaranteeing himself a solid alibi. When the actions were at night, he looked just like a young student from some private school in the upper-class areas of Barcelona. The actions were planned in detail: everybody's station, what each of them had to do if anything untoward occurred, escape routes. They had agreed that they would not surrender under any circumstances and to every action they carried homemade grenades that El Químico had designed and manufactured for the purpose of facilitating their getaway. None of their actions misfired. Even on that morning when they were waiting in front of a gun store for it to open up (which it was unusually tardy in doing that day). Víctor and the comrade were supposed to enter the store, armed, in order to rob it, but they were stopped by a couple of policemen, who asked to see their papers. Although they had to scrub the operation until a later date, they came through without any major problems.

One morning, though, Víctor reckoned that he was being tailed to the factory by a motorbike. He stopped, as he did every day, in front of the entrance gate, and once in his place of work, he could see that the biker was on the corner. When his day was done, he fell back on the agreed countersurveillance measures, and found his suspicions confirmed. He managed to shake off whoever was tailing him. He made it back to his lodgings and bade his comrades farewell. He would revert to living above the radar. His nighttime actions were over.

A few weeks later, Víctor received his call-up papers. He went off to the assigned barracks and was sent directly from there to a punishment company. Made up for the most part of youngsters with police records, whether due to criminal or political offenses. There seemed to be no obvious reason why he had been posted to it, but this just confirmed his suspicions over the preceding months. Even though he had never had a police record, he was on the list.

Months after that, while he was with that punishment company, one of his uncles popped downstairs from the Via Laietana police station to the cells. He wanted a word in person with one of Víctor's fellow group members, who was arrested and suffered brutal treatment from those brutes: "So you're one of my nephew's pals, eh?"

7.

THE DREAM LIVES ON

THE DREAM LIVES ON

After French doctors diagnosed him as sterile due to the tortures he had endured in a Civil Guard barracks in Vitoria back in 1984, Petit Loup is today the father of two wonderful boys. He is a recognized healer operating on the fringes of Western medicine.

A regular contributor to various libertarian media outlets, Sabata was one of several comrades who were spurred into action over the screening of the movie *Salvador*.

Roger is still living in the same farmhouse where he was born, surrounded by cattle, orchards and now highways as well.

Llengües is still connected to the communication of the libertarian ideas that brought him into activism. He was one of the people most agitated about the commercialization of *Salvador*.

Through gastronomy, agroecology, and cooking with local seasonal ingredients, Gerard strives to recapture the everyday pleasures he was also looking for as a youth, while at the same time defending the earth and helping to rescue farming species under threat of extinction.

José is another one who fled the city in search of the peace he was denied as a youth. He helps out at the ateneo in the town where he lives.

In the end, Dani was able to turn to literature and journalism, and has received praise for his work on several occasions.

Felipe lives in the mountains where he gets a better reception from fauna and flora than other animals offered him in his youth.

Juan is still linked to the autónomo libertarian movement.

These days, Paco is still organized and part of an assembly-based social center while turning his hand to market gardening and dedicating himself to the rescue of seeds under threat of extinction.

The other Paco, Paco from Madrid, is as much into music as ever, but rather than "tripping" with Om and Weather Report, he now listens to jazz on his travels.

Miguel lives with his partner in a little house on the outskirts of a small Catalan town. He has no need of the major service companies, water or power companies, and his main preoccupation is also the rescue of seeds under threat of extinction.

Juanjo still lives near the apartment where he was first arrested. He intends to work with his comrades on a written collective record of what he lived through as a youth.

Michel shares his time with everybody and remains the lynchpin. Just as he was thirty-five years ago.

Víctor, never having been arrested, is still part of the autónomo libertarian network.

My dream is that Julia, Pol, Pau, Aina, Iu, Joana, Ona, Llucia, Lila, Emma, Jairo, and upcoming generations may not have to live through similar history and may plant seeds without needing to rescue them.

CHRONOLOGY

Note: Neither MIL nor CAA actions are included here, but MIL operations in which other grupos autónomos took part are.

1972

11/18: Holdup at a Caja de Ahorros y Monte de Piedad branch in Barcelona.

11/19: Agustín Rueda Sierra and a couple from the mining settlement are arrested in Sallent, charged with "disturbing the peace."

11/28: Holdup at a Banco Central branch in Barcelona.

1973

1/27: Banco de Vizcaya branch held up in Barcelona.

3/20: Bail for provisional release of Agustín Rueda set at ten thousand pesetas (about sixty euros).

7/2: Holdup at the Telegraphs Office in the Central Post Office Building in Barcelona.

9/15: Roundup of MIL members starts.

9/25: Last arrests of MIL members.

1974

1/4: Device planted at the Sant Andreu police station.

1/9: Military tribunal considers the case against Salvador Puig Antich and another two MIL members.

1/11: Bombs at the Monument to the Fallen and branches of the Banco Popular Español and Banco de Vizcaya in Barcelona.

1/15: Attacks on banks in Madrid. Demonstration outside the Spanish consulate in Toulouse.

1/16: Four activists arrested in Paris making preparations for actions in support of Puig Antich; two of them will be sent to prison.

1/17: Two devices at the University of Bilbao.

1/19: Device at the Monument to the Fallen in Mataró. Molotov cocktail attacks on *La Voz de España* and *Unidad* newspapers in San Sebastián and at the Iberia offices in Barcelona.

2/8: Devices in Mataró police station and at the Monument to the Fallen in Badalona.

2/11: Demonstration at the Universidad Autónoma in Barcelona.

2/22: Operation closing off the main street in San Sebastián using chains.

2/23: The car of the Spanish consul is machine-gunned in Toulouse.

3/1: Demonstration in Barcelona.

3/2: Salvador Puig Antich murdered. Demonstrations in Barcelona.

3/3: Molotov cocktail attacks on banks in the Via Júlia; device at the Sant Andreu barracks. Demonstrations. Propaganda actions in six cinemas. All in Barcelona.

3/4: Universities across Spain brought to a standstill. Large demonstration in Barcelona with banks coming under attack.

3/5: Policía Armada vehicles come under Molotov cocktail attacks in Valencia; one youth arrested. Universities at a standstill nationwide. Demonstrations in Barcelona; attacks on *La Prensa* and *Solidaridad Nacional*. A Policía Armada patrol comes under attack.

3/22: Announcement that twenty-two youths responsible for actions in Barcelona and district have been arrested; the initials OLLA come to public notice for the very first time.

3/22: Attacks in France on a bridge and two railway lines leading to the border.

4/7: Arrest of three OLLA-linked activists in Barcelona on the high-speed train service from Geneva.

4/8: Agustín Rueda and the others arrested on 11/19/1972 are acquitted.

4/26: Propaganda action on an FGC train in Muntaner station in Barcelona.

4/27: Banco Central branch in Barcelona held up and Molotov cocktail attack on the Banco Guipuzcoano; both in Barcelona.

5/1: Molotov cocktails thrown at four bank branches in Poble Nou, in Barcelona.

5/3: Baltasar Suárez, director of the Banco Bilbao, is abducted in Paris.

5/7: Press conference in Barcelona regarding the abduction of Baltasar Suárez.

5/13: Six young people linked to the Catalan activists' network are arrested on the Lyon-to-Geneva motorway.

5/21: Premises of the French newspaper *L'Est Républicain* torched by the "Puig Antich Commando."

5/22: Baltasar Suárez released; seven activists arrested in France.

5/23: Two people arrested in connection with the Suárez abduction.

5/29: A further two arrests made in Paris.

7/7: Eight people arrested in Barcelona and elsewhere over the press conference on May 7; four of them will be imprisoned.

7/15: Devices used on several trans-Pyrenean power lines in Andorra and against the Paris-Irún train in Paris.

7/16: Thirteen coaches burned in Lourdes as well as several cars involved in the Tour de France.

7/17: Abduction in Madrid of Juan Antonio Astarloa, son of a leading businessman.

7/18: Astarloa released.

7/23: Military tribunal sits in judgment of Oriol Solé Sugranyes and other members of the MIL.

7/25: Device at the Nîmes branch of the Banco Popular Español.

7/27: Device at the Spanish consulate in Toulouse.

7/28: Two further devices at the Spanish consulate in Toulouse. Device in Hendaye train station. Two coaches destroyed in Paris. Devices in Le Perthus and Bourg-Madame.

7/29: A GARI member arrested in Toulouse.

7/30: Attacks on the port of La Grand Motte.

8/5: Three car bombs in Brussels, at the Iberia offices and two Banco Español premises.

August: The GARI decide to voluntarily disband.

9/14: Two members of the GARI arrested in Toulouse.

9/15: Another two members of the GARI arrested in Hendaye.

9/23: OLLA activist arrested in Barcelona on arrival from France. Two others were arrested days earlier.

10/9: Unarmed devices planted in the Stade de Paris ahead of the Paris v. Barça match.

10/14: The two people arrested on January 16 stand trial in Paris. An activist from the GARI arrested; in subsequent searches, a draft dodger in hiding is discovered and arrested.

10/15: Ten-month prison sentences announced for the two people tried the previous day. They are released from custody, but one of them is transferred to an army barracks, being a draft dodger.

10/17: It is announced that four activists with OLLA links are arrested in Barcelona.

11/2: Action mounted at the Wax Museum in Paris results in decapitation of the effigy of Juan Carlos.

11/6: It is announced that two young people with OLLA links have been arrested in Barcelona.

11/25: The two young people arrested on January 16 stand trial in Paris but are not jailed.

12/3: Three members of the GARI arrested in Paris.

12/12: Holdup at the Roca gun store in Barcelona's Calle Aribau.

12/27: Banco Hispano-Americano branch in Barcelona held up.

12/27: The GARI prisoners in La Santé prison in Paris begin a hunger strike.

1975

1/5: The Naval Museum in Paris comes under attack in a gesture of support for the comrades on hunger strike.

1/8: Tear-gas grenade tossed into the courthouse in Toulouse.

1/16: Attack on the courthouse in Paris.

1/23: One of the people arrested in Paris on December 3 is released.

2/27: The only person imprisoned in Toulouse over GARI actions launches a hunger strike and insists on being transferred to Paris.

3/3: Anniversary of the killing of Puig Antich. Device planted at the Monument to the Fallen in Madrid.

3/7: The only person imprisoned in Fresnes for GARI actions joins the hunger strike begun by the comrade down in Toulouse.

April: Another of those arrested on December 3, 1974, in Paris is released.

4/15: Another two GARI activists released.

4/22: Another activist set free.

5/1: Car bomb left at the Santiago Bernabeu stadium while Franco is attending a CNS rally in Madrid.

5/9: Holdup at the Sabadell Savings Fund office in Martorelles.

5/17: Three OLLA activists face trial before the TOP (Public Order Tribunal).

6/28: Molotov cocktail attack on the National Social Security Institute in Valencia.

7/2: Holdup at the Sagrada Familia Savings Fund in Barcelona.

7/9: Another GARI activist released, leaving three still in prison.

8/6: Three activists with links to Estudiants Llibertaris and OLLA arrested.

September: The military tribunal trying the ten OLLA activists in prison since 1974 is postponed.

9/16: It is announced that three young activists have been arrested in Barcelona.

9/27: The dictatorship carries out its last firing squad executions.

11/4: An office of the Sagrada Familia Savings Fund held up in Barcelona.

1976

1/3: The sentences passed on the four young people jailed in relation to the

May 7, 1974, press conference in Barcelona is revealed: they are sentenced to between three and five years in prison.

1/8: A young Catalan activist is arrested in Perpignan, as is Eduardo Soler; they each receive six-month sentences.

2/17: An activist is arrested in Valencia.

2/18: The Banco Hispano-Americano branch in Hospitalet is held up.

2/27: A bus and the offices of the Banco-Hispano-Americano in the Calle Pelai in Barcelona are torched.

3/2: Demonstrations in Barcelona; bank premises set on fire.

3/6: It is announced that two young Valencian activists being linked with members of the MIL and Catalan activists have been arrested in Valencia.

3/8: Activists Jaime Diego Ruiz Donales aka El Jebo (Madrid) and Robert Touati are killed while planting an explosive device in Toulouse.

4/5: Escape from Segovia Prison. Among the escapees are Oriol Solé Sugranyes and Josep Lluís Pons Llobet.

4/5: A Catalan activist stands trial in Switzerland.

4/6: Oriol Solé Sugranyes is killed.

4/19: Letter confirming that Agustín Rueda has arrived in Perpignan.

5/13: Arson attack in Barcelona at the German Hoechst firm in response to the death of Ulrike Meinhof.

5/25: One of the activists jailed as part of the OLLA case is released.

5/26: Another four OLLA activists released.

June: One of the people jailed for the May 7, 1974, press conference in Barcelona is released.

6/20: A copy machine is stolen from a school in Ceutí, Murcia.

7/14: Attacks on the Librería Española and L'Escletxa in Perpignan.

7/25: Six bank premises attacked in Madrid.

7/31: Rioting in Carabanchel demanding an amnesty for ordinary prisoners.

8/5: Savings Fund branch held up in Madrid; a security guard is killed.

8/10: Attack on the Civil Guard barracks in Playa de Aro, Girona.

9/7: A van from the Provincial Savings Fund is robbed in Barcelona.

9/13: Molotov cocktail attack on the Syndicates Delegation in Cornellà.

9/27: Molotov cocktail attack on the Telephone Exchange, Valencia.

9/28: El Corte Inglés department store in Madrid comes under Molotov cocktail attack.

9/29: Four Madrid Civil Guard barracks come under Molotov cocktail attack.

10/7: Gun store in Murcia held up.

10/8: A branch office of the Sabadell Savings Fund at the Universidad Autónoma in Barcelona is held up.

12/11: A Banco Central office in Cabezo de Torres, Murcia, is held up.

1977

1/30: Between forty-six and fifty-three arrests made in Barcelona for attempts to reorganize the FAI.

February: Four activists with links to those arrested in Barcelona are rounded up in Málaga.

2/4: The arrests continue—five in Huesca, three in Barcelona, two in Bilbao, two in Tarragona, and one in Iruña.

2/6: Seven arrests made during a demonstration in Barcelona.

2/8: The seven people arrested are released.

2/11–2/12: Arrest in Murcia of eleven activists linked to the arrests in Barcelona; they include Joaquín Gambín Hernández. Another arrest is made in Barcelona.

2/14: Another activist is arrested in Murcia.

2/16: An activist arrested in Barcelona on January 30 is released. Since that date, he had been held, unlawfully, at the Via Laietana police station. He makes a complaint about torture.

2/21: Two activists with links to the one arrested in Barcelona on February 11 or 12 are arrested in Barcelona.

2/21: Riots in Carabanchel Prison, COPEL's first action.

2/23: It is announced that another activist has been arrested in Málaga.

2/27: In Valencia, premises belonging to the Banco de Vizcaya, Banco Hispano-Americano, and the Levante Insurance Corporation come under Molotov cocktail attack.

3/1: Attack on the Justice Ministry in Madrid.

3/2: Molotov cocktail attacks on the police station in Santaló, the Liceu, and premises belonging to the Banca Catalana, Banco Bilbao, and Banco Español de Crédito. Demonstration held. All in Barcelona.

3/5: Molotov cocktail attacks on branches of the Banco Popular, Banco de Santander, and Banco de Vizcaya in Valencia.

3/9: Molotov cocktail attacks on branches of the Banco March, Banco Popular, Banesto, and Banco de Vizcaya in Madrid.

3/10: Molotov cocktail attack on a Banco Occidental branch in Madrid.

3/11: Military tribunal tries two of the people arrested in Barcelona on August 6, 1975.

3/13: A pro-amnesty demonstration in Barcelona is banned leading to serious clashes. One young man is shot while attacking a police patrol.

3/27: Clashes in Barcelona and an attack mounted on a group of FN members.

4/13: A van belonging to Autopistas del Mediterráneo is held up in Barcelona.

4/21: Attack on the Lufthansa offices in Barcelona.

5/2: Clashes during the Malasaña festival with an attempt made to attack the police station in that Madrid barrio. Twenty-nine arrests made.

5/3: Continuing clashes in Madrid.

5/25: The Court in Paris rules that the three GARI members still in custody should be released.

5/25: The final young person linked to the activities of the OLLA, arrested on August 6, 1975, is released.

6/1: Holdup at the National Social Security Institute in Badalona.

6/20: Holdup at the ONCE offices in Barcelona.

7/13: Explosive device found at the courthouse in Barcelona

7/15: Election day. Devices planted in the courthouses in Seville, Córdoba, and in electrical installations in Málaga and Madrid. Molotov cocktails thrown in Valencia.

7/18: Rioting in Carabanchel. Mass self-harming.

7/24: Five devices planted in Madrid in protest at the exploitation of prisoner labor; these include two at the Corte Inglés department store.

7/24: Nineteen CNT members arrested in Barcelona.

7/27: It is reported that fifty-seven inmates in Córdoba (twenty-seven of them COPEL members, plus eleven political prisoners transferred there from Carabanchel) have gone on hunger strike.

7/28: The Alcalá de Guadaira (Seville) branch of the National Social Security Institute is held up.

7/30: A transport agency in Madrid is held up.

August: Joaquín Gambín Hernández is released.

8/29: Clashes in Barcelona during a demonstration in support of Apala. Molotov cocktails thrown at the SEPU. One arrest made.

9/3: Clashes in Barcelona. Two public buses torched and a third crashed into a branch of the Banco Popular Español. Two arrests made.

9/7: The announcement is made that five people have been arrested in Valencia who have ties to the GAR, a "ghost" group linked to the police agencies.

9/13: It is announced that thirteen young people linked to actions carried out in Barcelona have been arrested; they are being linked to the FIJL.

9/27: Device attached to a pro-amnesty placard found on the motorway in Badalona.

October: Amnesty granted to those arrested in January and February 1977.

10/8: It is reported that twelve young people linked to actions in Barcelona and once again with ties to the FIJL have been arrested.

10/13: Holdup at the Central Fish Market in Barcelona.

10/14: It is announced that an activist has been arrested for a holdup, with which he had no connection. It subsequently came to light that he had been the victim of a police frame-up.

10/15: Agustín Rueda and his comrade are arrested after crossing the border with explosives.

10/20: Molotov cocktail attack on the German consulate in San Sebastián, as a response to the RAF "suicides."

10/28: Rioting in the Modelo.

10/31: Large printing firm held up in Madrid.

November: Device planted at the District High Court in Valladolid.

11/11: Molotov cocktail attacks on the Porsche dealership and the Mantequerías Alemanas company in Madrid.

11/19: Device plated at the German International School in Madrid.

12/3: Clashes in Barcelona; one person receives a gunshot wound.

12/24: Rioting in Basauri and in Murcia. Mass self-harming in Segovia Prison. Demonstrations in support of COPEL, with Molotov cocktails thrown in Barcelona and Valladolid.

12/28: Devices planted at the courthouses in Sant Feliu de Llobregat and Barcelona.

1978

January: Hunger strike in Girona Prison; Agustín Rueda and his comrade participate.

January: Four autónomo activists arrested in Valencia.

1/5: It is reported that the GAR has claimed responsibility for an attack in Valencia on a discotheque belonging to a member of the FN.

1/15: The CNT holds its first legally permitted demonstration to protest the Moncloa Agreements. Arson attack on the Scala nightclub.

1/18: It is reported that nine young people allegedly involved in the arson have been arrested.

1/20: It is announced that three of the young people have been released.

1/23: Devices planted at the courthouse in Granollers, the Modelo, and the Durán y Bas Home in Barcelona.

1/30: A Barcelona branch of the Banco Central is held up.

2/2: Agustín Rueda and his comrade arrive in Carabanchel.

2/3: It is reported that four members of the grupos autónomos have been arrested in Barcelona.

2/3: Eight Madrid autónomo activists linked to those above are arrested.

2/8: It is reported that five young people in charge of border crossings have been arrested in Girona, and another five autónomo activists in Barcelona.

2/17: Protests in the Modelo. Some libertarian activists ferociously beaten by prison officers.

3/9: FN members attack a CNT meeting in Valladolid.

3/11: Devices found in Valladolid in the Via Madrid–León. Responsibility is claimed on behalf of the Aid For COPEL Armed Groups.

3/14: Agustín Rueda murdered inside Carabanchel.

3/15: The four autónomo activists arrested in January go on hunger strike to press to be held together in the same ward.

3/16: In La Trinitad women's prison, Barcelona, eight political prisoners call a hunger strike in protest at Agustín Rueda's murder. Four people are arrested in Madrid for putting up placards. twenty-one arrests are made during the press conference on the AFAPE premises in Madrid.

3/17: The deputy governor, chief of services, and eight Carabanchel Prison officers are sentenced to prison. In Madrid, there is a violent demonstration with numerous clashes. Demonstration in Sallent. Those arrested on the AFAPE premises are released.

3/18: Agustín Rueda's funeral in Sallent.

3/19: The Policía Nacional barracks in Cornellà is machine-gunned.

3/21: Demonstration in Barcelona protesting the death of Agustín Rueda.

3/22: An explosive device is defused at the Civil Guard barracks in L'Hospitalet.

3/23: An explosive device is defused at the Madrid CNT's local.

3/23: The hunger strike in La Trinidad ends, except for the PCE(i) prisoners.

3/26: It is reported that an attack with explosives was carried out against the police station in Montpellier the previous Saturday by the "Agustín Rueda Libertarian Grupo Autónomo."

3/30: Four arrests made in connection with the machine-gunning of the barracks in Cornellà. A further five libertarians arrested over Molotov cocktails and expropriations.

4/8: Nine autónomo prisoners in Carabanchel declare a hunger strike.

4/12: The strike is joined by four libertarian prisoners in La Trinidad women's prison, seven in the Modelo, and two in Alcalá de Henares, making twenty-six libertarian prisoners on hunger strike across Spain.

4/16: A member of the ERAT is arrested.

4/17: Six young people with links to ERAT are arrested.

4/21: The news is released of the arrests above, as well as those of three other persons.

4/21: The comrade arrested with Agustín Rueda stands trial; he is sentenced to two years.

4/27: It is announced that one of the young people linked to the ERAT has been released.

4/27: Clashes in Barcelona. Two arrests made.

May: Eighteen arrests made in connection with the clashes in Barcelona.

5/1: Incidents in Valladolid; eighteen arrested.

5/2: A further arrest is made in Valladolid, while three of those arrested the previous day are freed.

5/4: A branch of the Catalonia Savings Fund in Barcelona is held up.

5/5: It is announced that nineteen of those arrested in Valladolid have been referred to the courts.

5/10: Demonstration outside the Modelo calling for the release of the ERAT prisoners. Clashes.

5/11: COPEL's day of struggle inside the prisons.

5/23: Rioting in Guadalajara.

5/24: French activist carrying a load of arms arrested on the French border.

5/26: Riots in Basauri and Segovia.

5/28: It is confirmed that seven prisoners have escaped from Carabanchel.

June: Seventeen of those arrested in January and February 1977 have their amnesty revoked.

6/1: Forty-four prisoners escape from the Modelo.

6/10: Rioting in Valencia prison in an attempt to thwart the discovery of a tunnel.

6/22: Arrests in Valladolid.

6/23: Molotov cocktail attack on the School of Economics at the Universidad Autónoma in Barcelona.

7/2: Eleven prisoners, it is announced, have begun a hunger strike in Valladolid against the Antiterrorist Law; seven of them are anarchists.

7/4: Three Madrid autónomos arrested in February are tried for the July 24, 1977, attack on the El Corte Inglés department store.

7/9: A Zaragoza branch of the Savings Fund is held up.

7/12: It is reported that the three Madrid autónomos tried on July 4 have been sentenced to four years.

7/28: A branch of the Banca Catalana is held up in Barcelona.

8/17: A branch of the Banco de Madrid and of the Caja de Girona in Lloret de Mar are held up. Three autónomo activists are arrested for the first holdup, while the two Caja de Girona raiders escape.

8/28: A member of the ERAT is arrested along with José Juan Martínez Gómez, El Rubio.

9/7: Demonstration in support of the gas station workers' strike. Clashes. Five arrests made.

9/10: Gas station workers' strike. Molotov cocktails thrown at two stations in Granollers and Barcelona.

9/11: Serious clashes in Barcelona. Gustau Muñoz Bustillo from the PCE(i) is killed.

9/22: There are reports of a tunnel having been uncovered in Segovia Prison and a second in the Modelo.

9/25: Two gas stations located between Rubí and Cerdanyola come under gunfire.

9/26: Explosive devices used on two service stations.

10/1: A hunger strike by five autónomo prisoners, ERAT prisoners and the Scala prisoners begins in the Modelo.

10/11: There are reports that the autónomo prisoners in the Modelo are still on hunger strike.

12/21: Banco Hispano-Americano branch in Barberá is held up.

1979

1/9: Four autónomo activists arrested in Valencia following the discovery of a tunnel headed for the prison. They are freed after a few days, except for one who is a deserter.

1/17: Rioting in the Yeserías women's prison in Madrid.

2/23: Eleven libertarian autónomo activists arrested in Barcelona.

3/1: Election day. Molotov cocktail attack on the Sant Josep de la Muntanya Civil Guard barracks. Attack on a strike-hit firm in Cerdanyola.

3/14: The courthouse in Barcelona is cleared after a suspicious package is found.

3/30: A Banco Popular Español branch in Montornès is held up.

5/21: Autónomo activist arrested in La Jonquera in a vehicle with weapons.

June: Three of those arrested on February 23 are released.

6/18: Agustín Valiente Martín is killed during a clash in Almería, and three activists are arrested. In Madrid, another nine activists are arrested, and in Barcelona, one more. They all have FIGA connections.

7/27: Failed holdup at a Banco Central branch in Barcelona; in the course of a shootout a guard is killed and one of the robbers and another guard are wounded.

7/31: An activist connected with the holdup on the 27th is arrested in Barcelona.

August: The two prisoners who have refused to drop the charges relating to Agustín Rueda's murder are transferred to Herrera de la Mancha.

8/5: It is reported that eleven autónomo activists linked to the holdup on the 27th have been arrested.

8/29: It is reported that a tunnel has been found in Figueres Prison.

9/15: A former autónomo activist linked to those arrested in August is sent to the Modelo.

10/13: The activist imprisoned on September 15 is released.

10/23: The Cale Vilamarí tunnel in Barcelona is uncovered. Links are made to ETA.

10/24: Arrests in Madrid related to the FIGA.

11/1: It is reported that three anarchists on the run from mainland Spain have been arrested in the Canaries. Among them is one from Valladolid.

11/12: Demonstration and clashes in Barcelona.

11/15: The trial before the National High Court of eight autónomos arrested in Catalonia in February 1978 is postponed.

11/16: Device planted in the courthouse in Valencia.

11/17: Failed escape attempt from Valencia Hospital, with two autónomos arrested.

December: Twenty libertarian prisoners go on hunger strike in Segovia.

12/7: Four autónomo activists arrested on the Valencia–Córdoba train.

12/16: The Calle Vilamarí tunnel is recognized as the handiwork of libertarians.

12/17: The three people arrested for the holdup at the Banco de Madrid in Lloret de Mar appear before the National High Court, as does a fourth person who will be acquitted.

1980

January: Jorge Benayas Manzanares arrested for embezzlement.

1/4: It is announced that three of those arrested for the Banco de Madrid holdup in Lloret de Mar were given sentences of seven years, two months, and one day.

1/29: Antifascist demonstration in Madrid; two people arrested.

1/30: The FN's premises in Valladolid is burned down.

6/30: The seven people charged in connection with the ERAT stand trial.

July: Jorge Benayas Manzanares found dead in Segovia Prison.

July: Raid on the office of the Banco Comercial Español in Barcelona, in solidarity with the ERAT members.

7/4: The National High Court hears the case against a Barcelona grupo autónomo.

8/18: Barcelona Zoo is held up.

10/12: Four activists reported arrested in Valencia.

10/17: It is reported that twelve libertarian activists have been arrested in Barcelona. Half of them will be released over the ensuing days.

10/29: The National High Court hears the case against six autónomo activists from Madrid arrested in February 1978.

11/22: Holdup at a car showroom in Barcelona.

11/25: Holdup at Cornellà post office.

11/26: It is reported that the six Madrid activists tried on October 29 have been acquitted.

December: Attack on the armed security guards at the Walden-7 building in Sant Just Desvern.

12/1: The Scala night club arson trial opens. Clashes in Barcelona.

12/2: Demonstrations over the Scala case trial.

12/3: The trial ends, and running battles (*saltos*) take place.

1981

January: Jacinto Avalos arrested in Terrassa.

1/6: Carrefour supermarket held up in Barcelona.

1/13: Banco de Santander branch in Hospitalet held up.

2/18: The Crédit Lyonnais offices in Barcelona are attacked by way of protest at the arrests made in France.

2/23: A Barcelona grupo autónomo stands trial before the National High Court.

3/18: It is reported that four Barcelona libertarians have been convicted in relation to actions during 1978.

3/26: A Civil Guard jeep comes under attack in Hospitalet.

4/22: The German firm Hoescht in Barcelona is attacked over the death of Sigurd Debus.

May: Trial held in Paris regarding GARI actions; all of the accused are acquitted.

5/16: Barcanova Bingo Hall in Barcelona is held up. One activist is arrested.

5/17: It is reported that five activists have been arrested in Madrid on charges of attempted escape from Carabanchel.

5/20: Two activists arrested in Bilbao.

5/23: José Juan Martínez Gómez, aka "El Rubio," raids the Banco Central in Barcelona.

5/31: It is reported that three activists have been arrested in Valladolid, one in Vitoria, two in Bilbao, one in Errenteria, and one in Barcelona. They are being linked with the arrests on the 20th.

6/6: Device found in a Banco Hispano-Americano in Barcelona.

6/8: Device found in another Banco Hispano-Americano branch in Barcelona.

6/29: Advertising agency in Barcelona held up.

8/14: Activist arrested on October 17, 1980, is released.

9/26: Holdup at the Banco Atlántico in Barcelona.

9/27: It is reported that the trial of seven of those arrested on January 30, 1977, has opened.

10/27: Attempting to escape from the Modelo, an autónomo activist arrested in August 1979 sustains a gunshot wound.

12/3: Joaquín Gambín is arrested in Valencia.

12/31: It is announced that four alleged members of the FAI have been arrested in Andalusia, another one in Lugo, one in Badajoz, and two more in Barcelona.

1982

2/6: The activist wounded while trying to escape from the Modelo on October 27 escapes from the Clinical Hospital.

4/26: A branch of the Banco de Europa in Premià is held up.

May: Four of the activists arrested in Barcelona between July 31 and August 5, 1979, stand trial before the National High Court. Three are sentenced to thirty years apiece and one to four years.

5/14: The trial before the National High Court of sixteen FIGA members is postponed.

7/16: Sentence is passed on one of those arrested in the Canaries on November 1, 1979.

7/20: It is reported that, in Barcelona, five activists with FAI connections have been arrested.

7/23: Three of those arrested released without charge.

7/24: Another is given a provisional release.

10/16: A branch of the Banco de Vizcaya in Mataró is held up.

11/16: The National High Court tries seven Valencian autónomos.

1983

1/24: Three activists arrested in Valencia.

1/25: Four activists with ties to the above are arrested in Barcelona.

1/29: One of the activists is freed on bail.

2/26: Another verdict brought in on one of those arrested in the Canaries on November 1, 1979.

3/16: Trial in Barcelona for the February 18, 1981, attack.

6/27: Two activists arrested between July 31 and August 5, 1979, over the October 8, 1976, holdup in Bellaterra stand trial.

9/16: An autónomo activist escapes from Carabanchel.

10/30: Jacinto Avalos found hanged in Carabanchel.

12/15: Joaquín Gambín stands trial for the arson attack on the Scala nightclub.

1984

1/25: Device found at the premises of the printing trades entrepreneurs' association in Zaragoza.

1/25: Two activists arrested in Barcelona.

2/5: It is reported that two young people linked to those arrested on the 23rd have been arrested in Premià de Mar.

3/16: Two activists arrested in Santa Coloma and Sant Adrià.

3/19: An activist arrested in Navarra.

3/21: It is reported that four activists have been arrested in the Basque Country. They are being linked with the arrests on March 16 and 19.

3/22: An ambush in Pasajes results in the killing of four members of the CAA and the arrest of another.

5/23: Two ex-members of the MIL and the OLLA arrested in Barcelona for check fraud

8/2: A French activist is arrested in Gijón.

8/6: Three of the activists arrested in January 1983 start a hunger strike.

10/4: The activist arrested on March 19 is released.

10/26: Two activists reportedly arrested in Oviedo.

11/28: The MIL activist arrested on May 23 is released under the terms of the 1977 amnesty.

1985

1/10: The verdict on those arrested in January 1983 is issued. One of them is acquitted.

1/16: The National High Court brings in its verdict on the FIGA members.

1/29: The two former members of the MIL and of the OLLA are rearrested for check fraud.

1/31: Both activists are imprisoned.

April: Two FIGA members arrested in Almería.

6/12: The court acquits the six people jailed on October 17, 1980.

6/15: Six FIGA members are arrested in Barcelona and another two in Almería.

1987

January: One of the people arrested on June 15, 1985, is released.

7/2: The trial of the FIGA members before the National High Court is suspended.

9/24: Six of the FIGA members are tried by the National High Court.

10/8: An activist is arrested in Finland.

12/9: The trial for the killing of Agustín Rueda opens.

1988

2/5: A fresh verdict on one of those arrested in the Canaries on November 1, 1979.

3/28: The activist arrested in Finland is extradited.

July: The activist extradited from Finland is released.

10/10: The activist arrested in Barcelona on May 16, 1981, is released.

10/14: The activist extradited from Finland and subsequently released is sentenced to seven years.

1989

3/22: A cabinet meeting pardons eight of the fifteen prisoners acknowledged as anarchists. They are freed five days later.

9/21: Those arrested in Barcelona on February 23, 1979, face the court. The charges are withdrawn.

1990

8/10: The last remaining autónomo prisoner, arrested on January 25, 1983, in Barcelona, is released.

ABBREVIATIONS

AAA – Alianza Apostólica Anticomunista / Anticommunist Apostolic Alliance
AD – Action Directe / Direct Action
AFAPE – Asociación de Familiares y Amigos de Presos y Ex-Presos /
PRISONERS and Ex-Prisoners' Families and Friends Association
CAA – Comandos Autónomos Anticapitalistas / Anticapitalist Autonomous
Commandos
CC.OO – Comisiones Obreras / Workers' Commissions
CGT – Confederação Geral dos Trabalhadores / General Workers' Confederation
(Portugal)
CGT – Confederación General del Trabajo / General Confederation of Labor
(Spain)
CIU – Convergencia i Unió / Convergence and Union
CNT – Confederación Nacional del Trabajo / National Confederation of Labor
CNT-AIT – The International Workers' Association-affiliated CNT
CNS – Central Nacional Sindicalista / National Syndicalist Center
COPEL – Coordinadora de Presos en Lucha / Prisoners-in-Struggle Coordination
COS – Coordinadora de Organizaciones Sindicales / Trade Union Organizations'
Coordinating Body
DI – Defensa Interior / Internal Defense
EAA – Escamots Autònoms Anticapitaistes / Anticapitalist Autonomous
Commandos
ERAT – Ejército Revolucionario de Ayuda a los Trabajadores / Revolutionary
Army for Aiding the Workers
ESB – Euskal Sozialista Biltzarrea / Basque Socialist Assembly
ETA – Euskadi ta Askatasuna / Basque Homeland and Freedom
ETAPM – ETA político-militar / ETA politico-military
ETAM – ETA militar / ETA military
FAC – Front d'Alliberament Català / Catalan Liberation Front
FAF – Fédération Anarchiste Française / French Anarchist Federation
FAI – Federación Anarquista Ibérica / Iberian Anarchist Federation

FIGA – Federación Ibérica de Grupos Anarquistas / Iberian Federation of Anarchist Groups

FIJL – Federación Ibérica de Juventudes Libertarias / Iberian Libertarian Youth Federation

FL – Front Libertaire / Libertarian Front

FN – Fuerza Nueva / New Force

FOC – Front Obrer Català / Catalan Workers' Front

FRAP – Frente Revolucionario Antifascista y Patriota / Patriotic Antifascist Revolutionary Front

FSLN – Frente Sandinista de Liberación Nacional / Sandinista National Liberation Front

GAAC – Grupos Armados de Ayuda a la COPEL / Armed COPEL Assistance Groups

GAC – Grupos autónomos de Combate / Autonomous Fighting Groups

GAI – Groupes Autonomes d'Intervention / Autonomous Intervention Groups

GAI – Groupes d'Action Internationaliste / Internationalist Action Groups

GAL – Grupos Antiterroristas de Liberación / Antiterrorist Liberation Groups

GALOP – Groupe Autonome Libertaire Occasionnellement Parieur / Occasional Libertarian Autonomous Gambling Group

GALUT – Groupe Autonome Libertaire des Usagers du Tribunal / Court Users' Autonomous Libertarian Group

GAR – Grupo Anarquista Revolucionario / Revolutionary Anarchist Group

GAR-5 – Grupo de Acción Revolucionaria 5 / Revolutionary Action Group 5

GARI – Groupes d'Action Révolutionnaires Internationaliste / Internationalist Revolutionary Action Groups

GAROT – Groupe Autonome Révolutionnaire Occasionnellement Terroriste / Occasionally Terrorist Revolutionary Autonomous Group

GIL – Grupo de Incontrolados en Lucha / Uncontrollables-in-Struggle Group

GOA – Grupos Obreros Autónomos / Autonomous Workers' Groups

GRAPO – Grupos Revolucionarios Antifascistas Primero de Octubre / First of October Revolutionary Antifascist Groups

HB – Herri Batasuna / Popular Unity

JGR – Joven Guardia Roja / Young Red Guard

JS – Juventudes Socialistas / Socialist Youth

KAP – Kol.lectiu Anti-Presons / Antiprisons Collective

KAS – Koordinadora Abetzale Sozialista / Nationalist Socialist Coordination

LAIA- Langile Abertzale Iraultzaileen Alderdia / Revolutionary Nationalist Workers' Party

LUAR – Liga de Unidade e Ação Revolucionaria / Revolutionary Action Unity League

MATRA – Mouvement Armé Terroriste Révolutionnaire et Anarchiste / Anarchist Revolutionary Terrorist Armed Movement

MC – Movimiento Comunista / Communist Movement

MIL – Movimiento Ibérico de Liberación / Iberian Liberation Movement

NAP – Nucleos de Acción Proletaria / Proletarian Action Cells

NAPAP – Noyaux Armés Pour l'Autonomie Populaire / Armed Cells for Popular Autonomy

OJE – Oganización Juvenil Española / Spanish Youth Organization

OLLA – Organització de Lluita Armada / Armed Struggle Organization

ORA – Organization Révolutionnaire Anarchiste / Revolutionary Anarchist Organization

ORT – Organización Revolucionaria de Trabajadores / Workers' Revolutionary Organization

PCE – Partido Comunista de España / Communist Party of Spain

PCE (i)- PCE Internacional / International PCE

PCE(ML) PCE Marxista Leninista / Marxist-Leninist PCE

PNV – Partido Nacionalista Vasco / Basque Nationalist Party

PSAN – Partit Socialista d'Aliberament Nacional / Socialist National Liberation Party

PSC – Partit dels Socialistes de Catalunya / Socialists' Party of Catalonia

PSE – Partido Socialista de Euskadi / Euskadi Socialist Party

PSOE - Partido Socialista Obrero Español / Spanish Workers' Socialist Party

PSUC -Partit Socialista Unificat de Catalunya / Unified Socialist Party of Catalonia

PT – Partido del Trabajo / Party of Labor

RAF – Rote Armee Fraktion / Red Army Faction

SIA – Solidaridad Internacional Antifascista / International Antifascist Solidarity

UCD – Unión de Centro Democrática / Union of the Democratic Center

UGT – Unión General de Trabajadores / Workers' General Union

USO – Unión Sindical Obrera / Workers' Trade Union Unity

BIBLIOGRAPHY

NEWSPAPERS

ABC, Madrid, various issues.
Diario 16, Madrid, various issues.
El Correo Catalán, Barcelona, various issues.
El País, Madrid, various issues.
La Vanguardia, Barcelona, various issues.
Los Sitios de Girona, Girona, various issues.
Punt Diari, Girona, various issues.

REVIEWS AND BULLETINS

Bicicleta, Madrid/Valencia, various issues.
BOE, Madrid, various issues.
CNT-Informa, Barcelona, June 1974
Cuadernos Jurídicos, November 1994
Cuadernos para el Diálogo, Madrid, various issues.
El Topo Avizor no. 6–7, Barcelona, January–February 1978
Enciclopèdic Noticiari, III Epoca, no. 33, Barcelona, December 2007, published by
    the Ateneu Enciclopèdic Popular.
Federación, Madrid, various issues.
La Lletra A, Reus, various issues.
La Voz Confederal, July 1978.
¡¡Libertad!! Madrid, CASPA, various issues.
Lloret Gaceta, Lloret de Mar, August 24 and 31, 1978.
Opción Libertaria no. 3, October 1974.
Revista de Girona no. 265, Girona, 2011.
Solidaritat, Comissions Civiques de Solidaritat, various issues.
Star, Barcelona, various issues.

BOOKS

113 crónica de la emboscada de Pasajes, (no publication information).
Absintia, J., et al. *La Barcelona rebelde: Guía de una ciudad silenciada*. Barcelona,
    Octaedro, 2003.

Alberola O. and Gransac, A. *El anarquismo español y la acción revolucionaria, (1961–1974)*. Barcelona, Virus, 2004.

Alcalde, J. J. *Los servicios secretos en España*. Madrid: Universidad Complutense, 2008.

Amorós, M., et al. *Por la memoria anticapitalista: Reflexiones sobre la autonomía*. Barcelona, Klinamen, 2009.

Andrés Edo, L. *La CNT en la encrucijada: Aventuras de un heterodoxo*. Barcelona: Flor del Viento, 2006.

Azagra, C. and Pardiñas, E. *A la revolución en gerundio*. Alicante: Edicions del Ponent, 2006.

Cañadas Gascón, X. *Entremuros: Las prisiones en la transición* democrática. Bilbao: Muturreko Burutazioak, 2000.

————.*El Caso Scala: Terrorismo de estado y algo más*. Barcelona: Virus, 2008.

Carmona Pascual, P.C. *Libertarias y contraculturales: El asalto a la sociedad disciplinarian—Entre Barcelona y Madrid (1965–1979)*. Madrid: Universidad Complutense, 2012.

Castillo, D., ed. *Barcelona: Fragments de la contracultural*. Barcelona: Ajuntament de Barcelona, 2010.

Castro, R., et al. *Diez años sin Franco: Desatado y bien desatado*. Barcelona: El Periódico de Catalunya, 1985.

Colectivo de Estudios por la Autonomia Obrera. *Luchas autónomas en la transición democrática*. Madrid: Zero, 1977.

Comandos Autónomos: Un anticapitalismo iconoclasta. Bilbao: Likiniano Elkartea, 1996.

Comunicados de la prisión de Segovia y otros llamamientos a la guerra social. Bilbao: MuturrekoBututazoiak, 2: MuturrekoBurutazoiak. El Lokal, 2000.

Comunicados de los presos autonomos encarcelados en la prisión de Segovia. Publication details listed.

Duhourcq, J.C and Madrigal, A. *Mouvement Ibérique de liberation: Mémoires de rebelle*. Toulouse: CRAS, 2007.

El grupo 1°de Mayo: Solidaridad revolucionaria internacional en los '60 y '70. Madrid: n.p., 2002.

Emboscada en Pasaia: Un crimen de estado. Barcelona: Virus, 2008.

Espai En Blanc, ed. *Luchas autónomas en los años 70*. Madrid: Traficantes de Sueños, 2008.

Lorenzo Rubio, C., *La revuelta de los communes*. Valencia: Desorden Distro, 2007.

Los incontrolados: Crónicas de la España salvaje, 1976–1981. Seville: Klinamen / Biblioteca Social Hermanos Quero, 2004.

Malvido, P. *Nosotros los malditos*. Barcelona: Anagrama, 2004.

Perez Puche, F. *La Valencia de los años 70*. Valencia: Carena 2001.

Quilez, C. *Atracadores*. Barcelona: Cossetània, 2002.

Ribas, J. *Los 70 a destajo: Ajoblanco y Libertad*: Barcelona: RBA, 2007.

Roglan, J. *Oriol Solé: El Ché català*. Barcelona: Edicions 62, 2006.

Rosés Cordovilla, S. *El MIL: Una historia política*. Barcelona: Alikornio, 2002.

Rouillan, J. M. *De memoria (I): Otoño de 1970 en Toulouse*. Barcelona: Virus, 2009.

—————.*De memoria (II): Un día de septiembre de 1973 en Barcelona*: Barcelona, Virus, 2011.

Sanz Díaz, B. *Rojos y Demócratas: La oposición al franquismo en la Universidad de Valencia, 1939–1975*. Valencia: Comisiones Obreras, 2002.

Sola, E. *La Vaquería de la calle Libertad: Crónica callejera (y al parecer sin políticos) de la transición hispana a la movida y a la democracia, que se suele decir*. Alcalá: n.p., 2006.

Tajuelo, T. *El MIL, Puig Antich y los GARI*. Paris: Ruedo Ibérico, 1977.

Téllez Solà, A. *El MIL y Puig Antich*. Barcelona: Virus, 1994.

—————.A, *Sabaté: Guerrilla urbana en España*. Barcelona: Virus, 1992.

Wilhelmi, G. *El movimiento libertario en la transición: Madrid, 1975–1982*. Madrid: Fundación Salvador Seguí, 2012.

Zambrana, J. *La alternativa libertarian: Catalunya 1976–1979*. Barcelona: Edicions Fet a Mà, 2000.

Zaragoza rebelde: Movimientos sociales y antagonismos 1975–2000. Zaragoza: Colectivo Zaragoza Rebelde, 2009.

Zirikatu. *Komando Autonomoak: Una historia anticapitalista*: Zaragoza: Colectivo Zaragoza Rebelde, 2009.

DOSSIERS

COPEL: Butrones y otras aportaciones de grupos autónomos: Valencia: Desorden Distro, 2004.

Dossier Agustín Rueda. Barcelona: Centre de Documentació Arran, 2003.

Dossier caso "ERAT." n.p.: 1981

Dossier GARI. Toulouse: Groupes d'entr'aide, 1975.

Insurrection. Organe d'expression de groupes et d'individus autonomes d'action. Toulouse: n.p., 1979.

ARCHIVES

Juan's personal archive.

Manel Tirado's personal archive.

Víctor's personal archive.

Associació d'Amics d'Agustín Rueda, Sallent.

Centre de Documentació de La Ciutat Invisible, Barcelona.

Fundación Salvador Seguí, Madrid.

FV documentary sources. Pavelló de la República (University of Barcelona), Barcelona.

Felip Solé personal archive. Pavelló de la República (University of Barcelona), Barcelona.

DOCUMENTARIES

Carles, Pierre and Minangoy, Georges. *Ni vieux ni traîtres*. France: Pages & Images, 2004.

Falconetti Peña nd Orsino Zefrí. *Autonomía Obrera*. Barcelona: Espai en Blanc, 2008.

Loher Rodríguez, Martina. *MIL: Historia de una familia con historia*. Switzerland: 2006.

Murcia Clavería, Oriol, *Setenta y dos horas*. Barcelona: Démode Produccions, 2012.

B. H. *Presos de la democracia*. Barcelona: 2006.

INTERVIEWS AND MISCELLANEOUS

Antonio, September 30, 2012, outskirts of Perpignan.

Dani, June 5 and 13, 2012, Barcelona.

Felipe, July 21, 2012, Alicante Province.

Gerard, June 21 and 28, 2012, Barcelona.

Gria, Andrés, June 14, 2012, Barcelona.

Inés, Hortensia, May 27, 2012, La Seu d'Urgell.

José, May 7, 2012, Barcelona.

Juan, February 3, 2012, Barcelona.

Juanjo, April 23, 2012, Madrid.

"Llengües," May 15, 2012, Barcelona.

Llimona, Francesc, various conversations throughout 2012, Barcelona.

Melich, Enric, May 27, 2012, La Seu d'Urgell.

Michel, April 19 and June 25, 2012, Barcelona.

Miguel, September 27, 2012, Tarragona Province.

Paco (from Madrid), October 3, 2012, Madrid.

Paco (from Valencia), July 19, 2012, Alicante Province.

Petit Loup, April 3, 2012, Chetumal.

Piñero, Miquel Didac, June 8, 2012, Peralada.

Pont, Daniel, e-mail dated December 20, 2012.
Roger, September 23, 2012, Barcelona Province.
Sabata, June 9, 2012, Girona Province.
Sebas, June 9, 2012, Barcelona Province.
Simal, Victor, September 30, 2012, outskirts of Perpignan.
Tirado, Manel, June 1, 2012, Moià.
Titina, April 11, 2013, Barcelona.
Víctor, February 14, 2012 plus subsequent conversations until January 2013, Barcelona.
Vigo, April 11, 2013, Barcelona.

INTERNET SITES (all accessed between January 2012 and January 2013)
ABC (digital newspaper archive): hemeroteca.abc.es/avanzada.stm.
Autonomía Obrera (digital archive): autonomiaobrera.net.
Centre de documentació antiautoritari i llibertari: www.cedall.org
Clandestine Political Press Archive, Universitat Autònoma de Barcelona: ddd.uab.cat/collection/ppc
El País (digital newspaper archive): elpais.com/diario
Girona City Council, Document Management Service, Archives and Publications: girona.cat/sgdap/cat/premsa.php#pandora.
La presse anarchiste (website): www.la-presse-anarchiste.net/
La Vanguardia (digital newspaper archive): archive: lavanguardia.com/hemeroteca
La Web Sense Nom (website on Spanish counterculture): lwsn.net
Los de la sierra: Dictionnaire des guerilleros et resistants antifranquistes, 1936–1975 (biographical dictionary of anti-Franco fighters): losdelaierra.info.
Website entry on María Mombiola: libcom.org/history/articles/1914-1999-maria-mombiola
Wikipedia, Spanish: es.wikipedia.org
Wikipedia, Italian: it.wikipedia.org/
Wikipedia, French: fr.wikipedia.org.

INDEX

What is the Kate Sharpley Library?

The Kate Sharpley Library is a library, archive, publishing outfit and affinity group. We preserve and promote anarchist history.

What we've got

Our collection includes anarchist books, pamphlets, newspapers and leaflets from the nineteenth century to the present in over twenty languages. The collection includes manuscripts, badges, audio and video recordings, and photographs, as well as the work of historians and other writers who have documented the anarchist movement.

What we do

We promote the history of anarchism by reprinting original documents from our collection, and translating or publishing new works on anarchism and its history. These appear in our quarterly bulletin or regularly published pamphlets. We have also provided manuscripts to other anarchist publishers. People come and research in the library, or we can send out a limited amount of photocopies.

Why we do it

We don't say one strand of class-struggle anarchism has all the answers. We don't think anarchism can be understood by looking at 'thinkers' in isolation. We do think that what previous generations thought and did, what they wanted and how they tried to get it, is relevant today. We encourage the anarchist movement to think about its own history—not to live on past glories but to get an extra perspective on current and future dangers and opportunities.

How we do it

Everything at the Kate Sharpley Library—acquisitions, cataloguing, preservation work, publishing, answering inquiries is done by volunteers. All our running costs are met by donations (from members of the collective or our subscribers and supporters) or by the small income we make through publishing.

How you can help

Please subscribe to our bulletin to keep up with what we're doing. There are four issues of the Bulletin a year. Or become a Friend, a KSL Friend subscription gets you the *Bulletin* and all our publications as they come out.

You can send us anarchist material that you don't need any more (from books to badges)—we can pay postage for large loads, but it doesn't have to be large. A couple of pamphlets will be as gratefully received as anything. Even if you send us duplicates we can trade with other archives for material we do not have. If you publish anarchist material, please add us to your mailing list!

You can send us money too. Details are on our website at: http://www.katesharpleylibrary.net/doc/donations

Keep in touch!

www.katesharpleylibrary.net | www.facebook.com/katesharpleylibrary

Kate Sharpley Library
BM Hurricane
London, WC1N 3XX
UK

AK PRESS is small, in terms of staff and resources, but we also manage to be one of the world's most productive anarchist publishing houses. We publish close to twenty books every year, and distribute thousands of other titles published by like-minded independent presses and projects from around the globe. We're entirely worker run and democratically managed. We operate without a corporate structure—no boss, no managers, no bullshit.

The **FRIENDS OF AK PRESS** program is a way you can directly contribute to the continued existence of AK Press, and ensure that we're able to keep publishing books like this one! Friends pay $25 a month directly into our publishing account ($30 for Canada, $35 for international), and receive a copy of every book AK Press publishes for the duration of their membership! Friends also receive a discount on anything they order from our website or buy at a table: 50% on AK titles, and 30% on everything else. We have a Friends of AK ebook program as well: $15 a month gets you an electronic copy of every book we publish for the duration of your membership. *You can even sponsor a very discounted membership for someone in prison.*

Email **friendsofak@akpress.org** for more info, or visit the website: **https://www.akpress.org/friends.html**.

There are always great book projects in the works—so sign up now to become a Friend of AK Press, and let the presses roll!